Obsession

A Chess Biography of Vsevolod Rauzer

Alexander Konstantinopolsky

Obsession: A Chess Biography of Vsevolod Rauzer
Author: Alexander Konstantinopolsky

Translated from the Russian by Alexei Zakharov
Edited and updated by Grigory Bogdanovich
Typesetting by Andrei Elkov
First published in Russian in 2022
© LLC Elk and Ruby Publishing House, 2023 (English version)
© Mark Konstantinopolsky and Andrei Elkov, 2022 (Russian version)
Follow us on Twitter: @ilan_ruby
www.elkandruby.com
ISBN 978-5-6047848-9-1 (hardback), 978-5-6047848-8-4 (paperback)

A note from the publishers

The author Alexander Konstantinopolsky died in 1990 before he was able to publish this book. Thanks to the efforts of his son, Mark Konstantinopolsky, it was eventually published in Russian in 2022, and now in 2023 it is published in English.

The articles by Alexander Konstantinopolsky, Mikhail Yudovich/Fedor Fogelevich, Efim Lazarev and Mikhail Botvinnik were included in the author's original manuscript.

International Master Grigory Bogdanovich updated the games analysis using modern chess engines.

The four games included in the Additional Games section (no. 75-78) were not part of the author's book. They were provided separately by Sergey Voronkov and Vlad Novikov from their own research efforts, for which we thank them. They are analyzed by Rauzer with updates by Grigory Bogdanovich. Game 4 against Zhuk was included in the original book without Rauzer's annotations. Thanks to the efforts of Sergey Voronkov and Vlad Novikov we have restored them.

Contents

Vsevolod Alfredovich Rauzer

Index of Games

Game	White	Black	Opening	Year
I1	Rauzer	Rokhlin	Queen's Gambit	1929
I2	Riumin	Rauzer	French Defense	1929
I3	Rauzer	Botvinnik	Fragment	1931
I4	Rauzer	Konstantinopolsky	Nimzo-Indian Defense	1932
I5	Rauzer	Konstantinopolsky	Four Knights Opening	1932
I6	Rauzer	Alatortsev	French Defense	1933
I7	Rauzer	Riumin	Ruy Lopez	1936
I8	Konstantinopolsky	Rauzer	Fragment	1940
I9	Rauzer	V. Makogonov	Sicilian Defense	1934
1	Rauzer	Bogdanov	Queen's Pawn Game	1924
2	Travin	Rauzer	Slav Defense	1925
3	Rauzer	Kosolapov	Slav Defense	1925
4	Rauzer	Zhuk	English Opening	1926
5	Rauzer	Grinberg	Slav Defense	1926
6	Kiev	Kharkov	French Defense	1927
7	Rauzer	Pogrebyssky	Queen's Indian Defense	1927
8	Rauzer	Ballodit	Queen's Gambit Accepted	1927
9	Rauzer	Kaspersky	Dutch Defense	1927
10	Rauzer	Pavlov-Pianov	Slav Defense	1927
11	Rauzer	I. Rabinovich	Queen's Indian Defense	1927
12	Vilner	Rauzer	French Defense	1928
13	Rauzer	Konstantinopolsky	French Defense	1929
13a	Pillsbury	Tarrasch	Fragment	1898
14	Botvinnik	Rauzer	French Defense	1929
15	Riumin	Rauzer	French Defense	1929
16	Rauzer	Grigoriev	French Defense	1929
17	Rauzer	Rokhlin	Queen's Gambit	1929
17a	Bogoljubov	Reti	Queen's Gambit	1923
18	Rauzer	Konstantinopolsky	Nimzo-Indian Defense	1930
19	Rauzer	Kofman	Nimzo-Indian Defense	1930
20	Rauzer	Selezniev	Queen's Gambit	1930
21	Rauzer	Freymann	Queen's Gambit	1930
22	Rauzer	Bychek	Slav Defense	1931
23	Rauzer	Moskalev	Queen's Gambit	1931
24	Gribin	Rauzer	Chigorin Opening	1931
25	Sorokin	Rauzer	Queen's Gambit	1931
26	Rauzer	Zamikhovsky	Queen's Gambit	1931
27	Kasparyan	Rauzer	English Opening	1931
28	Rauzer	Yudovich	Queen's Gambit	1931
29	Rauzer	Riumin	King's Indian Defense	1931
30	Rauzer	Ragozin	Four Knights Defense	1932
31	Lisitsin	Rauzer	Queen's Gambit	1932

Game	White	Black	Opening	Year
32	Rauzer	Alatortsev	French Defense	1933
33	Rauzer	I. Rabinovich	Caro-Kann Defense	1933
34	Rauzer	Savitsky	Ruy Lopez	1933
35	Rauzer	Chekhover	Sicilian Defense	1933
36	Sorokin	Rauzer	Reti Opening	1934
37	Rauzer	Levenfish	Ruy Lopez	1934
38	Chekhover	Rauzer	Queen's Gambit	1934
39	Rauzer	Alatortsev	French Defense	1934
40	Ragozin	Rauzer	Catalan Opening	1934
41	Riumin	Rauzer	Queen's Gambit	1934
42	Rauzer	V. Makogonov	Sicilian Defense	1934
43	Rauzer	Goldberg	Caro-Kann Defense	1935
44	Rauzer/ Belakovsky	E. Polyak/ Zhukhovitsky	Ruy Lopez	1935
45	Rauzer	Goldberg	Caro-Kann Defense	1936
46	Levenfish	Rauzer	Queen's Gambit Accepted	1936
47	Rauzer	Ilyin-Zhenevsky	Latvian Gambit	1936
48	Rauzer	Ragozin	Ruy Lopez	1936
49	Rauzer	I. Rabinovich	French Defense	1936
50	Freymann	Rauzer	Queen's Gambit	1936
51	Rauzer	Konstantinopolsky	French Defense	1936
52	Rauzer	Sozin	Caro-Kann Defense	1936
53	Rauzer	Mazel	Alekhine Defense	1936
54	Rauzer	Konstantinopolsky	French Defense	1936
55	Konstantinopolsky	Rauzer	Queen's Gambit	1936
56	Chekhover	Rauzer	Reti Opening	1936
57	Ragozin	Rauzer	Simagin-Larsen Opening	1936
58	Rauzer	Riumin	Ruy Lopez	1936
59	Riumin	Rauzer	Reti Opening	1936
60	Rauzer	Chekhover	Sicilian Defense	1936
61	Kan	Rauzer	Queen's Gambit Accepted	1936
61a	Pillsbury	Steinitz	Queen's Gambit Accepted	1895
61b	Showalter	Blackburne	Queen's Gambit Accepted	1896
62	Rauzer	Goglidze	Sicilian Defense	1936
63	Rauzer	Ragozin	Sicilian Defense	1936
64	Rauzer	Fine	Alekhine Defense	1937
65	Rauzer	Alatortsev	French Defense	1937
66	Rauzer	I. Rabinovich	Ruy Lopez	1937
66a	Em. Lasker	I. Rabinovich	Ruy Lopez	1925
67	Rauzer	Panov	Ruy Lopez	1937
68	Rauzer	Budo	Caro-Kann Defense	1937
69	Rauzer	Lilienthal	French Defense	1937
70	Levenfish	Rauzer	Queen's Gambit Accepted	1937

Game	White	Black	Opening	Year
71	Rauzer	Chekhover	Caro-Kann Defense	1937
72	Rauzer	Konstantinopolsky	Caro-Kann Defense	1937
73	Rauzer	Rovner	French Defense	1937
74	Rovner	Rauzer	Ruy Lopez	1937
75	Rauzer	Zinder	Fragment	1926
76	Rauzer	Romanovsky	Queen's Gambit	1927
77	Rauzer	Russo	Queen's Gambit	1928
78	Rauzer	Rosenstein	Queen's Gambit	1928
A1	Konstantinopolsky	Goglidze	Reti Opening	1936
A2	Konstantinopolsky	Smyslov	Fragment	1945
A3	Konstantinopolsky	Panov	Fragment	1946
A4	Keres	Konstantinopolsky	Caro-Kann Defense	1948

Vsevolod Rauzer as I Knew Him

Alexander Konstantinopolsky
(This article was first published in Shakhmaty v SSSR *nos. 7-9, 1989)*

Alexander Tvardovsky once wrote the following lines of poetry:

Of the things I know better than anyone in the world,
I would like to speak – and in my own manner.

It was this desire that grabbed hold of me when the *Shakhmaty v SSSR* editors asked me to share my memories of the prominent master and theoretician Vsevolod Alfredovich Rauzer (1908–1941).[1]

* * *

Kiev of the late 1920s, the city of my chess youth. The Moscow International Tournament caused an explosion of interest in chess among both young and old. We played in very modest conditions, usually in a room of some club or other. We organized competitions by ourselves, overseen by a committee of two or three people. They arranged the equipment and acted as arbiters – of course, *pro bono*, on a voluntary basis. Huge team matches, on 100–200 boards, were becoming fashionable – for instance, Trade Unions vs. University Students or Red Army vs. Education Workers. Friendships emerged there, the spirit of collectivism was nurtured, this was a school of mastery. So many analyses, debates, discoveries and refutations were born there!

Chess clocks were a rarity. In the days of big blitz tournaments, the clocks were often replaced by the Kiev fan favorite (chess player, checkers player, and giveaway checkers champion) Vasily Grigorievich Sherminsky. He acted as a timekeeper. As he counted loudly, "One, two, three, four, five, six, six, six!" you had to make a move, otherwise you lost on time. Sherminsky announced the results and the pairings for the next rounds. There were never any incidents.

---

[1] Actually, May 1942 is given in the martyrology of victims of the Siege of Leningrad as Rauzer's month and year of death, and more precise information is unavailable (see the article by Alexander Kentler "Poor Rauzer" dated 20 April 2020 on https://e3e5.com/article.php?id=1797), though 1941 is given in some other secondary sources. According to the official housing records that Kentler found, he died in 1942 (the month was not provided). So it is uncertain whether he died in 1941 or 1942 but 1942 seems more likely. According to the same records his mother died on 29 July 1942.

Our friendship with Vsevolod Rauzer blossomed during these old times. From his stories, I learned that he came to Kiev in 1924. Before that, he lived in Rostov-on-Don, and even earlier, in Kislovodsk. I didn't think to ask him where he was born.[2]

"Since I was first introduced to chess in 1920," Rauzer would recall 16 years later, "and up until now, I've been working on chess on my own. My first book was an almost unreadable Dufresne handbook; in addition, I copied all chess columns I found in the *Niva* magazine by hand."

The chess column in *Izvestia* first appeared on 29th October 1922. On 17th December that year, Grigoriev, the column editor who had a knack for discovering and encouraging young talents, published the 14-year-old Rauzer's chess problem. It showed that the young self-taught player had already mastered the basics of chess composition.

1.♕d8! The a7 pawn is necessary to eliminate a dual: 1.♕a4+ c4 2.♕a7#.

This problem has a tiny imprecision in that after 1...g4 white has two ways to mate the black king, but in fairness to the 14-year-old Rauzer 1...g4 is not the main black reply, as it's not an attempted defense and it would be cooperative.[3]

N. Grigoriev also publicized Rauzer's first notable practical success in his column on 26th April 1924: "Rostov-on-Don. The city-level competition ended with a brilliant victory of the 15 year-old V. A. Rauzer, who won all 7 games out of 7(!)."

I'm getting a bit ahead of myself here, but on 14th February 1925, N. Grigoriev published another problem by Rauzer – already a Kiev resident – with praise for the author: "The problem is not difficult, but elegant."

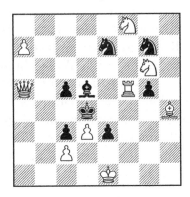

Mate in 2

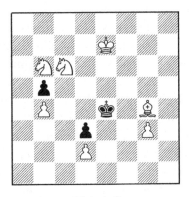

Mate in 3

---

[2] According to the housing records, both Rauzer and his mother were born in Kiev (*ibid.*).

[3] Comments in italics, both here and below, were added by Grigory Bogdanovich

1.♘a8! ♔d5 2.♗f5.

Still, problem composition was only a small detail in Rauzer's chess biography (as well as mine). Later, he would characterize his play in that period as follows: "I used to like and still like positional play. My first chess tastes, before I earned 1st category, can be stated thus: 'capture some pawns at the very least, hold on to them, defend and convert.' The first examples I used to hone my style were some games by Lasker, and later by Tarrasch... Tarrasch amazed me with his logic, the clarity of his positions. Still, until 1933, I did not have any concrete practical outlook on the issues of chess struggle."

* * *

Rauzer was a peer of mine, only slightly more than a year older. Still, he had a reputation as the most talented, knowledgeable and authoritative player among the young Kiev guys. I can definitely say that, in the period of 1926–1930, I was an attentive and loyal pupil of his.

Neither I nor Vova (or Ruzia), as friends used to call Rauzer, liked blitz too much, preferring friendly games, where we tested the craziest variations.

Rauzer's flat became a meeting place for the curious fans of chess analysis. He lived in the city center, on Engels Street (formerly Lyuteranskaya *[the historical name of Lyuteranskaya Street was restored in 1992])*. We would stay up late. Often, the only signal for us finally to leave was a voice from behind the curtain hung across the room, belonging to Rauzer's mother, Varvara Grigorievna, "Vova, it's time to stop the thumping!"

Chess immediately became Rauzer's calling and destiny. You could describe him with a poet's words, "He obeyed only one thought, one, but fiery passion."[4] And, alas, he could say about himself, "I haven't saved up a single ruble with my lines."[5] Only a few people could really earn a living with chess back then. Rauzer, impractical and maladjusted to life, most certainly could not.

He worked as a courier in the city's financial department. "I found Botvinnik in Kiev!" he joked once. It turned out that one of the carters to whom he delivered tax notices bore that glorious chess surname.

What features were characteristic for Rauzer as a person? Directness. Honesty. Integrity. A heightened sense of his own dignity. I remember one telling incident. During a Kiev championship, Rauzer turned up 5 or 10 minutes late to his game. As he entered, he saw that his clock had already been started, but there

---

[4]   A quote from Mikhail Lermontov's *The Novice*. – Translator

[5]   A quote from Vladimir Mayakovsky's poem *Out Loud*. – Translator

was no chair on his side of the board. "But I wouldn't have been able to play without a chair," he argued. And the arbiter admitted that he was right and turned his clock back. On that day, Rauzer had to face the only master that Kiev had back then, F. Bogatyrchuk; the organizers were a bit afraid of him and didn't want to spoil the relationship with him.

By the way, Bogatyrchuk recognized Rauzer very early as the main threat to his "supremacy" in Kievan chess, and he was very wary of his success.[6]

* * *

The first aspect of Rauzer's talent that got wide recognition was his endgame analysis.

---

[6]   Here the author wrote in the article "I remember the 1928 Kiev championship, where I made my debut at the city level. The tournament became a race between Rauzer and Bogatyrchuk. There was no doubt that the younger player would win, but, alas, the tournament was never finished". However, Sergey Voronkov in his two-volume biography of Bogatyrchuk (published only in Russian as of the date of publication of the current work) explains that in fact Bogatyrchuk withdrew from the 1928 tournament (which was indeed unfinished) after just two games, while the 1929 Kiev championship really was a race to the wire between the two players, with Bogatyrchuk winning by half a point (10.5/13).

Back then, the current theory, relying on Tarrasch's authority, evaluated this position (with white to move) as better for white. However, in 1926, Rauzer found an original and economical way for black to reach a draw. At first, black gives checks along the files, but when white threatens to hide his king on a7 (and indeed win), he plays ♜a4-f4 and begins to give checks along the ranks. For instance, 1.♔f2 ♔g7 2.♔e2 ♜a4 3.♔d3 ♜f4 4.♔c8 ♜a4 5.♜c6 ♔f7 6.♔c3 ♔e7 7.♔b3 ♔d7, with a draw.

(Simultaneously with Rauzer and independently from him, master I. Rabinovich, the author of the first Soviet endgame handbook (1927), came to the same conclusion. In the second edition of his work, published in 1938, the position was credited to two authors, I. Rabinovich and V. Rauzer.)

And then Rauzer, with his characteristic fanaticism, started to solve the secrets of a mysterious endgame.

"This interesting endgame," he wrote in an article published in *Shakhmatny Listok* (No. 7, 1928), "was never to my knowledge analyzed in print, despite its intricacy."

In Rauzer's opinion, white wins if he is to move: 1.♗h2! prevents the black king from reaching the drawing zone, which is limited by the squares a7, a8, h8, h6, f4, e5, d4. If black is to move (1...♚d6), white cannot do that, and so it's a draw.

If the black king is in the drawing zone, this doesn't guarantee a draw yet, because the white king is too close to the a-pawn, and the black king might not have enough time to reach a8. So it's worth remembering that if the white bishop stands on the h2-b8 diagonal, the black king that occupies the drawing zone must reach d7 immediately after the white king returns to b5.

However, several months later, A. A. Troitsky objected to Rauzer on the pages of the same magazine (No. 13). The famous endgame study composer named a long row of chess players who had studied that

endgame ever since 1851: J. Kling and B. Horwitz, M. Karstedt and A. Weiss, R. Teichmann and, finally, A. Troitsky himself. Troitsky posed a number of analytical doubts and asked Rauzer to revise his analysis.

Vsevolod got very worried and started to work on the controversial endgame even more eagerly. He came to my house to analyze, too; of course, I couldn't help him much in this difficult undertaking. I remember us sitting in my tiny room, forgetting about everything else, and checking Rauzer's subtlest lines; a street organ was playing in the yard, and we heard the lines of an old-time romance song:

But the withered flowers will not bloom again,

And love will not be revived.

Vova said ironically, "Alik, take this into account as well!"

Jokes aside, the refined (or, rather, more clearly worded) lines published by Rauzer in the 20th issue of *Shakhmatny Listok* were so convincing that Troitsky even named his reply article "Rauzer's Analysis Is Correct!" So, this means that all the old authorities were wrong! It's easy to imagine how inspired Rauzer was after such recognition.

Rauzer summarized his research of "bishop versus rook pawns" endgames in the second volume of the chess yearbook published in 1938. His classical analysis is still valuable today.

* * *

We keenly watched all the ups and downs in the career of our strongest peer. We were happy when Rauzer became the Ukrainian champion in 1927 (he took second place in the tournament after master A. Selezniev, who played *hors concours*), but we were sad when he suffered a major setback in his Soviet Championship debut that year (shared 18th–19th place in the 5th championship).

These passions reached their crescendo during the next, 6th Soviet Championship, which was played in 1929 using a complicated, three-tier formula. To learn the round results, we had to go to the train station and search for an Odessa newspaper that published them.

To our common joy, Vsevolod returned to Kiev as a master. He demonstrated his games to us (both best and worst!), as though it was his creative report before us.

Rauzer considered reaching the semi-final his main goal. The masters norm set there was quite feasible – 1.5 points out of 5. One could easily scrape up the masters title by agreeing a few draws. Some candidates did precisely that. Rauzer, however, loathed such calculations (he didn't agree to a single draw in the semi-final!). He won in the first round, while in the second, when he faced Y. Rokhlin, he came up with an interesting attack.

No. 11. Queen's Gambit
V. Rauzer – Y. Rokhlin (17)[7]
Odessa 1929

1.d4 d5 2.c4 e6 3.♘c3 ♘f6 4.♗g5 ♘bd7 5.e3 c6 6.a3 ♗e7 7.♕c2 h6 8.♗h4 0-0 9.♘f3 ♖e8 10.♗d3 dxc4 11.♗xc4 ♘d5 12.♗g3 ♘xc3 13.♕xc3 ♘f6 14.♗d3 ♗d7 15.0-0 ♕b6 16.♖ac1 ♖ec8 17.♘e5 c5 18.♘xd7 ♘xd7 19.dxc5 ♘xc5 20.♗b1 ♗f6 21.♕c2 ♗xb2 22.♕h7+ ♔f8 23.♖cd1 ♔e7 24.♗d6+ ♔f6

The last move was the point of black's plan. After escaping the checks, his king seems to be quite comfortable. But it's only an illusion. Objectively speaking, black needed to give up his queen: 24...♕xd6! 25.♖xd6 ♔xd6, with sufficient compensation.

Here, Rauzer could have crowned his plan with a brilliant

---

[7]   The number in parentheses refers to the games section of this book, where this game is annotated more thoroughly.

rook sacrifice – 25.♖d5! The threat of mate on f5 leaves black no choice – 25...g6, which is met with 26.♗xg6! ♕f8 27.♗xf7!, and if now 27...♕xd6 (the side-lines are pretty too: 27...♖g8 28.♗e7+; 27...♖xf7 28.♕xh6# – a "quiet" checkmate), then 28.♖xd6 ♖xf7 29.♕c2 with an easy win.

These lines were shown by Y. Rokhlin after the tournament. In the actual game, however, Rauzer got tempted by a queen sacrifice, planning to weave a mating net around the black king with e3-e4 and f2-f4, which looks inescapable at first glance.

25.e4!? ♘d7 26.♔h1 ♖h8 27.f4 ♖xh7 28.e5+ ♘xe5 29.fxe5+ ♔g5

30.♗xh7?

The correct continuation was 30.♖xf7! g6 31.♗e7+ ♔h5 32.♖d3 ♗xe5 33.♖h3+ ♔g4 34.♖h4#.

30...h5 31.♖xf7 ♔h6 32.♗e4

The bishop had a more secure square on b1. It would relocate there two moves later, anyway.

32...♖c8! 33.h4

With the idea of ♗e7 and ♗g5; however, black has a defense.

33...♕e3 34.♗b1 ♖c4??

This "unfortunate accident" became the fodder for many witty jokes. M. Botvinnik, for instance, called it "falling under a tram." The crude move 34...♗xa3! destroyed white's plans.

35.♖f6+!!

And instead of a full point, black got zero – 35...gxf6 36.♗f8# or 35...g6 36.♖xg6+.

However, Rauzer considered his win against the talented Moscow player N. Riumin his greatest achievement. In this game, as he put it himself, he managed to win by arranging the black pieces in graceful phalanx pairs. The game was played in the last round of the group stage and was therefore decisive for semi-final qualification. I hope that analysis of this charming miniature will give the readers great pleasure.

No. 12. French Defense
N. Riumin – V. Rauzer (15)
Odessa 1929

1.e4 e6 2.g3 d5 3.♗g2 dxe4
4.♘c3 ♗d7 5.♘xe4 ♗c6 6.f3 e5
7.♘e2 f5 8.♘f2 ♗c5 9.♘d3 ♗d6
10.0-0 ♘f6 11.♘c3 0-0 12.♕e2 ♕e7
13.♘f2 ♕f7 14.d3 ♘bd7 15.♗d2
♖ae8 16.♖ae1 ♕h5 17.♔h1 ♘c5
18.♘cd1 ♘e6 19.c3

19...♘f4!! 20.gxf4 exf4 21.♘e4
fxe4 22.fxe4 f3! 23.♗xf3 ♘xe4
24.dxe4 ♖xf3 25.♖xf3 ♖xe4
26.♖f8+ ♗xf8

White resigned.

* * *

And so, Rauzer became a master. He was only 21 years old. Back then, notably, there were only about thirty masters in our entire country.

Of course, Rauzer never thought about resting on his laurels. On the contrary, he considered joining the ranks of our chess guard as a starting point on his way to becoming a chess thinker.

As I already said, Rauzer was a chess classicist. He didn't approve of the fashionable views of "hypermodernism" (A. Nimzowitsch, R. Reti, S. Tartakower, in our country – P. Romanovsky). I, on the other hand, was a fan of "new ideas in chess", and our opinions on them were among our "creative differences" that didn't spoil our friendship.

In 1926, Tarrasch's magnum opus, *Die Moderne Schachpartie*, was published in Russian. It immediately became Rauzer's go to book. Rauzer was attracted by its logic, methodicalness, and literary form. On the other hand, Tarrasch's biases, which attracted a lot of polemical shots from modernists, also came to the fore. But time showed that classicism remained an unshakable value. Rauzer was right in his insistence that studying the classics was necessary, and this is still relevant even in our time.

I'll continue this topic later. Now I wish to point out that Rauzer's opening repertoire at the time was based on the "cult" of 1.d4. I experienced his excellent knowledge of the Queen's Gambit firsthand: it was a formidable weapon in his hands. It was hard to defend against him after 1.d4.

And then Rauzer was suddenly beset by creative doubts. The 7th Soviet Championship that took place in 1931 became the impetus for a re-evaluation of his chess outlook. His score itself was quite satisfactory: Rauzer shared 8th–9th place in the competition of the country's strongest masters, hence making it to the top ten. However, our hero never looked at chess solely through the prism of points and results. Creativity was his main goal. He set a very high bar for himself, saying ruefully, "I am not winning – it's my opponents who lose to me because of their mistakes." Another drawback of his play, according to Rauzer, was the fact that he "made disappointingly too many draws" (8 out of 17 games). And he was especially upset because his belief in 1.d4 was undermined.

In the tournament, Rauzer put his system with 6.♕b3 into practice (after 1.d4 d5 2.c4 e6 3.♘c3 ♘f6 4.♗g5 ♘bd7 5.♘f3 c6). Strictly speaking, the authorship of the move 6.♕b3 didn't belong to him – it was Steinitz who used it first in several games of his return match against Lasker, back in 1896/97. However, Rauzer put a very different meaning into this move, connecting it with an original plan. The direct purpose of 6.♕b3 is to prevent the Cambridge Springs system, which was popular back then: 6...♕a5 can now be met with the unpleasant 7.♗d2!. The move also has a more far-reaching aim, giving a new direction for the Queen's Gambit struggle. Instead of organizing a standard attack on the h7 square, white deploys his

forces under the slogan "Everyone to the center!": ♗e2, ♗f3, 0-0, ♖fd1, ♖ac1, ♘e5. And we have to say that in all games where Rauzer deployed his novelty (against B. Verlinsky, M. Yudovich[8], A. Zamikhovsky, and M. Botvinnik), the opening battle ended in his favor. However, after getting an obvious advantage against Botvinnik, Rauzer lost to the future tournament winner in a tactical struggle.

No. 13.

V. Rauzer – M. Botvinnik
Moscow, 1931

17.e4!

"A typical move for Rauzer's style – he always strove to seize

---

8   This game, where Rauzer executed his plan most consistently, was thoroughly annotated by him for the *64* magazine. However, the analysis was never published or returned to the author. Maybe somebody needed it for their own use? We shall see later that this was not the only such case in Rauzer's career...

the maximum possible space on the board." (M. Botvinnik)

17...♕c5+ 18.♔h1

"Black saw only now that the planned move 18...♕e3, threatening 19...d4 and 19...♕xf4, was not possible because of a rather obvious refutation, 19.♘xd5. He had to search for another continuation that still allowed him to muddy the waters."

18...♖cd8 19.exd5 ♕e3

"But even now white, of course, could still win with 20.♗f3! ♕xf4 21.dxc6 ♘c5 22.♕a3 ♗c8 23.♕xa7. White, however, thought that after winning the pawn, the position was purely technical, and so he made two mistakes in a row in his conversion."

20.♕c4 cxd5 21.♘xd5

"It was necessary to play 21.♕d4 ♕xd4 22.♖xd4 ♘c5 with slightly better chances in the endgame."

21...♗xd5! 22.♖xd5 ♘c5! 23.♗f3 ♘d3 24.h3 ♖xd5 25.♗xd5 ♕g3

"Some years after this game was played, an amateur player found that white could still save the game with 26.♗xf7+!! (Rauzer waited too long before delivering this tactical blow). After 26...♖xf7 27.e6! ♘f2+ 28.♔g1 ♘xh3+ 29.♔h1, black would have had to resort to perpetual check, because 29...♖xf4? leads to mate (30.e7+). The game move loses by force."

26.♖f1 ♘f2+ 27.♔g1 ♘xh3+ 28.♔h1 ♘f2+ 29.♖xf2 ♕xf2 30.♗xf7+ ♖xf7 31.e6 ♖xf4!

White resigned. "After 32.e7+ ♖xc4 33.e8=♕+ ♕f8 34.♕e6+ ♕f7, the c8 square is protected by the c4 rook!"

This loss discouraged Rauzer. Thankfully, it happened at the tournament's finish. My efforts to convince him that his opening play had nothing to do with his loss were futile. He stubbornly insisted that 1.d4 was the root of all evil...

After that, he started his search for "the absolute" – the ideal first move that "starts and wins!" Earlier, Rauzer thought that it was 1.d4, but now he placed his best hopes on 1.e4.

Unfortunately, my friend got fully obsessed with this idea. I tried to argue, "You, Vova, are trying to destroy our ancient game, dreaming to prove the so-called 'first-move advantage'. Why?" The answer was always the same: with a flourish, he would move the white king's pawn two squares ahead and exclaim, "Make your move! Defend!!"

And the argument continued over the silent squares of the chess board. I had to make moves and defend with the black pieces. It was not easy at times, because Rauzer's rationale was original and deeply thought-out. I wasn't always able to finish the discussion convincingly.

I said "unfortunately" a bit earlier. This word reflects my perception back then. Now, wise with experience of past decades, I'm inclined to look at things differently. Yes, the search for "the absolute", in chess or any other pursuit, is somewhat similar to chasing a bluebird, which is elusive and only allows a select few to catch it. But this search was the factor that made Rauzer the prominent theoretician and innovator who broadened the horizons of Chess Knowledge, discovered uncharted depths in it, and gave world renown both to himself and the entire Soviet theoretical school.

Rauzer did not abandon 1.d4 right away. But I bear some part of the

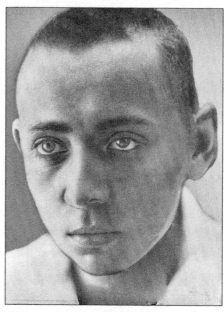

Vsevolod Rauzer in 1927

"blame" for completely shattering his faith in that move.

In summer 1932, the Leningrad youth team visited Kiev (V. Ragozin, A. Tolush, V. Lisitsin, L. Savitsky, and V. Chekhover). In addition to team matches, a ten-player training tournament was organized, including five Leningrad and five Kiev players. A game was played in this tournament that initiated analytical debates around a line in the Nimzo-Indian Defense which had been successfully introduced by A. Alekhine in his well-known game against M. Vidmar (San Remo 1930). Rauzer thought that this line was advantageous for white, while I had a contrary opinion. No wonder that the game turned out to be especially sharp.

No. 14. Nimzo-Indian Defense
V. Rauzer – A. Konstantinopolsky
Kiev 1932

1.d4 ♘f6 2.c4 e6 3.♘c3 ♗b4 4.♕c2 d5 5.a3 ♗xc3+ 6.♕xc3 ♘e4 7.♕c2 ♘c6 8.e3 e5!?

I believed in this Alekhine invention. Rauzer tried to refute it by force. Later, the line's author himself, referring to the continuation

9.cxd5 ♕xd5 10.♗c4 ♕a5+ 11.b4 ♘xb4 12.♕xe4 ♘c2+

which occurred in our game, wrote, "But subsequently, several new tournament games and their analysis cast some doubts as to the solidity of black's counterplay." However, five years later, R. Fine scored a quick win in this line against the Riga master M. Feigin (Hastings 1936/37).

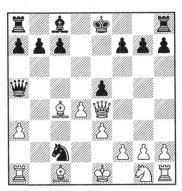

13.♔e2
13.♔d1? ♘xa1 14.♗b2 ♕a4+.
13...♕e1+ 14.♔f3 ♘xa1 15.♗b2
15.♕xe5+ ♗e6 16.♗xe6 0-0!
15...0-0 16.♕xe5?
This loses. White had to play 16.♔g3! h6 17.h4 or 17.h3 with unclear play.

16...♕d1+ 17.♘e2
17.♗e2 ♕b1!
17...♕xh1 18.d5 f6 19.♕h5
Or 19.♕e7 ♗h3. White is still hoping for mating threats – d5-d6, then ♘f4.

19...♕b1 20.♘f4 ♗f5 21.♗xa1 ♗e4+ 22.♔g3 ♕xa1 23.d6+ ♔h8 24.f3 ♕e5 25.♕xe5 fxe5 26.♘e6 cxd6 27.♘xf8 ♖xf8 28.fxe4 ♖c8 29.♗d5 b5 30.♔g4 g6
White resigned.

Modern theory prefers white in this line, agreeing with Alekhine and Rauzer. But on the whole, our game, even though it allowed us to penetrate a number of subtleties of the 8...e5 line, ended up as another "sacrifice to the altar of Theory" by Rauzer.

Still, he managed to take a very respectable 2nd place in the tournament.

This story had several important continuations. Rauzer completely eliminated 1.d4 from his opening repertoire. From then on, he played only 1.e4, and his goal was to prove that the fashionable defenses against this opening were unsatisfactory!

The analytical discussion spurred Rauzer to write a sharp and polemical, but very deep article "In Defense of Chess Classicism" (*Shakhmaty v SSSR*, No. 8, 1934). The point of the article was encapsulated in the following phrase: "My years of personal experience and the help from a group of Kiev players have led me to the conclusion that the classical style was a synthesis of positional and combinational play."

I was very flattered to be a part of that "group of Kiev players". But I had to admit that the editor's remark in the magazine had more than a grain of truth about it: "The same lines that, in his (Rauzer's) view, demonstrate the strength of Tarrasch-style moves, might as well be credited to Chigorin or Alekhine."

Finally, this is my duty – because only I know that – to tell you that around the same time (late 1933 or early 1934), Rauzer sent a long letter to the person whom he considered the head of the classical chess school – S. Tarrasch. He found the address, Reinstrasse 22, Munich, in our *Chess Player's Calendar 1926*. In his letter, Rauzer outlined his thoughts in defense of the classical school postulates, providing fundamental analysis that upheld and developed Tarrasch's principles. The fate of this letter is unknown – I don't even know if Tarrasch (who died on 13th February 1934) ever received it...

* * *

Rauzer started his analysis with his characteristic obsessiveness. "In the subsequent period," he wrote, "I worked hard and productively on opening theory. Outwardly, the change in my outlook resulted in abandoning 1.d4 in favor of 1.e4. In the 1933 Soviet Championship, I surprised my opponents by winning games that I played very consistently

from the very first moves. I can point to several such games in that tournament – against I. Rabinovich, Alatortsev, and Savitsky." Rauzer's 6th place was his best achievement in the national championships.

At first, Rauzer tried to solve his theorem "1.e4 and wins!" with the Four Knights Opening. In modern times, this opening is considered drawish, but for a long time, it was, as Tarrasch wittily put it, a "milch cow" for white, together with the Ruy Lopez. In the Kiev – Leningrad match (1932), Rauzer won a superb game against V. Ragozin in the Four Knights. However, he soon got disillusioned. The inadequacy of the Four Knights Opening as proof for his theories was demonstrated to Rauzer in a training game we played at the end of the same year 1932. My task, however, was quite easy because I followed a brilliant example – the game Tarrasch – Rubinstein (San Sebastian 1912).

No. 15. Four Knights Opening
V. Rauzer – A. Konstantinopolsky
Kiev 1932

1.e4 e5 2.♘f3 ♘c6 3.♘c3 ♘f6 4.♗b5 ♘d4 5.♗a4 ♗c5 6.♘xe5

White sometimes placed a lot of hope in this capture. However, the wise Akiba's ideas proved to be more convincing... At that moment, I saw a certain confusion or surprise in Vsevolod's gray-blue eyes: maybe he didn't expect his "examinee" to play so confidently?!

6...0-0 7.d3 d5 8.♗g5 c6! 9.♕d2 ♖e8 10.f4 b5! 11.♗b3 h6 12.♗h4 ♘xe4!

The exclamation marks belong to Rubinstein rather than me – I learned all that during the analysis of his games. If now 13.♗xd8 ♘xd2 14.♔xd2 ♖xd8 15.♘e2 ♘xe2 16.♔xe2, then 16...♖e8 17.♔d2 f6 18.♘xc6 ♗e3+ 19.♔e2!, and white can still fight – for a draw.

Our game finished quite suddenly and unexpectedly:

13.dxe4? ♕xh4+ 14.g3 ♕h5 and Rauzer resigned, explaining that the game had lost any theoretical interest for him. Quite a characteristic decision for him. Still, white needs to contend with the unpleasant threat of 15...♖xe5 and subsequent ♘f3+.

After this game, Rauzer redirected his efforts towards the Ruy Lopez. One of the first fruits of that labor was the aforementioned win against L. Savitsky in the 8th Soviet Championship (Leningrad 1933). His achievements in the Ruy Lopez crystallized in his game against N. Riumin, which I'll show the readers a bit later (game No. 17).

However, a player who challenges his opponent by moving the king's pawn two squares forward should also be prepared in case black chooses other defenses instead of the symmetrical e7-e5, as most often happens.

His first achievements in this area came in the French Defense. The rationale behind Rauzer's interpretation of the opening against V. Alatortsev from the same 8th Soviet Championship is quite revealing (it's annotated more thoroughly in the games section, No. 32).

No. 16. French Defense
V. Rauzer – V. Alatortsev (32)
Leningrad 1933

1.e4 e6 2.d4 d5 3.♘c3 ♗b4

Rauzer assigned a question mark to the move 3...♗b4: "It's hard to imagine that an opening where black pawns are developed on light squares, and then the dark-squared bishop, which is supposed to defend the squares between them, is brought out to be traded, can be considered acceptable!"

I can agree with those who think that this statement was exaggerated. As we shall soon see, Rauzer himself didn't disagree with that. However, his successes achieved from such a committal axiom look all the more impressive because of that!

4.e5 c5 5.a3 cxd4 6.axb4 dxc3

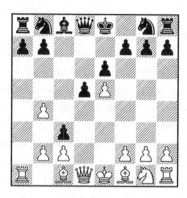

This position had a rather poor theoretical reputation for white because of the old game Lasker – Maroczy (New York 1924), which continued 7.bxc3 ♕c7. Rauzer said that he "noticed the lack of logic behind 7.bxc3: it's not beneficial for white to hold onto the c3 pawn at any rate; why then should he waste tempi to capture the c3 pawn? So I decided to spend that tempo on some beneficial move, specifically 7.♘f3: if black wants to get an extra pawn, he will have to gift white another tempo with 7...cxb2 8.♗xb2. However, it's clear that the weakness of all dark squares and black's lag in development cannot be compensated by the extra pawn on a7, which is placed on the white rook's open file in any case."

7.♘f3

Alatortsev sensed the danger and refused to accept the "Greek gift" of the b2 pawn, but this didn't save him from a quick rout.

7...♕c7 8.♕d4 ♘e7 9.♗d3 ♘d7 10.0-0 ♘c6? 11.♕xc3 ♕b6 12.b5 d4? 13.♕e1 ♘e7 14.♕e4 ♘g6

15.♖e1 0-0 16.b4 ♖d8 17.♗b2 f5 18.exf6 ♘xf6 19.♗xd4! ♕c7 20.♕e3 ♘d5 21.♕g5 ♘xb4 22.♗xg6 hxg6 23.b6 ♕d7 24.♖xa7 ♘xc2 25.♖d1 ♖b8 26.♖d2 ♕e8 27.♗e5

Black resigned.

"We should point out," Rauzer concluded, "that the seemingly easy victory in this game came to white only thanks to hard analytical work, which allowed him to steer the game in the right direction from the very beginning."

Interestingly enough, in the next two national championships, Rauzer and Alatortsev continued their theoretically significant discussion in this line of the French Defense. In 1934, Alatortsev gained his revenge (even though he was clearly worse out of the opening), while in 1937, Rauzer won again. "This game," he wrote then, "cannot be viewed as the final answer to the question of 3... ♗b4, it's only another test."

Here's another important remark by Rauzer concerning the move 3... ♗b4 (made in the same year 1937, analyzing a match game against D. Rovner): "A very fashionable move, which was declared by me in 1933 (to stir more controversy!) a 'blunder' that weakens the dark squares. I can attest that I managed to prove my paradoxical statement in important games. From this point of view, this game is theoretically significant. The entire match is theoretically significant, because

Rovner and I argued a lot in 1935 over whether a third move in the opening could be considered a mistake, especially such a move as 3... ♗b4. In such arguments, we couldn't agree on anything. Of course, it's possible that in the next few games black will take his revenge in this line, but I am deeply sure that white will have the last word!"

The same conviction served as the basis for Rauzer's research of the main lines of the most popular semi-open game, the Sicilian Defense, that also started in 1933. Rauzer experimented, sometimes got badly beaten, but never retreated – he came up with new ideas (his source was truly inexhaustible) and moved towards the truth – stubbornly, inexorably, determinedly. As a result, in all these lines, he came up with logical and harmonious systems that revolutionized the theory and practice of the Sicilian.

1) 1.e4 c5 2.♘f3 ♘c6 3.d4 cxd4 4.♘xd4 ♘f6 5.♘c3 d6 6.♗g5 e6 7.♕d2 ♗e7 8.0-0-0 (B64).

At first, Rauzer's opponents tried to defend with a7-a6 – immediately or after including the moves 8...0-0 9.f4. In this last branch, there's a forcing line 9...a6 10.♗xf6 ♗xf6 11.♘xc6 bxc6 12.♕xd6 ♕b6 13.♘a4 ♕e3+ 14.♔b1, tested by Rauzer in training games. He gave it a poetic name the "Caissa Variation", because white won in a logical and beautiful way. I was lucky to take a significant part in Rauzer's analysis and even

use its fruits in a correspondence game against the future master A. Chistiakov (1935–1936), which the reader can find in the [1985 Russian language 'Black Series'] book *Alexander Konstantinopolsky* number 22. A more complicated and sharp struggle arose after 8...0-0 9.f4 ♘xd4 10.♕xd4 ♕a5.

2) 1.e4 c5 2.♘f3 e6 3.d4 cxd4 4.♘xd4 ♘f6 5.♘c3 d6 6.♗g5 followed by 6...a6 7.♕f3 ♗e7 8.0-0-0 ♕c7 9.♕g3 (B95).

The forcing line 9...b5 10.♗xb5! axb5 11.♖he1! attracted Rauzer's particular attention. This positional sacrifice was used by Rauzer against V. Ragozin in a correspondence tournament organized to commemorate the 10th anniversary of the Ukrainian Physical Education Council (1934), but his opponent dropped out of the competition, and the game was never finished. My game against A. Akshanov, played around the same time in the Vinnitsa Oblast championship, wasn't printed in any contemporary chess publications either (see the book above, game 21; the move order was slightly different there – 9...♘bd7 10.f4 b5 11.♗xb5 axb5 12.♖he1). However, this line attracted much attention thanks to the game Rauzer – V. Makogonov (9th Soviet Championship, Leningrad, 1934/35); after 7.♕f3 ♘bd7 8.0-0-0 ♕c7 9.♕g3 b5 10.♗xb5 axb5, instead of 11.♖he1, Rauzer played 11.♘dxb5 ♕a5 12.♘xd6+ ♗xd6 13.♖xd6. A game with mutual chances ensued, which Rauzer ultimately managed to win.

3) 1.e4 c5 2.♘f3 d6 3.d4 cxd4 4.♘xd4 ♘f6 5.♘c3 g6 6.f3 ♗g7 7.♗e3 0-0 8.♕d2 ♘c6 9.0-0-0 (B76).

The Dragon Variation caused Rauzer the most trouble. In the 8th Soviet Championship, after playing the traditional line ♗e2, ♗e3, f2-f4, 0-0, Rauzer lost the opening battle against M. Botvinnik, G. Lisitsin and V. Chekhover. Only step by step, by making mistakes, did Rauzer give final shape to his innovative plan which became a dangerous weapon in white's hands for a long time. His idea was to hold control over the center and attack the opposing king with the g- and h-pawn push.

And again, I was lucky to be the first player to implement this plan, in the 10th Soviet Championship (1937). I credited my win against I. Kan (same book, game 23) not to myself, but to my friend.

These three "Rauzer attacks" alone (these designations, given by his contemporaries, stayed in the theoretical classifications forever) would have been enough to immortalize his name. However, Rauzer's thoughts illuminated, enriched, and fertilized almost all important semi-open games![9]

In the 1930s, Soviet chess stood among the best in the world. In the area of opening theory, this leadership, after Botvinnik, was largely epitomized by Rauzer. He had a special right to state proudly in 1937, "In the area of theory, we, the Soviet masters, have overtaken the foreign masters." But he added, "We need to improve our playing technique."

* * *

The career of Rauzer the theoretician was not paved solely with roses. I don't even mean what I called "sacrifices to the altar of Theory" earlier. It was disheartening to see misunderstanding from his own colleagues, the masters. "In Rauzer's play," Levenfish wrote in 1936, "opening system analysis has suppressed the main essence of chess art, and so the talented master has turned into a dry dogmatist." V. Panov also liked that word: "He (Rauzer) is harmed by his dogmatism, his biased attitude towards certain conceptions."

M. Yudovich, who was especially adept at sticking labels, tried to assign an "ideological base" to his unsightly activities. Back in 1933,

---

[9] In late 1934, Rauzer wrote an article "The Sicilian Defense as an Irregular Opening" based on his analytical research and sent it to the *Shakhmaty*

v SSSR magazine for publication. It was supposed to be printed in No. 4, 1935, but because of the impending 2nd Moscow International Tournament it was first delayed and then canceled altogether. The subsequent fate of this paper is unknown.

reviewing the outcome of the 8th Soviet Championship, he called Rauzer an original master who, however, adhered to a "reactionary chess ideology." He continued in the same vein, "His achievements stem from deep development of opening ideas, but his deliberately provocative sweeping statements (such as 'e2-e4 wins', '♝f8-b4 loses', and so on), are unconvincing, unjustified and essentially harmful. Rauzer's strength as an over-the-board player is clearly high, but it could have been even greater had he chosen another approach to chess struggle and chess theory."[10]

Thankfully, Rauzer didn't let these attacks deter him. He simply ignored them. Only once did Rauzer decide to answer his critics. "I think," he wrote with dignity, "that I am getting accused of dogmatism by those of my opponents who don't properly appreciate my approach to chess games. I think that you have to play soundly, scientifically, according to a plan." Great words that expressed Rauzer's true chess credo. They matched the progressive "chess ideology" of the Soviet chess school, of which he was a worthy representative.

---

[10] Thirty years later, the same author dedicated an article to Rauzer (*Shakhmatny Bulleten*, No. 5, 1965), praising him precisely for the things he criticized him for while Rauzer was still alive...

Of course, Rauzer would meet many more supporters than detractors. M. Botvinnik was the biggest among them, awarding the best game prize of the All-Union Young Masters Tournament (1936) to Rauzer; the victory in that tournament (shared with V. Chekhover) remained one of his best chess achievements. "I was greatly impressed," said Botvinnik explaining his decision, "by the consistent, logical play of Rauzer (white) against Riumin."

No. 17. Ruy Lopez
V. Rauzer – N. Riumin (58)
Leningrad 1936

1.e4 e5 2.♘f3 ♘c6 3.♗b5 a6 4.♗a4 ♘f6 5.0-0 ♗e7 6.♖e1 d6 7.c3 b5 8.♗b3 ♘a5 9.♗c2 c5 10.d4 ♕c7 11.♘bd2 ♘c6 12.a4 ♖b8 13.axb5 axb5 14.dxc5 dxc5

"Rauzer's opening play was rather consistent. It's now going to be very hard for black to defend the d5 square." (Botvinnik)

15.♘f1 ♗e6 16.♘e3 0-0 17.♘g5 ♖fd8 18.♕f3 ♖d6

19.♘f5

"An excellent idea. The trade on f5 is unavoidable; afterwards, the c2 bishop goes to e4 by force, occupying a most powerful position. In addition, the relocation of the e4 pawn to f5 prepares a pawn storm of black's kingside."

19...♗xf5 20.exf5 h6 21.♘e4 ♘xe4 22.♗xe4 ♗f6 23.♗e3 ♘e7 24.b4 c4 25.g3

"White pieces control the whole board. Black is defenseless before the looming attack."

25...♖d7 26.♖a7 ♕d8 27.♖xd7 ♕xd7 28.h4 ♔h8 29.g4 ♘g8

"The attack basically plays itself."

30.g5 ♗e7 31.♖d1 ♕c7 32.f6 ♗xf6 33.gxf6 ♘xf6 34.♗c2 ♖d8 35.♗xh6 ♖xd1+ 36.♗xd1 e4 37.♗f4 ♕d8 38.♕e2 ♘d5

Black resigned.

"Rauzer played this game like a true grandmaster."

To fully appreciate these words, you must remember that there was only one grandmaster among the Soviet chess players back then – Botvinnik himself.

This high praise resonates with what Botvinnik said about Rauzer recently (*Analytical and Critical Works, 1923–1941*): "Rauzer was one of the deepest chess researchers. He invented many opening systems for white that enjoyed great longevity. His analysis of Kling and Horwitz's "bishop + pawn vs. bishop" endgame was admired by everyone

and published in all handbooks. Unfortunately, he lacked a chess fighter's personality and a strong, efficient nervous system, which negatively affected his over-the-board results."[11]

There was also another encouraging voice, from another side. A. Alekhine watched the theoretical works of Soviet masters with great attention and interest, and, of course, he couldn't pass Rauzer's research by. Alekhine adopted the Rauzer Attack [as the Richter-Rauzer Attack is often termed in Russian] in the Sicilian Defense, and, according to him, achieved a 100-percent success in his games. I'll cite, among others, Alekhine – P. Frydman (Podebrady

---

[11] Rauzer's most important tournament results in Soviet Championships: 5th championship (1927) – 18th–19th; 6th championship (1929), semi-final – 3rd–4th; 7th championship (1931) – 8th–9th; 8th championship (1933) – 6th; 9th championship (1934) – 17th; 10th championship (1937) – 8th; All-Union Young Masters Tournament (1936) – 1st–2nd; Ukrainian championships: 1927 – 2nd (with champion's title); 1931 – 2nd; 1933 – 1st– 2nd; masters tournament of Ukraine, Transcaucasia and Uzbekistan (1930) – 1st; masters tournament featuring H. Kmoch (1934) – 3rd–5th; Russian SFSR championship (1935) – 4th; Leningrad masters tournament (1935) – 3rd; Leningrad championship (1936) – 2nd. We have to admit that this track record, while respectable in and of itself, did not fully reflect Rauzer's talent and creative potential.

1936) and Alekhine – Foltys (Margate 1937).

* * *

In 1934, Rauzer moved to Leningrad. His living conditions improved a bit. He got a room in the dormitory of the Physical Education Workers House, on Khalturin Street (by the way, not far from the Central Chess Club). Compared with Kiev, which did not have a chess club at all (it opened only in 1936), he had more opportunities for coaching work. Rauzer had a remarkable knack for teaching. L. Rudenko, the future first Soviet women's chess champion, was among his Leningrad pupils. And still, Rauzer's life was full of hardships. I remember being startled by the words in a letter I received from my friend: "I came to the game hungry, as usual."

It was hard to adapt to the unusual atmosphere of relationships between the Leningrad masters, who never acknowledged Rauzer as one of "their own". This especially showed during the first city championship in which he took part (1936). Three rounds before the finish, Rauzer had a two-point lead, winning both games against his main rival, V. Ragozin, in great style. However, Ragozin won all three remaining games, while Rauzer only managed to score a half-point. The "honor" of Leningrad chess was saved.

In the aforementioned article "In Defense of Chess Classicism",

Rauzer wrote that the classical style "requires great and continuous analytical work". First and foremost, he meant himself. This work did not have any psychological or emotional relaxation, he fully wore himself out.

Master A. Batuev described a rather colorful episode in his "Chess Novellas", published after his death. It happened at the 1935 Russian SFSR championship in Gorky.

"My functions as the captain of the Leningrad team included strictly watching over the team's fitness regimen, and Rauzer always caused me a lot of trouble. He was an obsessive chess analysis fanatic who eschewed sleep and food in his search for the correct continuation in whatever opening structure he was analyzing. He firmly believed that 1.e2-e4 won if both sides played correctly. Rauzer possessed a huge analytical talent and was an outstanding theoretician. His opening research and discoveries still remain a treasure of the Soviet chess school. The Ruy Lopez, Sicilian and French defenses, and many other openings, are still played according to his recommendations.

And so, Rauzer once played 1.e4 and lost. In the evening, he didn't show up for dinner, and we had to ask the restaurant management to deliver the caviar to his room. On the next day, he didn't show up for breakfast either. I thought that he was too tired after a night of analysis, so I decided not to disturb him.

Around lunch time I finally went up to his room. Our 'Ruzia', as we jokingly called him, sat on his bed, wearing only his undergarments. Chess pieces were scattered on the floor. It was complete chaos. The caviar sandwiches were left untouched.

'Get washed, get dressed and let's go to the restaurant immediately,' I said. Rauzer refused stubbornly. 'Look, as the team captain, I have no right to go to the playing hall without you. Do you want me to pull your trousers on you, like you're a baby? Don't forget that I also have a game to play.' Only with great effort did I manage to bring him to lunch."

I'll also quote Panov here: "I once asked about his (Rauzer's) work schedule, and when he answered, I was stunned by his fanaticism. 'You know,' he said, 'I usually get up at 6 a.m., get to my analysis board and work until night, with short breaks for eating. Unfortunately,' Rauzer sighed, 'I just can't make myself work on theory of the game for more than 16 hours a day! My head can't endure more.'"

Alas, Rauzer's head ultimately couldn't endure this punishing schedule. In the next Leningrad championship (1937/38), he had to drop out after the first round.

When I arrived in Leningrad a year later, I immediately visited my friend in the psychiatric hospital where he was being treated. It seemed that none of my stories or questions provoked any reaction from him. He lay there indifferently, wrapped up in a bed sheet. But when we met again after Rauzer got discharged from the hospital (this happened in Kiev in summer 1940, during the 12th Soviet Championship semi-final, where we both played), he touched upon the sad subject himself. "I understood everything you said," he told me, "and I can repeat it all verbatim."

In the last tournament of his life, Rauzer enjoyed a good start. The press happily wrote "this talented master is again in fighting form." However, the strain of the competition was too much to bear for his nervous system, and his performance deteriorated in the second half. Our encounter happened during that time, in the 13th round.

Rauzer got a notable advantage with black out of the opening (a Vienna Game), but then the struggle turned sharper.

No. 18.

A. Konstantinopolsky – V. Rauzer
Kiev 1940

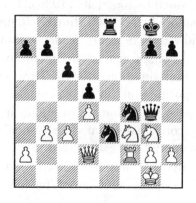

26...h5?

The simplest continuation was to prevent the white knight's jump to e5 with 26...♕g6.

27.♘e5

Now black can't play 27...♖xe5 28.dxe5 ♘exg2 29.♖xg2 ♘h3+ 30.♔h1 ♕f3 due to 31.♕e2 ♕xc3 32.e6+−.

27...♕g5

This hoping for 28.♕xe3 ♘h3+ is unrealistic.

28.♔h1 ♘g6?

And this is a miscalculation; black had to defend his queen – 28...♘e6.

29.♖f5 ♕h6 30.♖xh5

Black resigned.

Of course, we couldn't have known that this was our last encounter over the board. Over 15 years (1926–1940), we played 26 games, including 4 training games and 4 correspondence games. At first, Rauzer enjoyed a huge advantage, but later, after I became a master too, in 1933, the fights became more equal. Still, the overall score in tournament games was in Rauzer's favor (9.5–8.5, +8–7=3). Moreover, he won a game that could have become "the game of my life", in the 10th Soviet Championship; it was precisely this point that I lost in the penultimate round that prevented me from winning the championship. Of course, this did not sour our friendship. In the training and correspondence games I held the advantage: +5–0=3.

* * *

We do not have information about the last months of Rauzer's life. At my request, the well-known Leningrad chess player and organizer Y. Rosenstein, an old friend of Rauzer's, joined the search effort. According to his research, in late 1940, Rauzer was again hospitalized in a mental institution. He was discharged on 30th December and was never admitted again. We can only guess what happened to him afterwards. Quoting Shakespeare, "The rest is silence..."

900,000 Leningrad residents perished during the horrible siege. This sorrowful and heroic martyrology includes, among others, the name of the pride and joy of Soviet chess, Vsevolod Alfredovich Rauzer, as well as that of his mother, Varvara Grigorievna. I dedicate this article to their blessed memory.

The Opening Creations of Vsevolod Rauzer

Mikhail Yudovich and Fedor Fogelevich[12]

Opening theory in the USSR has developed with exceptional depth and precision. The analyses of Soviet theoreticians are at the center of attention of the world's chess press. The world's greatest theoreticians – Alekhine, world champion M. Euwe and others – widely use rich opening ideas that were introduced to chess theory by Soviet masters. Our analysts, especially the young ones, boldly create new ways of development, refuting long-established chess templates. Creative initiative, the will to win, boldness and precision – this is what characterizes the work of our young masters.

The leading position in modern theoretical development belongs to the Leningrad player V. A. Rauzer. The best Soviet masters play the openings very carefully and even with some degree of fear when they face Rauzer at the board, because it's impossible to know how deeply and up to which move their dangerous adversary has developed some new opening variation. In his analysis, Rauzer goes his own way, he organically eschews the templates. The brilliant analytical talent of the young Soviet theoretician has managed to resurrect quite a few opening problems that were relegated to the archives. Rauzer's tremendous advantage as a theoretician is that he manages to find entire coherent development systems in almost every modern opening, rather than just individual pretty and strong moves.

Since the game Lasker – Maroczy (New York 1924), the line 1.e4 e6 2.d4 d5 3.♘c3 ♗b4 4.e5 c5 5.a3 cxd4 has been considered better for black because of 6.axb4 dxc3 7.bxc3 ♕c7! with strong pressure along the c-file. Rauzer himself wrote that as he remembered that well-known game, he noticed the lack of logic behind

---

[12] The journal of publication and date of this article are unknown, but clearly in the period 1935 to 1937, as it refers to Euwe as being the world champion at the time. Fogelevich was born in 1909. He is mentioned by Vasily Smyslov as head of the Zamoskvorechye chess club in Moscow in the mid-1930s (see *Smyslov on the Couch* by Genna Sosonko, Elk and Ruby, 2018, p. 196), while the Russian-language *Jewish Chess Encyclopedia* (Russian Chess House, 2016, p. 267) provides a brief tournament biography. He went missing in action while serving in the Soviet armed forces in September 1941 during World War II (see records of the Central Archive of the Russian Defense Ministry https://poisk.re/loss/76329940).

7.bxc3. Since it's not beneficial for white to hold onto the c3 pawn, why then should he waste tempi on capturing the black pawn?

Rauzer drew very interesting conclusions from this seemingly unimportant detail. As a result, he found the famous continuation 7.♘f3!

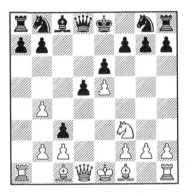

Sacrificing a pawn, but getting a very strong attack. If 7...cxb2 then 8.♗xb2, winning another tempo for development. Tournament practice shows that black's lag in development and weakness of the dark squares are not compensated by the extra pawn. Since 1933, following the game Rauzer – Alatortsev (Soviet Championship), the move 7.♘f3! has become one of the classical lines of the French Defense.

After the game Rauzer – I. Rabinovich (1933 Soviet Championship), the popular variation of the Caro-Kann, 1.e4 c6 2.d4 d5 3.♘c3 dxe4 4.♘xe4 ♘f6 5.♘xf6+ exf6, was positionally refuted. It seems that black had managed to solve the development problems in the opening

quite well, with the doubled f-pawns protecting the e5 and g5 squares. But here's what Rauzer managed to find in this position:

"After 5...exf6, white has got an extra pawn on the queenside, while black's kingside pawns are doubled. Thus, white's plan is as follows: castle short, push the queenside pawns and convert his essentially extra d-pawn. The plan is simple and clear. To implement this plan, it's very important to put the bishop on g2 to support the pawn onslaught, which should go as follows: c4, b4, a4, then c5 and b5 or (instead of c5) d5, depending on circumstances. By the way, the move g2-g3 kills the activity of black's dark-squared bishop along the d6-h2 diagonal, bolstering white's kingside and his king's position. If one carefully considers all the features of the move 6.g3!, it becomes clear that this is the best move in this position."

The flawless win in the game against Rabinovich brilliantly confirmed the correctness and concreteness of the intended plan, and the Rauzer system now holds an honorable place in Caro-Kann theory.

In one of the most fashionable lines of the Sicilian Defense that has given white a number of brilliant victories in international tournaments of the last few years, Rauzer, after 1.e4 c5 2.♘f3 ♘c6 3.d4 cxd4 4.♘xd4 ♘f6 5.♘c3 d6 6.♗e2 g6 7.0-0 ♗g7 8.♘b3 0-0 9.f4, proposed a bold and original idea based on the correct evaluation of the occurring position: 9...b5!.

Black, who threatens b4 and ♘xe4, gets excellent play in all lines. For instance: 10.♘xb5 ♘xe4 or 10.♗xb5 ♘xe4! 11.♘xe4 (or 11.♗xc6) 11...♕b6+ and ♕xb5 or ♕xc6; or 10.♗f3 (seemingly the best) 10...b4 11.♘d5 ♘xd5 12.exd5 ♘a5 or first 12...♕b6+ 13.♔h1 ♘a5.

"The move 9...b5, based on defending the c6 knight with ♕b6+, exploits all the disadvantages of white's position." (Rauzer in *Shakhmaty v SSSR*, No. 11, 1935.)

Of Rauzer's other numerous findings, a solid system in the same Sicilian Defense especially stands out, after 1.e4 c5 2.♘f3 ♘c6 (now black usually plays 2...d6 to avoid the Rauzer system) 3.d4 cxd4 4.♘xd4 ♘f6 5.♘c3 d6 6.♗g5! This system started a real revolution in the theory of the Sicilian Defense, and theoreticians are still hotly arguing about it.

The Opening Theory Classic

Efim Lazarev
(This article was first published in Shakhmaty v SSSR *No. 6, 1975)* [13]

...In spring 1925, at the age of 16, he achieved his first success, rather modest by modern standards: he shared 2nd–3rd place in the Kiev championship. Two years later, Vsevolod Rauzer became the champion of Ukraine. He took part in six Soviet Championships in 1927–1937; in 1929 he earned the master's title, and in 1933, he achieved his best success – 6th prize. He was one of the strongest chess players in our country at the time.

But these results do not reflect Vsevolod Rauzer's true value to chess. His theoretical contribution was so huge that even today Rauzer remains our contemporary. He made opening discoveries that outlived their times and their author for decades. Nevertheless, almost nothing was written about Rauzer. Old publications and memories of his contemporaries give only fragmentary information about this very talented chess player and his grim fate.

A Room in Apartment 48

Vsevolod Rauzer lived with his mother in Kiev, on Engels Street, which climbs steeply from Khreshchatyk Street to Pechersk Street, in building 13 (apartment 48), renting one room. This room certainly deserves to be remembered: it was a "chess club" of sorts, frequented by the young owner's peers. Four of them later also became masters (A. Konstantinopolsky, B. Ratner, A. Zamikhovsky, and E. Polyak).

"It was very interesting to take part in Rauzer's analysis," Zamikhovsky says. "He showed us a lot of things we never knew. Sometimes, however, we thought that he was going too far from what, in our opinion, was required by simple tournament practice. But it was hard to argue with him: Rauzer knew much more than we did. Only Konstantinopolsky could argue with him on any chess topics on equal terms..."

Rauzer's other friends of youth – B. Y. Ratner and E. I. Polyak – also told me about him. Their memories paint a picture of a fair-haired, gray-eyed young man, almost an albino, who belonged to a common type of quirky, absent-minded men. He was so

---

[13]   Efim Lazarev (1933-2013) was a Ukrainian Master of Sport at chess. Thanks to his friend Mykola Fuzik for finding the original publication.

engrossed with problems in chess that he was very impractical in mundane tasks, and so his friends had a hard time getting him even a modest job as a financial department's courier.

In 1934, Rauzer moved from Kiev to Leningrad, where he, already one of the strongest Soviet masters, obtained better working and living conditions.

The "club" in apartment 48 had existed for almost ten years. It left a small, but notable trace in some sections of chess theory.

Against Kling and Horwitz

Rauzer's first published article concerned a rare endgame, "bishop with rook pawns". It came out in 1928 in the *Shakhmatny Listok* magazine. The 20 year-old author analyzed the following position:

Even though the bishop does not control the promotion square, Rauzer proved that white won if he was to move (1.♗h2!), pushing the black king so far from the safe haven

that white manages to capture the a4 pawn and then make it to a8 first.

If black is to move, it's a draw. Rauzer established a "drawing zone" for the black king, limited by a polyline a8-h8-h6-f4-e5-d4-a7.

Later, the magazine published A. Troitsky's article that criticized this analysis. The legendary study composer correctly reproached Rauzer for his statement that this endgame was never properly analyzed, and cited the works of Kling and Horwitz (1851), Berger, Teichmann and his own as the proof. Troitsky came to the conclusion that the analyses of Rauzer's predecessors were more accurate.

The effect of this criticism was unexpected: three and a half months later, the same magazine published another article by Rauzer, where he admitted that he did not know about the previous analyses and then went on to refute those of them that disagreed with his conclusions. The editors showed Rauzer's manuscript to Troitsky before publishing. The famous master meticulously studied the arguments of his lesser-known opponent and had to admit that he was right. This admission was published together with Rauzer's new article, under the title "Rauzer's Analysis Is Correct!"

Thus, a very young chess player who didn't even know the works of endgame classics managed to refute generally accepted conclusions and contributed a new word to theory, showing his outstanding analytical skill.

Rauzer tried his hand in chess composition as well. He published his first endgame study, reflecting the ideas of his analysis, in *Shakhmatny Listok*.

White to play and draw

With subtle maneuvers, the white king manages to force the push a7-a6 and makes it to the drawing zone in time.

1.♔b5!

But not 1.♔c5?

1...♗f1+

After 1...♗b7, there's a good reply 2.♔c5!, winning a tempo to attack the bishop later.

2.♔c6 ♚d2

3.♔c7!

After 3.♔b7? a6, white is exactly one tempo late to the drawing zone.

3...a6

Otherwise 4.a6!

4.♔d6 ♗g2 5.♔e5 ♚e3 6.♔f5 ♗f3 7.♔g5!

7.♔e5? ♗e4! and wins.

7...♚e4 8.♔h4 ♚f4 9.♔h3 ♗c6 10.♔h2!

(A final subtlety: 10.♔h4? ♗d7!), and the white king is in the drawing zone.

Rauzer published a thorough analysis of this endgame in the 1936 *Chess Yearbook*.

Ariadne's Thread

We should first say that Vsevolod Rauzer's opening theory views were not fully consistent, and because of that, both his statements and his games received polar opposite evaluations from his contemporaries.

Rauzer's ideal was a style that he called "classical". Not everyone assigns the same meaning to this word. Rauzer, for instance, gave this name to the desire for objectively best play, for absolute truth in chess – for getting as close to it as humanly possible under tournament conditions.

Rauzer was convinced that a scientific approach to chess was the right way to achieve this goal. He thought that it was necessary to study the strategic content of the most important openings as deeply as possible, and he would search for ways out of the most complicated opening labyrinths with fanatical stubbornness, not deterred by any difficulties.

Steinitz's theory, which he unquestioningly trusted at first, served as his Ariadne's thread. And Tarrasch's *Die Modern Schachpartie*, captivating him with clarity of views and precise statements, became his go to book. The early Rauzer could have said in good conscience, "There's no chess god but Steinitz, and Tarrasch is his messenger."

In time, however, practical and theoretical discussions with other Soviet chess players who adhered to broader views helped Rauzer to overcome his excessive dogmatism.

His first games were immature. He followed Steinitz's advice too literally, "do not combine, but prevent combinations with the simplest means possible." Underestimation of concrete tactical factors cost Rauzer dearly in tournaments. As he understood it, Rauzer came to a conclusion that he had to learn from Tarrasch, who was more flexible in his play, without Steinitz's penchant to jump at polemical extremes in tournaments.

Here's how Rauzer argued, in his article "In Defense of Chess Classicism" (*Shakhmaty v SSSR*, 1934), against the conclusion

(published in the same magazine a bit earlier) that Tarrasch didn't understand our era in chess: "On the contrary, our era was not yet able to understand and appreciate Tarrasch, because it had moved away from the classical school that gives full scope to use the combinational element to any player who believes in the principles of this school and is able to discover all the resources of a position! My years of personal experience and the help from a group of Kiev players led me to the conclusion that classical style was a synthesis of positional and combinational play. You might ask, why then didn't it take hold if it's able to satisfy any demands, any tastes? It's not hard to understand. The classical style is too impractical... A chess player who cultivates it always faces the danger of getting lost in his own complications. The classical style requires a very deep knowledge of sharp opening lines, requires great and continuous analytical work, huge work by the memory. In exchange, it offers the master some inconsistent successes that sometimes hinge on the failure of some misunderstood opening line. No wonder that those contemporaries of Tarrasch who were not like the cowardly 'pacifists' Schlechter and Teichmann successfully adhered to this style. No wonder that international professional masters, who depended financially too much on their successes, who are too distracted from analytical work by various tours and simultaneous displays, adhere to a 'vulgarly practical' style rather than a 'classical' one, to a style of 'complications with a draw in the back pocket'. Who would dare to shoulder such a burden as the classical style?"

Even though these thoughts do have a grain of truth about them, they aren't all indisputable. For instance, one can argue that Alekhine, not Tarrasch, was the epitome of the "classical style" as defined by Rauzer... But Rauzer was blinded by the name of his idol, ascribing too much to him.

He harshly criticized Nimzowitsch's innovative ideas and opening novelties, thinking, for instance, that the move ♗b4 in the French Defense or after 1.d4 ♘f6 2.c4 e6 3.♘c3 was anti-positional, because it weakened the dark squares after trading that bishop for a knight.

He saw nothing good in a kingside fianchetto either. In 1937, Rauzer wrote, "My evaluation of Reti's teaching was always negative. I thought and still think that as soon as black gets his rook away from a8 and plays b7-b6 or b7-b5, the g2 bishop will be out of play. In addition, it's not beneficial to trade it because this would weaken the light squares."

Categorical and dogmatic – very Tarrasch-style. Too wide a generalization on too narrow a

base. Still, this talented master often managed to prove his ideas in practice. Why? Because his analytical talent, even based on shaky theoretical grounds, still allowed him to find some brilliant opening ideas!

How a Novelty Is Born

Let's take a glance into Vsevolod Rauzer's creative lab for a second.

Here he studies, with great interest, the games collection of the great tournament in San Remo (1930), published in 1932. The game Vidmar – Alekhine, won by the world champion in brilliant style, attracts his attention. Of course, he admires black's virtuoso play. But he wouldn't have been Rauzer if he hadn't tried to understand why white ceded the initiative to black so easily after some solid opening play.

Rauzer wasn't satisfied by P. Romanovsky's annotation of the move 5.a3 (after 1.d4 e6 2.c4 ♘f6 3.♘c3 ♗b4 4.♕c2 d5): "A Tarrasch-style move. It's based on rejection of the idea that trading the bishop for the knight might be useful. White wastes time on defending some abstract principles as black seizes the center with a series of aggressive moves." Rauzer, who grew up admiring Tarrasch, was offended by the implicit suggestion that the move might not be the best solely because it's "Tarrasch-style".

"In addition," Rauzer wrote, interested in the relationship between the first impression about a move and its true value (which is very important for an over-the-board player), "I couldn't help but notice this line and its description in the tournament book. My first impression after 5.a3 ♗xc3+ 6.♕xc3 was favorable: the dark squares seemed somewhat weakened, and I thought that if the position opened up (for instance, after c7-c5), the game would be favorable for white thanks to his bishop pair. To check this first impression thoroughly, I decided to elaborate on this position and analyze it."

What did Rauzer find? First and foremost, after 6...♘e4 7.♕c2 ♘c6 8.e3 e5

that the move 9.f3? was an almost a losing mistake. But he didn't agree with the commentator who wrote that 9.cxd5 was also better for black after 9...♕xd5 10.♗c4 ♕a5+ 11.b4 ♘xb4 12.♕xe4 ♘c2+

13.♔d1 ♘xa1, and the knight is not trapped. Rauzer found a "hole" in this line and proposed the bold move 13.♔e2! Now, after 13...♘xa1 14.♗b2, the black knight is doomed, and if black first checks on e1, then the e5 pawn is left defenseless, and the white king seems to be safe on f3...

Soon he got a chance to test this finding in the 1932 tournament of Kiev and Leningrad players. Alas! The game Rauzer – Konstantinopolsky continued: 13.♔e2 ♕e1+ 14.♔f3 ♘xa1, and then the author of the line, as he thought on his move, suddenly found that 15.♕xe5+ is met with 15...♗e6! 16.♗xe6 0-0!, and both white bishops are under attack. Confused, he played 15.♗b2 0-0 16.♕xe5, and after 16...♕d1+! 17.♘e2 ♕xh1 18.d5 f6 19.♕h5 ♕b1, black won.

A refutation? But then, Rauzer thought, it turns out that the "Tarrasch-style" move 5.a3 *is* bad after all. This cannot be, he decides, and eventually stops to analyze the position after 15.♗b2 0-0.

Here, instead of 16.♕xe5, white has the stunning move 16.♔g3!! He threatens 17.♘f3 ♕xh1 18.♘g5 or 17.h3 and 18.♔h2.

Even now, this move still stands the test of time! The whole line is considered beneficial for white.

The conclusions that Rauzer made from his discovery and published in *Shakhmaty v SSSR* (1934) are, however, another matter: "The lines I've shown illustrate well the strength of 'Tarrasch-style' moves." The editor's remark correctly states that the same lines could easily be credited to Chigorin or Alekhine.

What, then, do Rauzer's lines show us? Only that black didn't play in the best possible way in the game Vidmar – Alekhine either. Modern theory considers 7...♘c6 weaker than 7...c5.

From 1.d4 to 1.e4

For a long time, Rauzer only started the game with 1.d4. The game against M. Botvinnik in the 7th Soviet Championship [described on pages 16-17, in Konstantinopolsky's article] became the first step towards a re-evaluation.

Subsequent tournament practice showed that black had enough resources to equalize against Rauzer's plan. Who knows, perhaps this game was indeed the one that turned Rauzer off 1.d4. Later, he wrote that this move allows black, if he wants, to draw the game with 1...d5! easily.

Science knows quite a lot of naive fallacies that, nevertheless, benefited it in great ways because they pushed scientists towards new discoveries. A similar thing happened with Rauzer: after his disappointment in closed openings, he turned his attention to 1.e4, where his analytical work bore much more fruit!

He delivered his first blow in the French Defense, or, to be precise, in the system 1.e4 e6 2.d4 d5 3.♘c3 ♗b4 4.e5 c5, which was quite popular for black back then, because white couldn't find any better reply than 5.♗d2. The continuation 5.a3 was long considered unfavorable due to 5...cxd4 6.axb4 dxc3,

and after 7.bxc3 ♕c7! (Em. Lasker – Maroczy, New York 1924), black has a good game. However, Rauzer, in the first round of the 8ᵗʰ Soviet Championship (1933), played 7.♘f3! against Alatortsev.

Rauzer's idea was so unexpected for his time that it wasn't immediately appreciated. For instance, here's how V. Ragozin and V. Sozin commented on 7.♘f3 in *Shakhmaty v SSSR*:

"A novelty that Rauzer used to try and revive an old line that was mothballed a long time ago. It should be checked along the lines of whether the pawn sacrifice is correct, and so black should have played 7...cxb2 8.♗xb2 f5 9.♕d4 ♘h6 or 9...♘e7, and we think that black equalizes easily."

However, those who tried to follow these recommendations saw that white had more than enough compensation for the pawn. 8...f5 can be met in different ways by white: 9.♗d3 or 9.exf6 ♘xf6 10.♗d3 with a strong attacking position. In the game Panov – Verlinsky (Moscow 1934), black played 8...♘e7, but suffered a quick and crushing defeat. Rauzer's idea "buried" the entire line with 5...cxd4 and rehabilitated the move 5.a3.

We're speaking about the idea, rather than the move 7.♘f3 itself, because an even stronger continuation was discovered later: 7.♕g4!, with the same intentions. But this was already movement forward along an open road.

Operation Dragon

After the French, Rauzer turned his attention to the Sicilian Defense, where the Dragon Variation was popular in the early 1930s, with the following move order: 1.e4 c5 2.♘f3 ♘c6 3.d4 cxd4 4.♘xd4 ♘f6 (avoiding the Maroczy Bind – 4...g6 5.c4, which was rather feared by black players back then) 5.♘c3 d6 (avoiding 5...g6 6.♘xc6 bxc6 7.e5 as well) 6.♗e2 g6.

But there, things didn't go as smoothly as in the fight against the French Defense. Sicilian players struck quite a few blows against Rauzer in retaliation. Yet this didn't dishearten him – it only encouraged him to search even more. Rauzer's battle with the Dragon is somewhat similar to a well-known "missile versus armor" story-line; it can probably even be summarized as a thrilling short story, "Operation Dragon".

White's first strike. Instead of 6.♗e2, Rauzer finds 6.♗g5! Now the reply 6...g6 is more than dubious, and the Dragon players are in knockdown. It's now necessary to go for the Scheveningen with 6...e6, but in this case, Rauzer had a deeply thought-out plan with long castling and a direct attack in store.

His game against V. Makogonov (9ᵗʰ Soviet Championship, 1934) is characteristic in this regard; the Rauzer Attack arose after a slightly different move order:

No. 19. Sicilian Defense
V. Rauzer – V. Makogonov (42)
Leningrad 1934

1.e4 c5 2.♘f3 e6 3.d4 cxd4 4.♘xd4 ♘f6 5.♘c3 d6 6.♗g5! a6 7.♕f3 ♘bd7 8.0-0-0 ♕c7 9.♕g3 b5.

10.♗xb5!
This sacrifice has now become a typical technique.
10...axb5 11.♘dxb5 ♕a5 12.♘xd6+ ♗xd6 13.♖xd6 ♘h5 14.♕h4 h6 15.♗e3 ♘hf6 16.f3 ♖b8 17.♖d4 and white went on to win.

"Ever since this game was played, entire volumes of analytical research have been dedicated to the Rauzer Attack, there are hundreds of articles written about it, it's been tested in thousands of games... Decades of tournament practice has shown that the invention of the Ukrainian theoretician is organically connected with the positional essence of this line and will live on for years and years." (A. Kotov)

Black strikes back. A new move order was tested: **2...d6! 3.d4 cxd4 4.♘xd4 ♘f6 5.♘c3 g6.**

Now, white cannot avoid the Dragon Variation. Rauzer had to increase the strength of the "missile". At first, he tried the classical line, 6.♗e2 ♗g7 7.0-0 ♘c6 8.♘b3 0-0. However, he failed to find anything substantial for white. Moreover, when white deployed a new attacking plan in the game Romanovsky – I. Rabinovich (Moscow International Tournament, 1935): 9.f4 (before developing the bishop to e3) 9...♗e6 10.f5 ♗xb3 11.axb3 with an advantage for white, Rauzer came up with the reply 9...b5!, which he published in *Shakhmaty v SSSR*.

10.♗xb5 is met with 10...♘xe4! Therefore, the whole plan with 9.f4

was shot down by Rauzer. "The refutation of the Dragon Variation," he wrote in that article, "will be found in some other way."

White's second strike. Still, even after 5...g6, white plays **6.♗g5**, implementing the same plan with long castling as in the Scheveningen. In the game against Ragozin at the Young Masters Tournament (Leningrad 1936), there followed:

6...♗g7 7.♕d2 ♘c6 8.0-0-0.

A principled move and a subtle trap at the same time.

8...♘xe4 9.♘xe4 ♘xd4?

9...♗xd4 was the lesser evil.

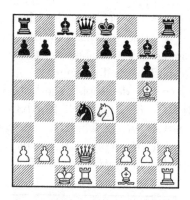

10.♘f6+! exf6 11.♕xd4 0-0 12.♗f4 with a positional advantage.

Black strikes back again. In the same tournament, Kan avoided 8...♘xe4 against Rauzer, preferring **8...0-0**. As it turned out, Rauzer had also prepared a tactic here, but it quickly became clear that his plan was not the best: after **9.♘xc6 bxc6 10.e5 ♘e8 11.exd6 ♘xd6 12.♗xe7 ♕xe7 13.♕xd6 ♕g5+** white had won a pawn, but fallen under attack.

White's third strike. The same tournament, the game against Chekhover: **5...g6 6.f3! ♗g7 7.♗e3 0-0 8.♕d2 ♘c6 9.0-0-0.**

It was later found that 9.♗c4, preventing d6-d5, was stronger. But that's nothing other than a technical detail. Rauzer's line, which bears his name, still remains a formidable weapon against the Dragon.

Rauzer opened an entire chapter in opening theory. His opponent, who was forced to become the first critic of that new plan, failed to find the strongest counterplay, and after **9...♘xd4 10.♗xd4 ♗e6 11.♔b1!** (preventing 11...♕a5 due to 12.♘d5!) **11...♖c8 12.h4 ♘h5 13.♗xg7 ♔xg7 14.♘d5!** (implementing centralization, which serves as the main weapon against the Dragon in the usual lines) **14...♗xd5 15.exd5,** got into a difficult position.

Was Levenfish Right?

In the Young Masters Tournament (1936), Rauzer shared

first place with Chekhover. Both sporting and creative-wise, this tournament, despite several setbacks and sometimes poor technique in converting the advantage he got after his novelties, was probably the pinnacle of Rauzer's chess career.

And yet, Rauzer's performances at the time drew some criticism. Here's what G. Levenfish wrote in his article "The Ways of the Soviet Masters" (*64*, 5th November 1936):

"In Rauzer's play, opening system analysis has suppressed the main essence of chess art, and so the talented master has turned into a dry dogmatist."

Rauzer got very offended after reading these words. He was already criticized for his analysis, he had already got the ironic nickname of "Debutmeister" ["Opening Master"], and then this article came out... And so, in the same newspaper (15th January 1937), he called Levenfish's words "not thoughtful enough". Rauzer wrote:

"The All-Union Young Masters Tournament clearly showed me that my weakest side is endgame play, and I play most precisely in the middlegame... The opening is not even my strongest side... The reason for my partial success in the middlegame, in my view, is that I have internalized the middlegame principles as described by Tarrasch in his book *Die Modern Schachpartie* and firmly believe in them. I also think that, in the middlegame, you

can develop and widely use positional intuition that can extend even to tactics (for instance, using intuition to determine the strength and tempo of the attack or the strength of a certain threat)."

We have already seen how contradictory Rauzer's views were, despite the seeming consistency. Now we see how this contradictoriness prevented even renowned experts from correctly evaluating his play, separating the important from the nonessential. The somewhat dogmatic interpretation of general strategy was one of those "nonessentials", rightfully highlighted by Levenfish. In our time, it's easy to see that Rauzer's dogmatism, stemming from overestimation of Tarrasch's views, indeed most often manifested itself in the middlegame, which he erroneously considered his strongest side and where he so often spilled the advantage he got out of the opening, which damaged his results.

But these drawbacks of Rauzer have been forgotten – together with the tournament tables where he would sometimes get more zeroes than he deserved. On the other hand, his opening research has retained its long-term value. A. Kotov was correct in his assessment in the book *Work, Talent, Victory* (1969):

"Ukrainian master Vsevolod Alfredovich Rauzer was an outstanding opening theoretician. His straightforwardness and principled approach were best encapsulated in his catchy slogan: white plays 1.e4 and wins! Rauzer was a strong over-the-board master, even though his contribution to opening theory was much greater than his tournament achievements. Rauzer played 1.e2-e4 and methodically refuted all defensive methods that are possible in reply to this move... It was hard to play against the man whose conviction in the unquestioned strength of 1.e4 inspired him to find brilliant ideas. This was probably the first case when the masters got literally befuddled, not knowing what opening to choose against Rauzer... This selfless dedication to an idea gave a great impulse to the development of chess openings. The thankful chess world will never forget Vsevolod Rauzer – one of the world's best theoreticians."

The Special Prize

In 1937, Rauzer took 8th place in the 20-player Soviet Championship. An honorable performance. As before, he could have probably done even better had his play been more practical. For instance, in the game against Ilyin-Zhenevsky, who decided to go for the Philidor Defense instead of well-known plans, Rauzer, after **1.e4 e5 2.♘f3 d6 3.d4 exd4 4.♘xd4 ♘f6**, played a poor novelty, **5.f3?** The idea is clear: white wants to play c2-c4, seizing the d5 square. But this novelty, invented over the board (in home analysis, Rauzer would have surely rejected it outright: it's

unlikely that he seriously spent time on lines such as the one used by black), was flawed.

After **5...d5! 6.e5 ♘fd7 7.f4 ♘c6 8.♘xc6 bxc6 9.♗d3 ♕h4+ 10.g3 ♕h3 11.♕f3 ♗c5 12.♗e3 0-0 13.♘d2 f6,** white's center fell apart like a house of cards...

Still, Rauzer remained true to himself in his favorite work, and he submitted three of his games for the theoretical novelty competition organized by *64*.

Against Budo and Konstantinopolsky, Rauzer deployed novelties in the Caro-Kann Defense: 1.e4 c6 2.♘f3 d5 3.♘c3 (Rauzer's favorite weapon against the Caro-Kann) 3...dxe4 4.♘xe4 ♘f6 5.♘xf6+ gxf6 6.g3. Unlike many other Rauzer innovations, this plan didn't stay in tournament practice for long, giving way to the simpler 6.d4.

The game against I. Rabinovich was an entirely different matter, however:

1.e4 e5 2.♘f3 ♘c6 3.♗b5 ♘f6 4.0-0 ♗e7 5.♖e1 d6 6.d4 ♗d7 7.♘c3 exd4 8.♘xd4 0-0 9.♗xc6 bxc6

Master Rauzer. Friendly cartoon by Galba

"This whole line has been known for a long time, but the subsequent game plan developed by Rauzer," N. Riumin wrote in his review, "is very interesting. With the next three moves, white threatens to play e4-e5 and forces black to make the weakening move c6-c5."

10.♗f4 ♖e8 11.h3 h6 12.♕f3 c5 13.♘b3 ♖b8 14.e5!

with an advantage for white. Even today, Rauzer's plan (albeit in a different technical interpretation) remains a strong weapon against the Steinitz Defense.

In addition, Alexander Konstantinopolsky confirmed Rauzer's authorship of the system used by black in the game Ilyin-Zhenevsky – Konstantinopolsky: 1.e4 c5 2.♘f3 d6 3.c3 ♘f6 4.♕c2 ♕c7.

So, four theoretically valuable games in total. Even though the *64* award went to S. Belavenets and M. Yudovich for an even more striking discovery, the editors still gave Rauzer a special prize "For a Set of Valuable Theoretical Novelties."

16 Hours per Day...

And so, our hero became a renowned author of lots of opening innovations at the age of just 29. Obviously, hard work was the main source of them. According to Rauzer himself, he studied chess for up to 16 hours per day. This led the talented master to a premature exhaustion of energy. After winning a match against D. Rovner in summer 1937 (10–6), Rauzer fell ill and stopped playing.

After 1937, Rauzer hardly ever played in tournaments. The semi-final of the 12th Soviet Championship (Kiev 1940) was his last performance. But this was not the same Rauzer anymore... He enjoyed a good start, winning two games and drawing six, but a loss completely threw him off balance, and Rauzer lost another five games in a row. The end result: shared 13th–15th place out of 17. But, what's more important, he didn't show anything brilliant in the opening. His strength was depleted.

After this tournament, Rauzer completely quit over-the-board chess. And in 1941, he perished during the Siege of Leningrad, aged just 33...

Big Things Are Best Seen at a Distance

Vsevolod Rauzer was one of those players whose work allowed Soviet chess thought to overtake that of foreigners in the 1930s. His original personality was characterized by the spirit of search and creativity, exerting certain influence on the new generation of Soviet masters who reached world class level in sporting competitions. Vsevolod Rauzer's research work is not only a monument to his period: it still largely belongs in the modern day.

The classic of opening theory (today, we can say that this is no exaggeration), Vsevolod Rauzer certainly deserves a monograph written by a strong master who was his contemporary and comrade in arms.

Vsevolod Rauzer

Mikhail Botvinnik
(This article was first published in 64 – Chess Review, *1990)*

We first met at the Soviet Championship in Moscow [in 1927]; I was 16 years old, he was 19.

Lean, young, with an angelic face – there was something childish, naive in his image. While his opponents were thinking, Rauzer walked around the hall clasping his hands behind his back, to avoid slouching.

Rauzer shared a room with the Leningrad player Perfilyev in the Liverpool Hotel in Stoleshnikov Lane. Berman, the chairman of the Leningrad chess section, attended the tournament, and all the Leningrad players gathered in Perfilyev's room. They found a single room for Rauzer and asked him to move, so that Berman could join Perfilyev... Rauzer refused adamantly: "I am already used to this room. If I move, this might affect my game..."

I liked that reply, and looked at the young Kiev player with respect. However, the cunning Model decided to test the young man's sense of humor: "If you don't move out, then Perfilyev will, Berman will move in, and he's a loud snorer..."

Alas, Rauzer immediately agreed to move!

His play at that tournament was somewhat weak and passive – it seemed that he was too inexperienced.

Two years later, at the Soviet Championship in Odessa, he was unrecognizable. In the last round of the quarter-final, he crushed none other than Riumin with black, qualified for the semi-final and earned his masters title. Another two years later, we met in Moscow again, at the next Soviet Championship. At the end of the tournament, he defeated Riumin again, which allowed me to win the title.

Vsevolod Alfredovich's play was uneven, his mood would suddenly change, even during the course of a single game. Until a certain moment, he played with exceptional strength, and then abruptly crumbled and allowed his opponent to take him out basically with his bare hands. He was uncompromising – if he thought that his position was better, he wouldn't settle for a draw. For instance, in our well-known game in Leningrad (1933), he avoided a draw and was punished for that...

His opening analysis was tremendously deep. However, he was completely convinced that 1.e2-e4 won the game... Still, his systems in the Ruy Lopez, Sicilian Defense and other openings have withstood the test of time.

Unfortunately, his quirkiness slowly grew into an illness, and his chess skills declined before the war. Poor Rauzer perished during the Siege of Leningrad.

His opening research (and not only openings – he also produced some brilliant endgame analysis), with linked middlegame plans, gives us every reason to place V. Rauzer among the founders of the Soviet chess school, which defined the development of chess thought for many years.

At the 5th Soviet Championship, playing against Mikhail Botvinnik. Watching the game (left to right): V. Makogonov, Pavlov-Pianov, Rokhlin, and Model

No. 1. Queen's Pawn Game
Rauzer – Bogdanov
Inter-Circle Tournament
Kiev 1924
Annotated by V. Rauzer

1.♘f3 g6 2.♘c3 d5

It was better to play 2...d6, preparing c7-c5.

3.d4 ♗g7 4.♗f4 c6

4...♘f6 was more natural, preventing 5.e4.

5.e4 dxe4 6.♘xe4 ♗g4

Like in the Caro-Kann opening, the c8 bishop has no good squares.

7.♗c4 ♘f6

Black can't win the d4 pawn: 7...♗xf3 8.♕xf3 ♕xd4? 9.♗xf7+ ♔xf7 10.♗e5+ or 8...♗xd4? 9.♗xf7+ ♔xf7 10.♗c7+.

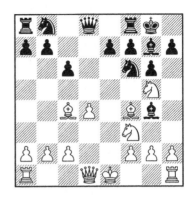

9.♘xf7! ♖xf7 10.♗xf7+ ♔xf7 11.♘e5+ ♔e8 12.♘xg4 ♘xg4 13.♕xg4 ♕xd4 14.0-0

Avoiding the complications after 14.♕c8+ and 15.♕xb7.

14...♘d7 15.♖ad1 ♘f6 16.♕xg6+ hxg6 17.♖xd4 ♘d5 18.♖e4 ♗xb2 19.♗g5 ♔f7 20.♖b1 ♗f6 21.♗xf6 ♘xf6 22.♖c4 ♖d8 23.♔f1 ♖d7

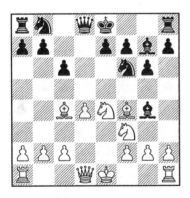

Now white cannot execute the combination 8.♗xf7+ ♔xf7 9.♘e5+ ♔f8 10.♘xg4 due to 10...♘xe4.

8.♘eg5 0-0

8...e6 is also bad: 9.♘xf7 ♔xf7 10.♘e5+ and 11.♘xg4; or 9...♗xf3 10.♘xd8 ♗xd1 11.♘xe6.

24.a4

White wants to ruin black's queenside with a2-a4-a5, which black prevents with ♘e8-d6; however, a new weakness then emerges – the g6 pawn, and the main play now switches to the kingside.

24...♘e8 25.♖b3 ♘d6 26.♖d3
♖c7 27.♖f4+ ♔g7 28.♖g3 ♘f7
29.h4 ♖d7 30.♖fg4 ♖d6 31.h5 g5
32.f4 ♖h6 33.♖e3 ♔f6 34.fxg5+
♘xg5 35.♖f4+ ♔g7 36.♖xe7+ ♔g8
37.♖xb7 ♖xh5 38.♖xa7

Black resigned.

Black wants to double rooks along the d-file, preventing d4-d5, and then exert pressure on the weak d4 pawn.

22.♘e5 ♘fd7 23.♘g4 ♘f6
24.♘e5 ♘fd7 25.♘d3 ♘f6 26.♘c5
♘c4

Now black need not fear d4-d5: after cxd5, the white knight on c5 is undefended. Black is planning to play b7-b6 and ♖cd7.

27.b3

No. 2. Slav Defense
Travin – Rauzer
4th Soviet Intercity Championship
Leningrad 1925
Annotated by V. Rauzer

**1.d4 d5 2.♘f3 ♘f6 3.c4 c6
4.e3 ♗f5 5.♘c3 e6 6.♗d3 ♗xd3
7.♕xd3 ♘bd7 8.0-0 ♗e7 9.e4 dxc4
10.♕xc4 0-0 11.♗g5 ♖c8 12.♖ad1
♕a5 13.♕b3 ♕b6 14.♕xb6 ♘xb6**

15.♖fe1

15.d5 ♗b4 16.d6 ♗xc3 17.bxc3
♘xe4 18.d7 ♘xg5 19.dxc8=♕
♘xf3+ 20.gxf3 ♖xc8 was dubious:
despite the equal material, white's
pawn structure is totally ruined.

**15...h6 16.♗h4 ♖fd8 17.h3
♔f8 18.♔f1 ♖c7 19.♘e5 ♘fd7
20.♗xe7+ ♔xe7 21.♘g4 ♘f6**

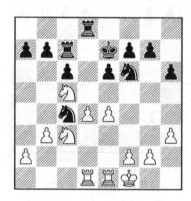

27...♘a5

This is better than 27...♘a3, because in the line 28.♖e2 b6 29.♘a6 ♖cd7 white has a brilliant defense: 30.♘b4.

28.♔e2 b6 29.♘5a4 ♖cd7 30.♔e3 g5 31.♘b2 b5 32.b4 ♘c4+ 33.♘xc4 bxc4 34.a3 h5

Intending to play h5-h4, ...♘h5 and ...♘f4.

35.g3 ♘e8 36.f4 f6 37.fxg5 fxg5 38.♖e2 ♘c7 39.a4 e5 40.♖ed2 ♘a6 41.b5 ♘b4

42.d5

After 42.dxe5 ♖xd2 43.♖xd2 ♖xd2 44.♔xd2 ♔e6, black regains the pawn and gets a drawn position.

42...cxd5 43.♘xd5+ ♘xd5+ 44.exd5 ♔d6 45.♖c2 ♖c8 46.♔e4

After 46.♖f2!? white is clearly better.

46...c3

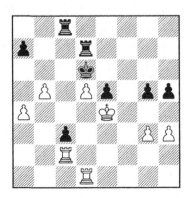

47.♔f5?

It was necessary to play 47.♖d3 with a probable draw.

47...♖f7+ 48.♔xg5

48.♔e4 g4 49.hxg4 hxg4 50.♖d3 ♖c4+ 51.♔e3 ♖f3+ 52.♔e2 ♖e4+ also lost.

48...♖g7+ 49.♔h4 ♖c4+ 50.g4 hxg4 51.♔g3 gxh3+ 52.♔h2 ♖g2+ 53.♖xg2 hxg2 54.♔xg2 c2 55.♖c1 ♔xd5 56.♔f3 ♔d4 57.♔e2 ♔c3

White resigned.

No. 3. Slav Defense
Rauzer – Kosolapov
4th Soviet Intercity Championship
Leningrad 1925

1.d4 d5 2.c4 c6 3.♘f3 ♘f6 4.cxd5 cxd5 5.♘c3 ♘c6 6.♗f4 e6 7.e3 ♗e7 8.♗d3 0-0 9.♖c1 ♘h5 10.♗g3 f5 11.♘e5 ♘xe5 12.♗xe5 ♘f6 13.0-0 a6 14.♘a4 ♗d6 15.♕c2 ♗xe5 16.dxe5 ♘g4 17.♕c3 ♕h4 18.h3

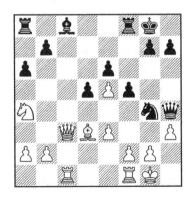

18...♘xe5?

A psychological mistake. 18...♘xf2 19.♘b6 ♘xh3+ drew the game. But could an old player be satisfied with such a result against a 16 year-old youngster?

After 20.gxh3 ♕g3+ 21.♔h1 ♕xh3+ 22.♔g1 ♕xe3+, black wins. White could equalize with 19.♗c2!? or 19.♖xf2!?

19.♘b6

19.♕xe5!? ♕xa4 20.♖c7+−

19...♘xd3   20.♕xd3   ♖b8 21.♕c3 ♕d8 22.♕e5 ♕xb6 23.♖c7 ♖f6 24.♖fc1 ♗d7

24...h6 25.♖xg7+.

25.♖xd7 ♖d8 26.♕d4 ♕a5 27.b4 Black resigned.

I managed to find the following two games in the contemporary newspaper *Proletarskay pravda ("Proletarian Truth")*. In both of these miniatures, Rauzer firmly (and prettily!) punished his opponents for tactical oversights.

No. 4. English Opening
Rauzer – Zhuk
Inter-Trade Union Tournament
Kiev 1926
Annotated by V. Rauzer

1.♘f3 e6 2.c4 ♘f6 3.♘c3 ♗b4 4.♕c2 0-0 5.e4 b6 6.e5 ♗xc3

A poor move. The black bishop is needed to protect the kingside. 6...♘e8 was better.

7.dxc3 ♘e8 8.♗d3 h6 9.♗e4

9.♗h7+! ♔h8 10.♗e4 ♘c6 11.♗xh6!+−.

9...♘c6 10.g4 f6

10...d5!? was better

11.h4 f5

This move was the reason for black's quick defeat. 11...fxe5 was a bit better.

12.gxf5 exf5 13.♗d5+ ♔h7

14.♗g5! hxg5

After this move black gets mated in six.

15.hxg5+ ♔g6 16.♘h4+ ♔xg5 17.f4+

Black resigned. *17...♔g4 18.♕g2+ ♔xf4 19.♘g6+ ♔e3 20.♕e2#. Proletarskay pravda, 8 April 1926.*

No. 5. Slav Defense
Rauzer – Grinberg
Kiev championship, 1926

1.d4 ♘f6 2.♘f3 d5 3.c4 c6 4.cxd5 cxd5 5.♘c3 ♘c6 6.♗f4 e6 7.e3 a6 8.♗d3 ♗d6 9.♗g3 0-0 10.♖c1 ♕e7?

After this, black falls under a deadly pin.

11.♗h4 ♗d7 12.0-0 ♖ac8 13.e4 dxe4 14.♘xe4 ♘b4 15.♘xf6+ gxf6 16.♗b1

The immediate 16.♘e5!? was stronger: 16...♖xc1 17.♕g4+ ♔h8 18.♖xc1 ♘xd3 19.♘xd7 ♖g8 20.♗xf6+ ♕xf6 21.♕xg8+ ♔xg8

22.♘xf6+ ♔g7 23.♘e8+ ♔f8
24.♖c8+–

16...♗b5

17.♘e5
17.♘d2!?
17...fxe5
17...♗xf1 was better, retaining some hopes for resistance.
**18.♗xe7 ♗xe7 19.♕g4+ ♔h8
20.♖xc8 ♖xc8 21.♕e4!**

Black resigned.

No. 6. French Defense
Kiev – Kharkov
1927

This game was published in the magazine *64. Shakhmaty i Shashki v Rabochem Klube* (1927, No. 11) under the headline "The World's First Radio Match". Later, meticulous chess historians dug up some cases of radio being used to broadcast chess moves in games between ships on the open sea. However, the consultation game between the teams of the two biggest Ukrainian cities was indeed a pioneering event in the history of public chess games.

The honor of Kiev was defended by master F. Bogatyrchuk, the future masters V. Rauzer, I. Pogrebyssky and E. Polyak, and also A. Grinberg. The Kharkov team did not feature such illustrious names, but it was strong enough: Alexei Alekhine, D. Grigorenko, N. Oistrakh, A. Port and I. Yanushpolsky. It was organized by the Ukrainian SSR Highest Education Council together with the Radioperedacha ("Radio Broadcast") society.

Even though consultation games are by definition played by a collective, this historical game left its trace in Rauzer's biography. So I thought that including this game in the collection of Rauzer's best games would be justified.

Until move 14, the opponents followed the famous game Em. Lasker – Maroczy from the 1924 New York tournament, which served as a beacon for theoreticians back then.

1.e4 e6 2.d4 d5 3.♘c3 ♗b4 4.e5 c5 5.a3 cxd4 6.axb4 dxc3 7.bxc3 ♕c7 8.♘f3 ♘e7 9.♗d3 ♕xc3+ 10.♗d2 ♕c7 11.0-0 ♘d7 12.♕e2 ♘g6 13.♖fe1 0-0 14.♕e3

The white players have sacrificed a pawn, but they have got hefty compensation for this small price – an active attacking position. Now the black players have to take care of their a7 pawn.

Maroczy's defense was unsophisticated – 14...♘b6, and then 15.♕g5 ♘c4 16.♗c3 h6 17.♕g4 ♘e7. Black got a clear advantage out of the opening, repelled all of his opponent's attacks with energetic and ingenious play, and got a winning position. However, at a critical moment he made several mistakes in a row and even lost.

The Kharkov players chose another defensive plan.

14...f6 15.exf6 ♘xf6

Perhaps the black players were now counting on the straightforward capture of the a7 pawn? After 16.♖xa7, they had prepared 16... ♘g4 17.♕d4 ♖xa7

18.♕xa7 ♘h4!, with a dangerous attack.

In this case, instead of 18.♕xa7, white has to play 18.♗xg6!? with somewhat better chances for black. It's better for white to go for the line

16.♗xg6 hxg6 17.♖xa7 ♘g4 with unclear play.

However, black got outwitted: there followed

16.♕d4!

The chess press of the time wrote, "Kiev's 16th move was not anticipated by Kharkov, and the consultants searched for a satisfactory reply to the unexpected move until late in the night. The clocks showed that they thought for 1 hour and 42 minutes until they came up with a good move."

16...♘e4

After this move, it became clear that in view of numerous weaknesses in the black players' position (a7, e6, g6), they could not hold onto their extra pawn. So black decided to go for a draw – they even sacrificed a pawn themselves to get opposite-colored bishops.

17.♗xe4

It was worth trying 17.♖xe4! dxe4 18.♕xe4 with the threats h2-h4 or ♘g5 and ♗c4. After such a sharp continuation, the white players could have cast doubt on their opponents' plan. After they miss this opportunity, however, they cannot prevent a draw.

17...dxe4 18.♕xe4 e5 19.♘xe5 ♘xe5 20.♕xe5 ♕xe5 21.♖xe5 ♗f5 22.c4 a6 23.h3

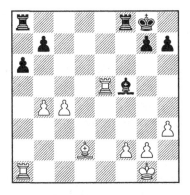

The playing time was over, and the result was adjudicated by a trio of judges – Leningrad masters A. Ilyin-Zhenevsky, I. Rabinovich and P. Romanovsky. Their verdict was easy to predict: a draw. While black is a pawn down, the opposite-colored bishops guarantee this outcome.

It seems that this game influenced Rauzer and helped him to find the strong idea 7.♘f3!!, which was slowly maturing prior to the 8th Soviet Championship. In the starting round of that career-defining competition, Rauzer caused a sensation when he brilliantly used this move against V. Alatortsev (see game 32).

No. 7. Queen's Indian Defense
Rauzer – Pogrebyssky
4th Ukrainian Championship
Poltava 1927
Annotated by V. Rauzer

1.d4 ♘f6 2.c4 e6 3.♘c3 b6 4.e4 ♗b7 5.♗d3 d6 6.♘ge2 ♘bd7 7.f3 ♗e7 8.♗e3 0-0 9.0-0 c5

10.b3

Intending to meet 10...cxd4 11.♘xd4 ♘e5 with 12.♗c2; however, the game move is a waste of time, because the immediate 10.♗c2 was just as good.

10...d5?

Black should have played 10...e5. Now white gets an advantage.

11.cxd5 cxd4

This frees the important d4 square for the white pieces.

12.♗xd4 exd5 13.e5 ♘e8 14.f4 ♘c5 15.♘g3

Preventing ♘e4 with the subsequent f7-f5.

15.f5!? was worthy of consideration, preventing both f7-f5 and ...♘e6.

15...♘e6 16.♘ce2

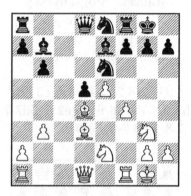

16...♘xd4

A pointless trade – the white knight on d4 is stronger than the bishop.

17.♘xd4 ♗c5 18.♘ge2 ♘c7 19.b4 ♗xb4

Too risky. It was better to retreat to e7 with the bishop.

20.♕b1 ♗c5 21.♗xh7+ ♔h8 22.♖f3 ♘e6?

It was necessary to play 22...♗c8; it seems that black missed white's 24th move.

23.♖h3 ♗xd4+

24.♔h1!

Of course, not 24.♘xd4 due to 24...♘xf4!, parrying the threat 25.♗g8+ because black takes the h3 rook with a check. Now, however, black cannot save the game.

24...♖e8

24...g6 was also hopeless.

25.♕f5 ♘g5

White threatened both 26.♗g6+ and, if the opportunity arose, ♕h5.

26.fxg5 ♕e7

26...♕c7 would have been met with 27.♖f1 and an easy win.

27.♗g8+

Black resigned due to mate in two moves.

No. 8. Queen's Gambit Accepted
Rauzer – Ballodit
4th Ukrainian Championship
Poltava 1927
Annotated by V. Rauzer

1.d4 d5 2.c4 dxc4 3.♘f3 c5 4.e3

The game Capablanca – Zubarev from the 1st Moscow International Tournament did the move d4-d5 no favors.

4...e6 5.♗xc4 ♘f6 6.0-0 ♘c6 7.dxc5

White wouldn't have gotten an advantage here in case of black's correct play.

7...♗xc5 8.♕xd8+ ♔xd8

The king should go to e7 – it stands nicely there.

9.a3

9...a6

Black chooses a poor plan – he doesn't take into account the fact that white hasn't developed his knight to c3 yet.

Now, white seizes the c-file and the c5 square with the maneuver ♘b1-d2-b3-c5. Black should have played 9...♔e7 with the subsequent e6-e5.

10.b4 ♗d6 11.♗b2 b5 12.♗e2 ♗b7 13.♘bd2 ♔e7 14.♖ac1 ♖ac8 15.♘b3 ♘a7 16.♗d4 ♘c6 17.♘c5 ♘xd4

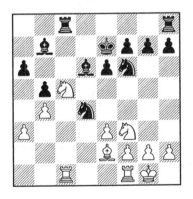

18.♘xd4

If 18.exd4, then 18...♖c7 19.♘xb7 ♖xb7 20.♖c6 ♖a8 with the subsequent a6-a5.

18...♗xc5 19.bxc5 ♗d5 20.f3 g6 21.e4 ♗c6 22.a4

Winning a pawn.

Analysis shows that black can retain the pawn with 22...♘d7!?.

22...bxa4   23.♗xa6   ♖c7 24.♘xc6+   ♖xc6   25.♗b5   ♖c7 26.♗xa4

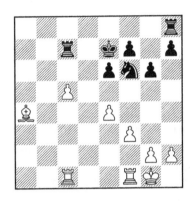

Black, sure that he can make a draw by any means, subsequently makes several small mistakes and gradually reaches a hopeless position.

26...♖a8 27.♖c4 ♘d7 28.♗xd7 ♔xd7 29.♖d1+ ♔e7 30.e5 ♖a5 31.♖dc1 ♖a2 32.c6 g5 33.h4 h6 34.hxg5 hxg5 35.♔h2 f6 36.exf6+ ♔xf6 37.♔g3 ♖d2 38.♖c5 ♖d4 39.♖1c4 ♖d6

39...e5 would have been met with 40.♖c2 and ♔f2, and then ♔e3, ♖2c4 and ♔e4.

40.♔g4 ♖d2 41.g3 ♖d5

If 41...♖g2, then 42.♗e4 ♖h7 43.f4! etc.

If, however, 41...♖d6, white wins with the simple 42.♖xg5.

42.♖xd5 exd5 43.♖c5 d4 44.♖xg5 ♖xc6 45.♖d5 ♖c4 46.♔f4

♕e6 47.♖e5+ ♔d6 48.♖f5 ♖c5
49.♖f8

49...♔d5?

After 49...♔e7 50.♖a8 ♖c3, black could still put up stubborn resistance.

50.♖d8+ ♔c4 51.♔e4

Black resigned.

No. 9. Dutch Defense
Rauzer – Kaspersky
5th Soviet Championship
Moscow 1927

The price of an opening mistake made in the first few moves can sometimes be huge. The following game is a great example of that. The move 4...♘c6 (instead of the correct 4...d5 and subsequent c7-c6) allowed white to seize the initiative, which he consolidated with 9.♘d4!. In a difficult situation, where it was hard to defend from the threat ♗xg6!, black made a decisive mistake. Rauzer played most energetically in the final stage.

1.d4 e6 2.♘f3 f5 3.g3 ♘f6 4.♗g2 ♘c6? 5.0-0 ♗e7 6.c4 d6 7.d5! exd5 8.cxd5 ♘b8 9.♘d4! 0-0 10.♕c2 g6 11.b4 ♘a6 12.a3 ♖e8 13.♗b2 ♗f8 14.♘d2 ♗g7 15.♖fe1 ♖e7 16.e4! fxe4 17.♘xe4 ♘xe4 18.♗xe4 ♕e8 19.♖e2 ♗d7 20.♖ae1 ♗f6

21.♘c6! ♖xe4 22.♖xe4 ♕f8 23.♘e7+

After 23...♔h8 (or 23...♔g7 24.♘xg6!), the killing blow 24.♖h4 comes, so black resigned.

No. 10. Slav Defense
Rauzer – Pavlov-Pianov
5th Soviet Championship
Moscow 1927
Annotated by V. Rauzer

1.d4 ♘f6 2.♘f3 d5 3.c4 c6 4.cxd5 cxd5 5.♘c3 ♘c6 6.♗f4 ♗f5 7.e3

7.♕b3 ♘a5 8.♕b5+ ♗d7 gives white nothing.

7...♕b6

If 7...e6 then 8.♕b3 is quite unpleasant. The game move gives white a tempo to transfer the knight to c5.

Modern practice shows that black retains equality after 8...♗b4.

8.♗b5 ♗d7

Black will regain the tempo by kicking the b5 bishop back to d3.

9.♕e2 e6 10.0-0 ♗e7 11.♖fc1 0-0

12.a3

Intending to prepare the maneuver ♘c3-a4-c5 with b2-b4. The immediate 12.♘a4!? was also possible.

12...a6!

But not immediately 12...♘a5, which would have been met with 13.♗xd7 ♘xd7 14.♘xd5 exd5 15.♗c7, winning a pawn.

13.♗d3 ♘a5! 14.♘d2 ♘b3!

Not 14...♕xb2 due to 15.♘d1 ♕b6 16.♗c7 etc.

15.♘xb3 ♕xb3 16.♗c2

Now white has to lose too many tempi to carry out the maneuver b2-b4 and ♘c3-a4-c5.

16...♕b6 17.♗a4 ♖fc8 18.♗xd7 ♘xd7 19.b4

19...♕a7(?)

It was better to play 19...♕c6, preventing ♘a4. For instance, 20.♕d1 ♘b6 21.♘e4 ♘c4 22.♘c5 b6!

20.♘a4 b5 21.♘c5 ♘b6 22.♖c2 ♖c6 23.h3 ♖ac8 24.♖ca2

White is worse, because black can trade his c5 knight; the black knight on c4, on the other hand, would be invincible, so white searches for compensation by trying to open the a-file.

24...♗xc5 25.dxc5 ♘a4?

The move a3-a4 was not so much of a threat for black to give up the superb position on c4 for his knight.

26.♖c2 ♕e7 27.♗e5

Preventing ...♕f6.

27...f6 28.♗d6 ♕d7?

Losing an important tempo. It was better to play 28...♕f7 immediately with the threat ♘a4-b6-c4, and if white plays 29.♖ac1, then 29...♕g6. Also note that black was in time trouble.

**29.♖ac1   ♕f7   30.♕d3   ♕g6
31.♖d1 ♕xd3 32.♖xd3 ♔f7**

Threatening ...♖xd6, winning a piece, which was impossible before, because after cxd6 ♖xc2 there followed d6-d7 and the pawn promoted.

Nor could black play 32...♘b6 due to 33.cxb6 ♖xc2 34.b7, winning a piece.

33.♗g3 ♖a8

Black has nothing left now. White, however, will try to put his bishop onto the a1-h8 diagonal (through d4), after which he would basically obtain a free piece on the kingside

34.♖cd2 ♖a7 35.♔f1 ♔e7

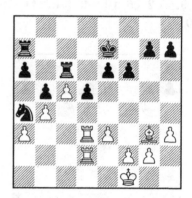

36.♖b3

One of those positions where you can afford to lose a tempo.

36...♖d7 37.♖bd3

Black threatened e6-e5.

37...♖a7 38.♔e2 ♖b7

Not 38...e5 due to 39.♔e1, winning a pawn.

39.h4 ♖a7 40.h5 ♖b7 41.♗h4 ♔e8 42.h6

Missing black's next reply. White easily won with 42.g4 ♖c8 43.f4 ♔e7 44.♔f2 ♖d7 (otherwise f4-f5 etc.) 45.e4 ♖cd8 46.h6 etc.

42...g5 43.♗g3 ♔f7?

Black should have played 43...g4!, to meet 44.f4 with 44...f5, closing off the white bishop.

Even this wouldn't have saved black. After 44.e4, his position is hopeless.

44.f4

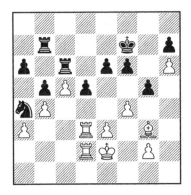

44...gxf4

Now 44...g4 is met with 45.f5 ♖c8 46.♔f1 ♖d7 47.e4 ♖cd8 48.fxe6+ ♔xe6 49.c6, winning easily.

45.exf4 f5 46.♗f2 ♖b8 47.♖g3 ♖g8 48.♖xg8 ♔xg8 49.♗d4

Now it's time for black to resign.

49...♔f7 50.♖d3 ♔g6 51.♖g3+ ♔xh6

Desperation! Now white has a mate in five:

52.♗g7+ ♔h5 53.♖g5+ ♔h4 54.♔f3

Black resigned without waiting for 55.g3+ ♔h3 56.♖h5#.

No. 11. Queen's Indian Defense
Rauzer – I. Rabinovich
5th Soviet Championship
Moscow 1927
Annotated by V. Rauzer

1.d4 ♘f6 2.♘f3 e6 3.c4 ♗b4+ 4.♘c3 c5 5.♗d2

Now white usually plays 5.d5 immediately, trying to seize space in the center. – **A. K.**

In modern times, the main lines are 5.e3 and 5.g3.

5...0-0 6.d5

White is too behind with development of the f1 bishop and opens the e-file for his opponent himself.

6...b6 7.♕b3 exd5 8.♘xd5 ♗xd2+ 9.♘xd2 ♘xd5

It was better to play 9...♘c6 10.e3 ♖e8, and if 11.0-0-0, then 11...♘g4. Now white gets a very pleasant game.

10.cxd5 ♖e8 11.e4 ♕g5

Black wins a pawn, but lags in development and falls under attack.

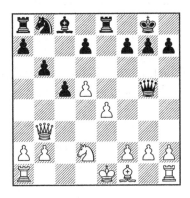

12.0-0-0 ♖xe4 13.♗d3 ♖e8 14.♖he1 ♖f8 15.h4 ♕h6 16.g4 ♗b7 17.g5 ♕d6 18.♘e4 ♕f4+ 19.♔b1 ♘a6

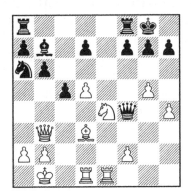

An oversight. However, it might still be the best move, otherwise white's attack is unstoppable due to black's inability to develop the a8 rook, b8 knight and b7 bishop. Now the attack stops, black gets three connected pawns, and white still needs to play very precisely to keep the d5 pawn, his last winning chance.

20.♗xa6! ♗xa6 21.♕a4 b5

White threatened ♘f6+, winning the queen. – **A. K.**

22.♕xa6 ♖ae8 23.♘xc5 ♕f5+ 24.♔a1 ♕xf2 25.♘d3 ♕xh4 26.♕xb5 ♕xg5 27.♕xd7 ♖d8 28.♖e5 ♕g2 29.♕f5 g6 30.♘e1 ♕g1 31.♕f6 ♖c8 32.a3 ♖c2 33.♖e7 ♖f2 34.♕d4

Black resigned due to the threat of d5-d6-d7 and a lack of counterplay.

No. 12. French Defense
Vilner – Rauzer
5th Ukrainian Championship
Odessa 1928

1.d4 d5 2.♘c3 ♘f6 3.♗g5 e6

Knowing that the Odessa master had a lot of experience playing the Queen's Pawn Game with 2.♘c3, Rauzer offered to transpose into a French.

4.e4 dxe4 5.♘xe4 ♗e7 6.♗xf6

Back then, this trade was considered white's best plan to keep the initiative.

6...♗xf6

Capturing with the pawn would have posed more difficult problems for both opponents.

7.♘f3 ♘d7 8.c3

8...0-0

A. Alekhine, who dedicated a lot of effort to the development of this playing system for black, preferred to develop the bishop to b7 immediately – 8...b6 9.♘xf6+ gxf6 (not 9...♕xf6 in view of 10.♗b5!) 10.♗d3 ♗b7.

After the immediate castling, black relies on the e6-e5 pawn push, opening another diagonal for the light-squared bishop and harassing the opponent's central pawn.

9.♗d3

9.♕c2 e5 10.0-0-0 exd4 11.cxd4 ♘b6 12.♗d3 ♘d5! 13.♘xf6+ ♘xf6 14.♘g5 h6 15.h4 ♕d6 16.♔b1 ♗d7 was worse, with good prospects for black.

9...e5 10.♕c2

White weakens his d4 pawn, but accelerates the development of his pieces. After long castling, his threats to the vulnerable h7 square will be very dangerous.

10...exd4 11.cxd4 ♖e8 12.0-0-0

12...♞f8!

Even back then, the young Kiev player knew the defensive power of the f8 knight well. On the other hand, Vilner thought it was necessary to play 12...h6, and after 12...♞f8, he thought that 13.♞xf6+ ♛xf6 14.♛xc7 ♝f5 15.♛g3! ♜ac8+ 16.♚b1 ♝xd3+ 17.♜xd3 ♛f5 18.♞e5 was very beneficial for white, but only after post-game analysis!

"Over the board, I thought that opening the c-file was so risky that I didn't even consider this line," he admitted.

Intuition served Vilner well: after 16...♜e2! his position could have become critical.

As we see, black avoided 12... h6 out of principle, although, objectively speaking, after 12...♞f8, the continuation 13.♞xf6+ ♛xf6 14.♛xc7!? ♝g4! 15.♛g3 ♝xf3 with the subsequent ♞e6 or g7-g6 was quite sufficient.

13.h4 ♝e6 14.♞eg5 g6 15.♚b1 ♝d5

The light-squared bishop has seized the dominant square in the center. It defends the f7 pawn, and after c7-c6 and ♛a5 it will take part in the attack on the king as well. Realizing that the situation was deteriorating, white immediately brought his king's rook into play.

16.♜h3 c6 17.♜g3 ♛a5 18.b3 ♛a3

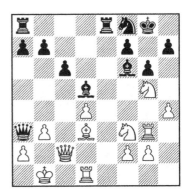

White cannot hesitate anymore. Anticipating his opponent's threat a7-a5-a4, he tries to breach the black king's armor.

19.h5! ♜e7!

Covering the vulnerable h7 point again. Still, master Vilner, a strong tactician (and problem composer!), tries to break through black's defenses with a complicated combination.[14]

---

[14] A chess biography of Vilner, including his fascinating but tragic life story, best games and compositions, called *Yakov Vilner, First Ukrainian Chess Champion and First USSR Chess Composition Champion*, by Sergei Tkachenko, was published by Elk and Ruby in 2019.

Analysis shows that 19...♛d6!?, with better chances for black, was stronger.

20.♘xh7! ♞xh7 21.hxg6 fxg6 22.♗xg6

The black king's position is quite suspect. After 22...♚h8, white is ready to deliver checkmate – 23.♗xh7 ♜xh7 24.♛xh7+! ♚xh7 25.♜h1+ and 26.♜xh4#! Only the knight can help its king.

22...♞f8!   23.♗h7+   ♚f7 24.♗g6+ ♚g8 25.♗h7+

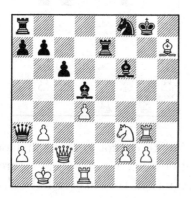

Draw agreed.

So, the "Achilles heel" proved to be invulnerable this time.

No. 13. French Defense
Rauzer – Konstantinopolsky
Kiev Championship 1929

1.d4 e6 2.e4 d5 3.♞c3 ♗b4 4.e5 c5 5.♗d2

Back then, this simple developing move was seen more often than 5.a3, which was universally accepted later (partly thanks to Rauzer's games and analysis).

5...♞c6

6.♞b5

The point of white's fifth move – the knight attacks the weak d6 square. However, even then players had already found a good rejoinder.

6...♗xd2+   7.♛xd2   ♞xd4 8.♞xd4 cxd4 9.♞f3 ♞e7 10.♞xd4 ♗d7

Here, of course, it was more energetic to play 10...♞c6, attacking the e5 pawn and preparing to trade the dangerous white knight.

11.c3 0-0 12.♗d3 ♞c6 13.♞f3! f6 14.exf6 ♛xf6 15.0-0 h6 16.♜ae1 ♗e8

Black is planning to play ♗h5 and e6-e5, but the d5 pawn requires defense nonetheless. The black king's position is not too comfortable either. I realized that my position was difficult, but placed hopes on some tactical subtleties.

17.♗c2   ♜d8   18.♛d3   ♗h5 19.♜e3 e5 20.♛h7+ ♚f7

21.♕f5!

My opponent was more experienced in positional struggle and evaluated the ensuing endgame better.

21...♕xf5 22.♗xf5 ♔f6?

Here, the king will soon fall under attack from the knight, all the more so as black is dreaming of pushing the d5 pawn. 22...♗xf3 23.♖xf3 ♔e7 was more prudent.

23.♗c2 d4(?) 24.cxd4 exd4 25.♖b3 ♖d7

26.♘d2!

This underscores black's mistakes.

It is now necessary for him to get his king to safety, for instance, with 26...♔f7!?.

26...b6 27.♘e4+ ♔e7 28.♖g3 g5?

A mistake that could have been punished by white with 29.♖e1! (preventing black's next text move) 29...♔d8, and only now 30.♖h3. After 28...♔d8!?, white had only a small advantage.

29.♖h3?! ♗e2

Even though white threatened both ♗a4 and ♖xh6, I had placed my hopes on this bishop lunge combined with the d4 pawn push. However, the forced line was not in my favor.

30.♖e1 d3 31.♗xd3!

Analysis shows that 31.♗a4!? was much stronger.

31...♖xd3 32.♖xd3 ♗xd3 33.♘c5+ ♔f6

Or 33...♔f7 34.♘xd3 ♖d8 35.♖d1 ♔f6 36.♔f1, and white has good winning chances.

Now, however (after 33...♔f6), instead of playing 34.♘xd3 ♖d8 35.♖d1 ♘b4 or 35.♘c1 ♖d2 (as I intended when playing 29...♗e2), Rauzer replied

34.♘d7+! ♔f7 35.♘xf8 ♔xf8 36.♖e6 ♘e7 37.♖xh6

And the rook with a passed pawn turned out to be stronger than two minor pieces. Black soon resigned.

During the post-mortem, my opponent asked in surprise: "How could you not know that the rook is much more active than two minor pieces in such endgames?" He immediately showed me the ending of the game **Pillsbury – Tarrasch** (Vienna 1898), where white got a technically won endgame after an elegant trading combination.

Here's this instructive endgame, which every chess player should know.

No. 13a.

21.♞xd7 ♛xd7 22.♛xd5+! cxd5 23.♝xd7 ♝xg3

After 23...f4!, black actually wins, so white's 22nd move was a mistake. The subsequent play of both white and black is rife with inaccuracies.

24.♝c6 ♝d6 25.♝xd5+ ♚h8 26.♝xa8 ♜xa8 27.♜ad1 ♝f8 28.♜d4 g6 29.♜ed1 ♞b7 30.♜d7 ♜b8 31.♜1d5 ♚g8 32.♚f1 ♞c5 33.♜a7 ♜c8 34.g3 ♝g7 35.b3 ♝f8 36.h4 ♜c6 37.♜d8 ♜f6 38.♜b8 f4 39.♜b6 ♜f5 40.g4 ♜d5 41.♚g2 ♜d4 42.♜b8 ♜d7 43.♜xd7 ♞xd7 44.♜b7 ♞c5 45.♜xb4 ♝d6 46.♜b6 ♝e7 47.b4 ♞a4 48.♜xa6 ♝xb4 49.♜a8+ ♚f7 50.a6

Black resigned.

I remembered this lesson forever. In particular, I learned that sometimes endgame knowledge is more important than tactical tricks.

No. 14. French Defense
Botvinnik – Rauzer
6th Soviet Championship (group stage)
Odessa 1929

1.e4 e6 2.d4 d5 3.♞c3 ♞f6 4.♝g5 dxe4 5.♞xe4 ♝e7

Rauzer honed this system for a long time and successfully used it in important competitions. Back then, we called it "Triple A", because it was developed and introduced to international practice by AMOS Burn, AKIBA Rubinstein and ALEXANDER Alekhine.

Em. Lasker also often used that system, but mostly as a psychological experiment (a kind of odds game, because the pawn trade dxe4 on move 3 or 4 had a poor reputation). The most telling game in this regard was the 6th game of his match against S. Tarrasch (1908), where, after 3.♘c3 dxe4 4.♘xe4 ♘f6? 5.♘xf6+ ♛xf6 6.♘f3 ♗d7 7.♗g5 ♛g6 8.♗d3 f5, black got a rather difficult position. However, Lasker himself thought that only 6...♗d7 was a mistake, deeming 6...h6 a sufficient defense, but this, of course, was not too convincing. Still, Tarrasch failed to win the game – he got into severe time trouble and missed a win in the endgame.

As far as I remember, Rauzer was convinced that the 4...dxe4 system was solid thanks to some games played by A. Alekhine, where he managed to keep the balance with great skill.

6.♘c3

This position was analyzed by theoreticians back then, as well. Avoidance of the trade on f6 became known after the game Tarrasch – Tartakower (Ostrava 1923), where, after 6...0-0 7.♘f3 b6 8.♛d2 ♗b7 9.♗e2 ♘bd7 10.0-0 ♘d5, black got roughly equal chances. Still, the maneuver outlined some kind of new game plan. As S. Tartakower wrote, "Like is cured by like. Tarrasch was trying to counter black's anti-scientific fourth move with something even more 'anti-scientific'! He looked at the position with the boldness of the new-generation players and came to the conclusion that the trade 6.♘xf6+ would have given his opponent a "dynamic tempo" for development. He also rejected the retreat to the right, 6.♘g3, because he intended to use all his forces for the impending battle in the center (around the d5 square!). All these considerations convinced him to do away with routine and make the strange-looking game move."

Perhaps it was the eloquent "Homer of Chess" who convinced the future world champion that the unexplored maneuver 6.♘c3 was promising.

6...0-0 7.♘f3 ♘bd7 8.♗e2 c5

After trading away the d-pawn, black wants to get rid of its neighbor as well.

9.0-0 b6 10.♛d2 ♗b7 11.♖ad1

Anticipating the possible d4 pawn trade, white is ready to seize the d-file. Black, however, had one more trump up his sleeve – seizing the d5 square.

11...♘d5! 12.♘e4

Again avoiding the knight trade, but what should he do about the dark-squared bishops?

12...h6 13.♗xe7

Only the sacrifice 13.♗xh6!? could shake black's defenses, but white wants to play in the center.

13...♕xe7 14.c4 ♘5f6 15.♘c3!

"Every single time, in this same place..." Now the d4-d5 push is prepared, and white gets a passed pawn in the center.

Actually, this well-known quote is a bit out of place here.[15] The author himself rightly assigned an exclamation mark to the game move, which, jointly with 15.♘xf6+, was the best choice.

---

[15] This is a quote from Ivan Gorbunov's short story "At the Postal Station". A coachman boasts that he knows every hillside in this area, and then proceeds to crash the coach in the night. When accosted by his passenger, he says, "What do you know! Every single time, in this same place..." – *Translator*

15...♖ad8! 16.d5

As we shall see shortly, this was a poor move.

16...exd5 17.cxd5 ♕d6

Even though the queen is not considered a particularly good blocking piece, the d5 pawn is nevertheless already under attack. The mutual positional threats are parried very precisely by the opponents.

Black could have refuted the hasty d-pawn push with 17...♘xd5!?

18.♖fe1 a6 19.a4! ♖fe8 20.♘h4

The f5 square attracts the white knight, but its black counterpart will be active enough on e5 and then on g6.

20...♘e5 21.♘f5 ♕f8

Now the black king's position has been bolstered; 22.d6 is met with 22...♘g6.

22.f4   ♘g6   23.♗c4   ♖xe1+ 24.♖xe1 ♗c8

It's time to harass the knight.

25.♘g3 ♕d6 26.♖f1 ♗d7!

This actually was not the best move; white could have

demonstrated that black's idea was dubious.

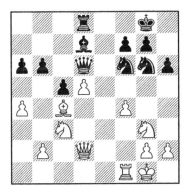

Black has prepared the push b6-b5, trading his b-pawn for his opponent's d-pawn. He intends to meet 27.♗xa6 with 27...♘e7!, eliminating the d5 pawn (28.♗c4 ♗c8 and ...♗b7). The same goal could be reached in another way: 27...♖a8 28.♗b5 ♗xb5 29.axb5 ♘e7! 30.♖d1 ♖d8, and the d5 pawn falls.

In the first line (after 27...♘e7), black simply cannot take the pawn because it's sufficiently protected, and in the second (after 27...♖a8), it would be rather difficult to get rid of the pin along the d-file.

M. Botvinnik preferred a quiet, consolidating move, after which b6-b5 leads to simplifications.

27.b3 b5! 28.axb5 axb5 29.♘xb5 ♗xb5 30.♗xb5 ♕xd5 31.♕xd5 ♘xd5

It turns out that black does not fear the pin, as 32.♖d1 ♖b8 33.♗c4 ♘e3 gives white nothing. So the opponents agreed to a draw.

No. 15. French Defense
Riumin – Rauzer
6th Soviet Championship
(group stage)
Odessa 1929
Annotated by A. Model

1.e4 e6 2.g3

If one avoids the usual continuations with 2.d4, it's probably better to choose the Chigorin defensive system: 2.♕e2 with the subsequent g2-g3 and ♗g2.

2...d5 3.♗g2 dxe4 4.♘c3 ♗d7 5.♘xe4

5.d3 leads to easy equalization; for instance, 5...♗c6 6.dxe4 ♕xd1+ 7.♔xd1, etc.

A poor recommendation that leads to black's advantage: 5...exd3 6.♗xb7 ♘c6 7.♗xa8 (7.♕f3 ♘e5!?) 7...dxc2 8.♕xc2 ♕xa8∓.

5...♗c6

Now, thanks to the threat f7-f5, black has a great position.

6.f3 e5 7.♘e2 f5 8.♘f2 ♗c5 9.♘d3 ♗d6 10.0-0 ♘f6 11.♘c3 0-0 12.♕e2

12...♕e7

Preventing the liberating maneuver 13.♘b4 ♗xb4 14.♕c4+.

13.♘f2 ♕f7 14.d3 ♘bd7 15.♗d2 ♖ae8 16.♖ae1 ♕h5 17.♔h1 ♘c5! 18.♘cd1 ♘e6 19.c3

19...♘f4!!

The knight has finally reached its desired square! White's position, already compromised by the misplayed opening, is destroyed in a few moves.

20.gxf4 exf4 21.♘e4

21.♗e3 fxe3 22.♘h3 f4 led to a hopeless position as well.

21...fxe4 22.fxe4

22.dxe4 is met with 22...♘xe4! 23.fxe4 f3! and then like in the game.

22...f3! 23.♗xf3

Forced, because of the threat 23...♕xh2#.

23...♘xe4! 24.dxe4

After 24.♗xh5, black mates in two: 24...♘f2+ and 25...♘h3#, while 24.♗xe4 is met with 24...♗xe4+ 25.dxe4 ♖xf1+, winning the queen.

24...♖xf3

24...♖xe4! was even more spectacular.

25.♖xf3 ♖xe4 26.♖f8+ (a last-gasp check) **26...♗xf8**

White resigned.

Winning this last-round encounter allowed Rauzer to advance to the semi-final.

No. 16. French Defense
Rauzer – Grigoriev
6th Soviet Championship
(semi-final group)
Odessa 1929
Annotated by V. Rauzer

1.d4 e6 2.e4 d5 3.e5 c5 4.♘f3 ♘c6 5.♗d3

By sacrificing a pawn, white gets an opportunity to attack his opponent's cramped kingside with all his might. ·

White's opening strategy is similar to the ideas of A. Nimzowitsch, who introduced the lines with sacrificing the d4 pawn, the trade e5xf6 (after f7-f6) and subsequent blockade of the center with pieces on d4 and e5.
– A. K.

5...cxd4 6.0-0 f6

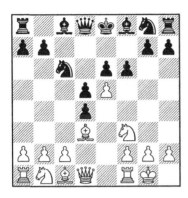

7.♕e2

In the well-known game Alekhine – Euwe (Nottingham 1936), there followed 7.♗b5 ♗d7 8.♗xc6 bxc6 9.♕xd4 fxe5 10.♕xe5 with a very complicated struggle. – **A. K.**

7...fxe5 8.♘xe5 ♘f6

It made more sense to play 8...♘xe5 9.♕xe5 ♘f6 10.♗b5+ ♔f7, even though after 11.♕xd4 ♗d6 12.♗f4 white's prospects seem better. – **A. K.**

9.♗g5 ♗d6 10.f4 0-0 11.♘d2 ♕c7 12.♖ae1

Black cannot develop his queenside: 12...♗d7 is met with 13.♘xd7 and 14.♕xe6+.

12...♗b4 13.a3

This loss of tempo allowed black to equalize. The correct move was 13.♖f3, and then:

13...♗xd2 14.♕xd2 ♗d7 (14...♘e4 15.♗xe4 dxe4 16.♖xe4±) 15.♖g3±;

or 13...♘e4 14.♘xe4 ♗xe1 15.♖h3 ♘xe5 (15...dxe4 16.♕xe4 ♖f5 17.♕xf5 exf5 18.♗c4+ ♔f8 19.♖xh7+−) 16.♖xh7+−.

13...♗xd2 14.♕xd2 ♗d7 15.♕f2

15...♖ae8?

Loses by force. 15...♘e4 equalized.

16.♗xf6 ♖xf6

If 16...gxf6 then 17.♗xh7+!, winning.

17.♘g4 ♖ff8 18.♕h4 h6 19.♖f3 ♖e7 20.♘xh6+ gxh6 21.♖g3+ ♖g7 22.♕xh6 ♖ff7 23.♕h7+ ♔f8 24.♕h8+ ♔e7 25.♖xg7 ♕xf4?

This loses another piece.

26.♖f1 ♕e3+ 27.♔h1 ♖xg7

If 27...♗e8 or 27...♘e5, then 28.♖gxf7+, 29.♕f6+ and 30.♕xf7.

28.♕f8#.

No. 17. Queen's Gambit
Rauzer – Rokhlin
6th Soviet Championship
(semi-final group)
Odessa 1929

1.d4 d5 2.c4 e6 3.♘c3 ♘f6 4.♗g5 ♘bd7 5.e3 c6

Black clearly shows his intention to play the Cambridge Springs system, which came into fashion after the memorable Capablanca – Alekhine match (1927). White answers with a relatively quiet development system that most often leads to Orthodox Defense structures, which proved its solidity in the aforementioned match.

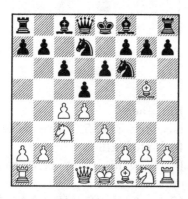

6.a3

This move attracted some attention during the world championship match, but it became especially popular after the beautiful game Reti – Spielmann (Trencianske Teplice 1928): 6...♗e7 7.♘f3 0-0 8.♕c2 a6 9.♖d1 ♖e8 10.♗d3 h6 (the immediate 10...dxc4 11.♗xc4 ♘d5 is simpler) 11.♗h4 dxc4 12.♗xc4 ♘d5 13.♗g3

♕a5 14.0-0! ♘xc3 15.bxc3 b5 16.♗a2 ♘f8 17.♘e5 ♗b7 18.f4 ♗f6 19.f5 ♗xe5 20.♗xe5 ♕d8 21.fxe6 fxe6 (21...♘xe6 22.♖xf7!) 22.♖xf8+ ♖xf8 23.♗xe6+ ♔h8 24.♗a2! ♕g5 25.♗b1 ♕g8 26.♕h7+ ♔f7 27.♗xg7! ♕xe3+ 28.♔h1 ♕e2 29.♗e5+ ♔e6 30.♕g6+ ♔d7 31.♕d6+, and black resigned.

6...♗e7 7.♕c2

In this way, white avoided the Cambridge Springs "danger" and transposed into a position from the Rubinstein System in the Orthodox Defense with ♕c2, which is quite beneficial for white.

7...h6

7...0-0 was more precise. The rook pawn move is only advisable after black finally decides which structure (Capablanca system or the extended fianchetto) he goes for. Alekhine later wrote an article on the strategic problem of the move h7-h6 in the Queen's Gambit, basing it mostly on materials from the 1931 Bled tournament (see *Shakhmaty v SSSR*, No. 8, 1932; *Central Chess Club Bulletin*, 1987, No. 30).

8.♗h4 0-0 9.♘f3 ♖e8

It was better to play 9...a6, preparing the immediate extended fianchetto. The b7-b5 thrust is sometimes possible in this system, forcing white to decide the "intentions" of his c4 pawn. The role of the e8 rook is unclear yet. At first, black used the game Bogoljubov – Reti (see No. 17a below) as the model for his play, but soon deviates from the correct path.

10.♗d3 dxc4 11.♗xc4 ♘d5

So, black has steered the game towards the Capablanca system, but now the bishop gets a very good position on g3.

12.♗g3! ♘xc3 13.♕xc3 ♘f6

Threatening an exchange operation, ♘f6-e4xg3, but white easily counters this plan.

14.♗d3 ♗d7 15.0-0 ♕b6

Not the best square for the queen, but black plans to play ...♖ec8 and ...c6-c5.

16.♖ac1 ♖ec8 17.♘e5 c5

Prematurely opening up the game. M. Chigorin and Em. Lasker used to play ...♗e8 successfully in similar positions, even though such a waiting strategy requires restraint and foresight.

18.♘xd7 ♘xd7 19.dxc5 ♘xc5

In view of the threat along the b1-h7 diagonal, it was more solid to play 19...♖xc5 and 20...♘f8, protecting the h7 square.

20.♗b1 ♗f6

Of course, not 20...♘b3? 21.♕xc8+ ♖xc8 22.♖xc8+ ♗f8 23.♖d1, and it's time to resign.

21.♕c2! ♗xb2

But not 21...♕xb2? 22.♕h7+ ♔f8 23.♗d6+ ♔e8, and then simply 24.♗xc5. Capturing the b2 pawn with the bishop complicates matters somewhat, but it's still risky. Perhaps black was counting on 22.♕h7+ ♔f8 23.♗h4, and then 23...♗f6 24.♗xf6 gxf6 25.♕xh6+ ♔e7 with the subsequent ...♖h8.

It was worth considering 21...g6 22.b4 ♘d7 23.♕xc8+ ♖xc8 24.♖xc8+ with an advantage for white, but black still retained some chances of a successful defense.

22.♕h7+ ♔f8 23.♖cd1

An interesting continuation for the attack: 23.♖c4!?

23...♔e7 24.♗d6+ ♔f6

The last move was the point of black's plan. After escaping the checks, his king seems to be quite comfortable. But it's only an illusion. Objectively speaking, black had to give away his queen: 24...♕xd6! 25.♖xd6 ♔xd6, with sufficient compensation.

After the game move, Rauzer could have crowned his plan with a brilliant rook sacrifice – 25.♖d5!! The threat of mate on f5 leaves black no choice – 25...g6, which is met with 26.♗xg6! ♖f8 27.♗xf7!, and if now 27...♕xd6 (the branches are pretty too: 27...♖g8 28.♗e7+; 27...♖xf7 28.♕xh6# – a "quiet" checkmate), then 28.♖xd6 ♖xf7 29.♕c2 with an easy win.

These lines were shown by Y. Rokhlin after the tournament. In the actual game, however, Rauzer got tempted by a queen sacrifice, planning to weave a mating net around the black king with e3-e4 and f2-f4, which looks inescapable at first glance.

25.e4!? ♘d7 26.♔h1 ♖h8 27.f4 ♖xh7 28.e5+ ♘xe5 29.fxe5+ ♔g5 30.♗xh7

30.♖xf7! was more precise.

30...h5

Providing a temporary hiding place for the king. But its sufferings were not over yet.

31.♖xf7 ♔h6

32.♗e4

After this bold (perhaps overly bold?) combination, white has two centralized pieces and a number of threats to the opposing king for the queen. 32.♗b1 was also interesting, to provide protection to the attacking bishop (see white's 34th move).

32...♖c8 33.h4

With the idea of ♗e7 and ♗g5#; but even here, black has a refutation.

33...♕e3 34.♗b1 ♖c4?

The crude 34...♗xa3! destroyed all the charm of white's combination. Of course, 34...♖c1? led to checkmate after 35.♖f6+, but 34...♕g3 35.♗e7 ♗c1 also saved black.

35.♖f6+!!, and black resigned (35...g6 36.♖xg6+ or 35...gxf6 36.♗f8#).

A dramatic game, especially considering its career implications for the players. "The 'accident' that happened to me (as Botvinnik liked to joke, I 'fell under the tram') was quite notorious," Rokhlin said, finding some strength for self-irony after the game. This loss cost him a point and the master's title...

On the other hand, this unexpected lucky break secured the coveted title for Rauzer ahead of schedule.

The next game with the successful wandering black king could have served as a model for both players. It was widely known back then.

No. 17a. Queen's Gambit
E. Bogoljubov – R. Reti
Carlsbad 1923

1.d4 d5 2.♘f3 ♘f6 3.c4 e6 4.♘c3 ♗e7 5.♗g5 ♘bd7 6.e3 0-0 7.♖c1 c6 8.a3 a6 9.♕c2 ♖e8 10.♗d3 dxc4 11.♗xc4 b5 12.♗a2 c5 13.dxc5
13.0-0!

13...♘xc5 14.0-0 ♗b7 15.♘d4 ♖c8 16.f3 ♕b6 17.♗b1

17...h6
"A fearless move" – S. Tartakower.
18.♗xf6 ♗xf6 19.♕h7+ ♔f8 20.♖cd1 ♖ed8 21.♔h1 ♔e7 22.♘ce2 ♖h8 23.♕c2 a5 24.b4 axb4 25.axb4 ♘a4 26.♕d2 ♖hd8 27.♗d3 g6 28.f4 ♗d5 29.♗xb5 ♗xd4 30.♘xd4 ♘c3 31.♗d3 ♘xd1 32.♖xd1 ♖a8 33.♕e1 ♖a2 34.♕h4+ ♔f8!

This move actually gives white a chance to save the game (which he missed). Only 34...f6 still gave black winning chances.

35.♕xh6+?

The decisive mistake. Only a "cold-blooded" computer could find the saving move 35.♗b1!!

35...♔g8

The black king is now safely home, and white's position is ruined.

36.♖g1 ♗xg2+ 37.♖xg2 ♖a1+ 38.♖g1 ♕b7+, and white resigned.

No. 18. Nimzo-Indian Defense
Rauzer – Konstantinopolsky
Kiev Championship, 1930
Annotated by V. Rauzer

1.d4 ♘f6 2.c4 e6 3.♘c3 ♗b4 4.♕c2 c5 5.dxc5 ♘c6 6.♘f3 ♗xc5 7.♗f4 0-0 8.e3

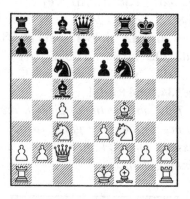

8...b6?

Since the move d7-d5 is necessary, there was no need to waste time and weaken the position (the c6 square) by fianchettoing the c8 bishop. Thus, it was better to play 8...d5 9.♖d1 ♕a5, and white would have regretted playing ♗f4 instead of ♗g5.

Modern theory is still undecided where the bishop is placed best – on g5 or f4. – **A. K.**

9.♗e2 ♗b7 10.0-0 d5 11.♖fd1

Thanks to the deferred d7-d5 move by black, the white rooks have enough time to get into the "classical" position on d1 and c1.

11...♕e7 12.cxd5 ♘b4 13.d6!

This trading tactic gives white several extra tempi.

13...♘xc2   14.dxe7   ♗xe7 15.♖ac1 ♘b4 16.♘b5

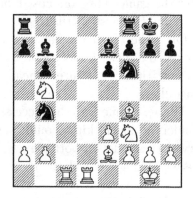

16...♘fd5

Black is experiencing some difficulties. If, for instance, 16...♖fd8, then 17.♖xd8+ ♖xd8 18.♘xa7, and 18...♘xa2 is met with 19.♖a1 and ♗c7, or 18...♖a8 is met with 19.♖c7 ♖xa7 20.♖xe7 ♘bd5 21.♗b8 ♘xe7 22.♗xa7 ♘d7 23.♘d4, then ♗b5, and the bishop on a7 is eventually freed.

In the first line, the situation after 19.♖a1 is unclear, for instance, 19...♘b4 20.♗c7 ♖a8 21.♗xb6 ♘fd5 22.♗d4 ♘c2 23.♖a2 ♘xd4 24.♘xd4 ♗c5 25.♘db5 f5, and white is uncomfortably pinned along the a-file.

17.♗d6 ♗xd6?

The losing trade. The correct continuation was 17...♘xa2 18.♖a1 ♘ab4 19.♗xe7 ♘xe7 20.♖d7 ♗xf3 21.♗xf3 ♘ed5 22.♖axa7 ♖xa7 23.♘xa7, and white's positional advantage is not so noticeable.

18.♘xd6 ♗a6

If 18...♖ab8, then 19.♘xb7 ♖xb7 20.a3, and white wins.

19.♗xa6 ♘xa6 20.♘e5 ♘c5

If 20...♖ad8, then 21.♘dxf7 ♖xf7 22.♘xf7 ♔xf7 23.e4 ♘f4 24.♖xd8 ♘e2+ 25.♔f1 ♘xc1 26.♖d7+, and white should win.

21.♘c6!

A peaceful conference of four empires. Black's heavy artillery is silent (disarmament!). In such conditions, technique makes all the difference.

21...a5 22.a3 a4 23.g3

After getting a clear advantage, white starts to rest on his laurels and plays rather poorly – and the disarmament of his opponent clearly doesn't happen. It was necessary to play 23.e4! and meet 23...♘f4 with 24.♖c2.

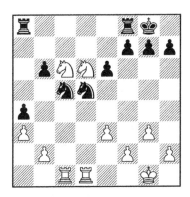

23...f5! 24.♖c4

Defending from ...♘e4 and stubbornly trying to keep the knights on d6 and c6. But now this doesn't lead to anything, because e3-e4 is impossible, and the position of the black knights is equally good.

24...♘f6 25.f3 g5 26.h3

To keep the black knight off g4 after e3-e4 and the trade on e4. However, the awkward position of the white pawns speaks for itself.

26...♘d5 27.♔f2

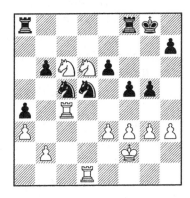

27...f4?

As though out of pity for white's pathetic attempts, black makes a losing move again. After 27...♖f6 with the subsequent ...♖h6, white's advantage evaporates.

28.gxf4 gxf4 29.e4 ♘e3 30.♖g1+ ♔h8 31.♘e5! ♖a7 32.♖d4

18.♘d5! exd5 19.♕xf5 dxc4

A blunder. 19...fxe5 20.♕xe5 ♕xe5 21.♘xe5 ♘f6 was necessary, leaving some hope for survival.

20.♕e4 fxe5 21.♗xc4+ d5 22.♗xd5+ ♔h8 23.♘h4 ♗f5 24.♘xf5 ♘f6 25.♕b1 ♖ad8 26.♗e4 ♖xd1 27.♖xd1 ♘xe4 28.♕xe4 ♕f7 29.g4 g6 30.♕xe5+ ♔h7 31.♖c1 gxf5 32.♖c7 and white won.

32...♖g7?

Black could have prevented checkmate (yes, checkmate!) by sacrificing an exchange: 32...h6 33.♘g6+ ♔g7 34.♘xf8+.

After 32...♖g7, white delivered a mate in six:

33.♘df7+ ♔g8 34.♘h6+ ♔h8 35.♘ef7+ ♖gxf7 36.♘xf7+ ♖xf7 37.♖d8+ ♖f8 38.♖xf8#.

No. 19. Nimzo-Indian Defense
Rauzer – Kofman
Kiev Championship, 1930

1.d4 ♘f6 2.c4 e6 3.♘c3 ♗b4 4.♕c2 c5 5.dxc5 ♘c6 6.♘f3 ♗xc5 7.♗g5 ♗e7 8.e4 ♕c7 9.♗e2 a6 10.0-0 ♘g4? 11.♕d2 0-0 12.♗xe7 ♘xe7 13.♕g5 ♘f6 14.e5 h6 15.♕g3 ♘e8 16.♖ad1 ♘f5 17.♕f4 f6?

It was necessary to play 17...d6.

No. 20. Queen's Gambit
Rauzer – Selezniev
Masters tournament of Transcaucasia, Ukraine and Uzbekistan
Tbilisi 1930
Annotated by A. Model

1.d4 ♘f6 2.c4 e6 3.♘c3 d5 4.♗g5 ♘bd7 5.e3 c6 6.♘f3 ♕a5 7.cxd5

Tarrasch's move that doesn't give white any advantage. 7.♘d2 is stronger, but 7.♗xf6 is probably the most solid here.

7...exd5

A weak move; 7...♘xd5 was better. Now the move ...♕a5 turns

out to be simply a loss of tempo, and white has better piece play.

8.♗d3 ♗d6 9.0-0 h6 10.♗h4 0-0 11.a3 b5

Black goes for complications because he's already worse; the standard continuation 11...♖e8 won't allow him to liberate his position.

12.e4! dxe4 13.♘xe4 ♘xe4 14.♗xe4 ♕c7?

Why not 14...♕b6 ?

15.♖c1 ♗b7 16.♗xc6

This move, which turns the weak d4 pawn into a strong one on c6, was, of course, impossible if the black queen were on b6.

16...♗xc6 17.d5 ♘b6

Or 17...♘e5 18.♘d4 etc., with an advantage for white.

18.dxc6 ♘c4 19.♘d4

Unnecessary complications. After 19.♕d5 a6 20.♖cd1, white had a winning position.

19...♗xh2+ 20.♔h1 ♗f4 21.♖c3 a6

21...g5!? with an unclear position was worthy of consideration.

22.♕g4 ♗e5

Black could have equalized chances with 22...h5 23.♕xh5 ♕e5!

23.♗g3 ♕d6

After 23...♗xg3 24.♖xg3, white has an unstoppable attack.

24.♘f5 ♕f6 25.♗h4 ♕e6

25...g5 wouldn't save black either – white had a strong, albeit somewhat risky reply 26.f4! For instance, 26...♗xc3 27.fxg5 hxg5 28.♗xg5 ♕h8+ 29.♗h6+, with a mate in five moves at most; or 27...♘e5 28.♕g3 ♗e1 29.♕xe1 etc., with a likely unstoppable attack.

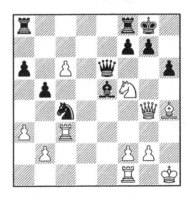

26.♖e1 ♔h7 27.♖xe5! ♕xe5 28.f4 ♕xc3 29.bxc3 g6 30.♗f6

Black resigned, because the move ♘xh6 with a mating attack cannot be prevented.

No. 21. Queen's Gambit
Rauzer – Freymann
Masters tournament of
Transcaucasia, Ukraine and
Uzbekistan
Tbilisi 1930
Annotated by V. Sozin

1.d4 ♘f6 2.c4 e6 3.♘c3 ♗b4 4.♕c2 d5 5.♘f3 0-0 6.♗g5 ♘bd7 7.e3 c5 8.cxd5 exd5 9.♗d3 ♕a5

White threatened 10.♗xh7+. The game has transposed from the Nimzo-Indian Defense into a well-known Queen's Gambit line often used by Spielmann.

10.0-0

10...c4

Such pawn advances, showing black's intentions to exploit his queenside pawn advantage, are always highly committal, because they allow the foundation of the pawn chain to be undermined with e3-e4. Black could have made the waiting move 10...♖e8, then h7-h6 and ♗xc3, leaving the pawn on c5.

The continuation 10...♖e8 11.♘xd5!? is better for white.

11.♗f5 ♖e8

If 11...g6, then 12.♗xd7 ♘xd7 13.e4! ♗xc3 14.bxc3 ♖e8, and now 15.e5! (instead of 15.exd5, Grunfeld – Spielmann, Merano 1926) with a better position for white.

12.♘d2

A good move, preparing e3-e4. However, it seems that 12.a3 was even stronger, retaining the possibility to put the knight on e5. The game Bogoljubov – Spielmann (Dortmund 1928) continued: 12...♗xc3 13.♕xc3! ♕xc3 14.bxc3 ♘b6 15.♗xc8 ♘xc8 16.♗xf6 gxf6 17.♘d2 etc., with an advantage for white. 12...♗e7(d6) was somewhat better, but even then, as Bogoljubov pointed out, after 13.♖ad1 white's position is preferable.

12...♗f8

Not 12...♘e4 due to 13.♗xe4!
dxe4 14.♗f4! 12...♗e7 was perhaps
somewhat better than the game
move.

**13.♖ae1 g6 14.♗h3 h6 15.♗h4
♗g7 16.f3**

This allows black to free himself
gradually. It was necessary to
continue the plan with 16.e4.

If now 16...g5, then 17.e5 ♘h7
18.♗g3 ♘df8 19.♗xc8 ♖axc8 20.f4±
etc.

*After 17...gxh4, the position is
unclear. Therefore, the piece sacrifice
17.♗g3!? g4 18.♗xg4! ♘xg4
19.♘xd5 with great compensation
was worthy of consideration.*

**16...♘f8 17.♗xc8 ♖axc8 18.♗f2
♘e6 19.♔h1 b5**

Black finishes his development
and returns to queenside play.

20.a3 ♕b6 21.♗g1? ♕c6 22.e4

Finally! But here, it actually
made more sense to spend one
more tempo on 22.g3, preventing
♘f4.

**22...♘f4 23.e5 ♘d7 24.♗e3
♘d3 25.♖e2 a5 26.a4**

26...b4

26...bxa4!? was better

27.♘b5

Threatening ♘d6 and ♘a7.

**27...♖b8 28.b3! ♘b6 29.♘d6
♖ed8 30.bxc4 dxc4 31.♘6xc4**

It was simpler to play 31.♘2xc4,
because the knight wouldn't have
been pinned.

31...♘xe5?

With 26...b4, black didn't just let
the white knight penetrate his camp
– he also took away the last escape
square from the d3 knight.

*Black probably didn't see how he
could save the knight and decided
to sacrifice it. The correct move was*

31...♘xc4 32.♘xc4 ♖bc8 with equal chances.

32.dxe5 ♖xd2 33.♖xd2 ♕xc4 34.♖c1

34...b3

If 34...♕xc2 35.♖dxc2 b3, then 36.♖c6 b2 37.♖b1 ♘xa4 38.♗d4! ♖d8 39.♖c4 with good winning chances.

35.♕xc4

After 35.♕d1! white won easily, for instance, 35...♕xa4 36.♖d8+ etc.

35...♘xc4 36.♖xc4!

After 36.♖e2 b2 37.♖b1 ♗xe5 38.♗c5 (black threatened ♘a3) 38...♖b3 black gets his rook to c1 and wins. White now returns the exchange and gets an extra pawn.

36...b2 37.♖xb2 ♖xb2 38.f4 ♖e2 39.♗b6 ♖e1+ 40.♔g1 ♗f8

After 40...f6!, black should have survived. Now, however, the fight flares up again.

41.g3 ♗b4 42.♔g2 g5 43.♖c8+ ♔h7

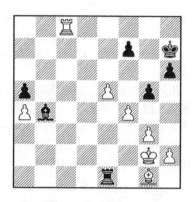

44.f5! g4

Not 44...♖xe5 due to 45.♗d4 ♖xf5 (45...♖e2+ 46.♔f3) 46.♖h8+ ♔g6 47.♖g8+ ♔h5 48.h3! ♖d5 49.g4+ and 50.♗f2#.

45.♗d4 ♖e4

45...♖d1 was somewhat better, forcing white to reply 46.♖c4, since 46.♖d8 is bad due to 46...♗c5! 47.e6 ♗xd4 48.h4! (48.exf7? ♖g1#) 48...♖d2+ with a draw.

Instead of 46.♖c4, white should play 46.♗e3!?, which likely wins.

46.♖d8 ♗e7 47.♖d7 ♔g8 48.h4 gxh3+ 49.♔xh3 ♗g5 50.♔g2 h5 51.♔f3 ♖e1 52.e6!

Black resigned.

No. 22. Slav Defense
Rauzer – Bychek
7th Soviet Championship
(group stage)
Moscow 1931

1.d4 d5 2.c4 c6 3.♘c3 ♘f6 4.♘f3 e6 5.♗g5 ♘bd7 6.♕b3

A possible method of combating the Cambridge Springs system.

The idea of 6.♕b3 is to protect

the c4 pawn, temporarily leaving the c1-h6 diagonal open for the bishop. If now 6...♕a5, then 7.♗d2. In addition, the queen on b3 puts some pressure on the d5 square.

6...dxc4

The wrong system. The correct development method for black in this line was shown in the game Rauzer – Botvinnik, played in the final tournament. That game, which was won by the future Soviet champion, can be found in the first volume of M. Botvinnik's *Analytical and Critical Works*. The opening was handled in the following way: 6...♗e7 7.e3 0-0 8.♗e2 b6 9.cxd5 exd5 10.0-0 ♗b7.

See also Rauzer – Zamikhovsky (game 26) and Rauzer – Yudovich (game 28).

7.♕xc4 h6 8.♗h4 ♕a5 9.e3

9.♖c1 was also possible, to meet 9...♘d5 with 10.a3! and the subsequent e2-e3.

9...♘d5! 10.♗d3 ♗b4

If 10...♘xc3?, then 11.♕xe6+ fxe6 12.♗g6#.

11.♖c1 ♘7b6 12.♕b3

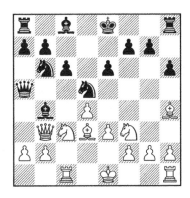

If now 12...♘a4, then 13.0-0 with the following possible lines:

I) 13...♘xb2 14.♘xd5 ♘xd3 15.♘xb4 ♘xb4 16.♘e5 ♘d5 (16... ♘a6 17.♘c4 ♕b4 18.♕c2 0-0 19.♖b1+−) 17.e4+−;

II) 13...♘axc3 14.bxc3, and black cannot win the pawn because this loses a piece;

III) 13...♘dxc3 14.bxc3 ♗xc3 15.a3 b5 16.♘e5+−;

IV) 13...♗xc3 14.bxc3 ♘dxc3 15.♕a3 ♘d5 (15...f6 16.♗g6+ ♔d8 17.♖xc3+−) 16.♖c5! ♕b4 17.♖xd5, and white wins.

12...♕a4 13.♗c2 ♕xb3 14.♗xb3 a5 15.a4

Necessary, because after 15.a3 ♘xc3 16.axb4 a4 17.♖xc3 axb3 18.♔e2 e5! 19.♖xb3 ♖a2 20.♘xe5 ♗e6 21.♖a3 ♖xb2+ 22.♔d3 ♖xb4 the position is equal.

15...♗e7

To seize the weakened b4 square with the knight.

16.♗g3 ♘b4 17.♔e2 0-0 18.♘e5 ♘d7 19.♘e4 ♖d8 20.♖hd1 ♘xe5 21.♗xe5 ♔f8 22.g4

After 22.♗c7 ♖d7 23.♗b6

♘d5 24.♗xd5 exd5 25.♘c5 ♗xc5
26.♖xc5, white wins a pawn, but gets
opposite-colored bishops.

*In addition, it's unclear how white
can even hold onto that extra pawn
after 26...♖a6 27.♗xa5 ♔e8!*

22...b5

A counter-attack against white's
pressure on the kingside.

23.♘c5 ♗xc5

24.dxc5

24.♖xc5 was also possible.

24...♗a6 25.♗d6+ ♔e8 26.f4?

It was necessary to prepare the
kingside pawn advance with 26.♔f3!?,
preventing the complications that
arose in the actual game.

26...bxa4+ 27.♗c4

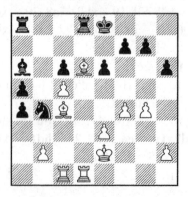

27...♖a7

After 27...♘a2 28.♖c2 ♘b4,
white would have had to settle for
a threefold repetition, because after
29.♗xa6 ♘xc2 30.♗b7 ♘b4, white's
kingside attack wouldn't have been
as strong given that one of the rooks
would have been traded.

**28.f5 ♘a2 29.♖c2 ♘b4 30.♖cc1
♘a2 31.♖c2 ♘b4 32.♖cc1 ♘a2
33.♖c2 ♘b4 34.fxe6**

The only possible way to decline
the draw. The exchange sacrifice
doesn't pose white any risk of
losing.

34...♘xc2

If 34...fxe6, then 35.♗xa6 ♘xc2?
(35...♘xa6 is better) 36.♗d3 ♘b4
37.♗g6+ ♔d7 38.♗b8+, winning.

35.exf7+ ♖xf7 36.♗xa6

36...♖f6

Defending from 37.♗d3 and
38.♗g6+. If 36...♘b4, then 37.♗c4
♖f6 (37...♖b7 38.♖f1 ♖xd6 39.cxd6
with the subsequent advance of
the e-pawn) 38.e4 with enough
compensation.

37.♗c4 a3?

By playing 37...♖fxd6!?, black would have gained the better chances in the ensuing endgame.

38.♗b3 ♘b4 39.bxa3 ♘a6

Or 39...♘d5 40.♗xd5 cxd5 41.♖xd5.

40.e4

40.♗a4!? was worth considering

40...♖dxd6 41.cxd6 ♖f4?

If 41...♘c5, then 42.e5 ♖f4 43.♗c2 ♖xg4 44.♔f3 ♖g5 45.♖e1 ♔d7 46.h4, ultimately winning the rook.

The correct move was 42...♖g6, with drawing chances.

42.♔e3 ♖xg4 43.♗e6 ♖g6

Otherwise 44.d7+ and then ♖f1.

44.♗f7+

Black resigned.

No. 23. Queen's Gambit
Rauzer – Moskalev
7th Soviet Championship
(group stage)
Moscow 1931

1.d4 d5 2.c4 e6 3.♘c3 c6 4.♘f3 dxc4

Long ago, this move was most often labeled as "ceding the center". With time, the move has served as a small seed for two or three systems which are not entirely correct, but still harbor some hope of success.

Without a doubt, 4...♘f6 is more solid.

5.e3 b5 6.a4

6.♘e5 ♘f6 7.♕f3 was also strong.

6...b4

Theoreticians also studied 6...♗b4 7.♗d2 ♕b6 8.axb5 cxb5 9.♘e5 ♗b7 (or 9...♘f6 10.b3 ♘d5 11.♘xb5! c3 12.♘xc3! and then ♕c2 – this is better for white) 10.b3 ♗xc3 11.♗xc3 cxb3 12.♗a5, and the b3 pawn doesn't help black – 12...b2 13.♖a2 ♕d6 14.♗xb5+ etc.

7.♘e4 ♗a6

7...♘d7 8.♗xc4 ♗b7 with the subsequent c6-c5 was more logical.

8.♕c2 ♕d5

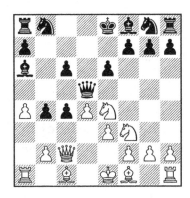

9.♘fd2(?)

Later, Rauzer demonstrated a better plan – 9.♘ed2! c5 10.e4 ♕d8 11.♗xc4, immediately regaining the pawn.

9...♘f6 10.♘xf6+ gxf6 11.♘xc4 ♗xc4

Black is glad to trade pieces and forgets to stop e3-e4.

12.♕xc4 ♕xc4

This was the last chance to organize play in the center – 12...a5 13.f3 f5!

13.♗xc4

13...a5

Rauzer analyzed two worse lines for black:

a) 13...f5 14.f3 ♗g7 15.♔e2 ♔e7 16.♖d1 ♖e8 17.a5 with threats ♗d2 and ♖a4;

b) 13...♗d6 14.e4 ♘d7 15.♔e2 ♔e7 16.f4! c5 17.d5 ♘b6 18.♗b5 exd5 19.a5. The game move is relatively better.

14.e4 ♗d6 15.♗e3 ♘d7 16.♖c1

Rauzer thought that this move was poor, and that the correct continuation was 16.♔e2 with the subsequent ♖hc1 and ♖c2, thereby not weakening the a4 pawn. However, the game move essentially doesn't spoil anything.

16...♔e7 17.♔e2 ♖hc8 18.♖c2 c5 19.d5 ♘b6

Of course, Rauzer was correct in thinking that the simple 16.♔e2 ♔e7 17.♖hc1 easily led to the main goal. But even now, white's pressure was considerable. For instance, 20.dxe6 ♘xc4 (20...fxe6 21.♗b5 ♖c7 22.♖hc1 ♖ac8 23.f4, with the threat of e4-e5 looming again) 21.♖xc4 fxe6 22.♖hc1 or 21...♔xe6 22.♖d1, then f2-f4 with the threat e4-e5.

The "crude" reply 20.b3 also kept the advantage, because black's forces are tied up, and white has numerous prospects involving a kingside pawn push and getting the king's rook into play.

Only the next ill-advised bishop retreat made white's task more difficult.

20.♗b3? c4! 21.♗xb6 cxb3 22.♖c6 ♖xc6 23.dxc6

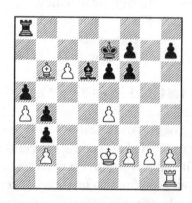

23...♖c8?

This loses. Only 23...♗e5!, attacking the b2 pawn, opened up the path to a draw. The main line was: 24.c7 ♗xb2 25.♖b1 ♗c3 26.♖xb3 ♔d7 27.♖b1 e5 28.♖d1+ ♗d4 29.♗xd4 exd4 30.♖xd4+ ♔xc7

31.♖d5 ♖b8 32.♖xa5 b3 33.♗c5+ ♔d6 34.♗c1 ♖b4 (V. Rauzer).

24.♗c1 ♗c7

There were still some hopes after 24...♗e5 25.♗xa5 ♗xb2 26.♗xb4+ ♔e8 27.♖b1 ♗e5 28.♖xb3 ♖xc6.

The plan in the subsequent endgame is rather simple. The trade of bishops and rooks makes black's loss all the quicker.

25.♗xc7 ♖xc7 26.♔d3 ♔d6 27.♔d4

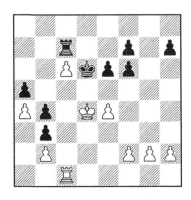

27...e5+

Or 27...♖xc6 28.♖xc6+ ♔xc6 29.g4 ♔d6 30.f4 ♔c6 31.♔c4 (31. g5? e5+!–+) 31...♔b6 32.f5 with a won pawn endgame.

28.♔d3 h6 29.g4 ♔e6 30.♖c5 ♔d6 31.♔c4 ♖xc6 32.♖xc6+ ♔xc6 33.f3 f5 34.gxf5 h5 35.h3 f6 36.h4 ♔c7 37.♔b5 ♔d6 38.♔b6 1-0.

Winning this game was much easier for Rauzer than annotating it for the first fundamental work by Soviet chess players – the tournament book of the 7th Soviet Championship edited by M. Botvinnik. Rauzer always treated such work with

special thoroughness, or, should I say, a certain "holy trepidation".

This was precisely the case here: the lines, both in the opening and in the very complicated endgame, were honed with great detail and precision by the young master. He spent many hours studying the various types of endgame that came up in the process of analysis, refining his evaluations and conclusions again and again.

While the opening stage of this game is, obviously, evaluated very differently several decades later, Rauzer's various analyses of this rather complicated endgame still remain a full-weight and instructive specimen of his play and researching talent.

In view of that, as I prepared the game for this collection, I had to omit some of Rauzer's opening theory findings, keeping, however, the valuable analysis of a rather unique endgame.

No. 24. Chigorin Opening
Gribin – Rauzer
7th Soviet Championship
(group stage)
Moscow 1931

1.e4 e6 2.♕e2

One of those "ways into the unknown" that facilitated the development and practical molding of the King's Indian structure. This opening "whim" by Chigorin, as perceived by his contemporaries, contained a seed of truth that later gave birth to a lush garden. In addition to the game move, white can meet the direct 2...d5 with 3.d3, strengthening the e4 pawn, or open up the position – 3.exd5 ♕xd5 4.♘c3 ♕d8 5.♘f3 or 5.f4 c5 6.♘f3 ♘c6 7.g3 ♘f6 8.♗g2 with a good position.

2...c5

Sometimes Rauzer played 2...♗e7 3.d3 d5, which also gave black a solid foundation in the center.

3.g3 ♘f6

Black also played 3...♗e7 here, and only then d7-d5. However, in this case white can meet d7-d5 with the e4-e5 push, cramping the position of the g8 knight. After the game move, however, 4.e5 is not good for white due to 4...♘d5 and then d7-d6 (in the vein of the Alekhine Defense), attacking the central white pawn.

4.♗g2 d5 5.exd5

Play is more exciting after 5.e5 ♘fd7 6.f4 ♘c6 7.♘f3 or 5.d3 ♘c6 6.♘f3.

5...♘xd5 6.♘c3

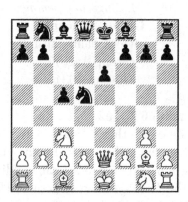

White speeds up the development of his pieces at the cost of assuming doubled pawns. However, black could calmly reply 6...♗e7. If white tried to win the pawn with 7.♘xd5 exd5 8.♕e5, then, after 8...0-0! 9.♕xd5 ♗d6 10.♘e2 ♖e8, he would have gotten into a difficult situation.

After the trade on c3, black has good prospects for the endgame: an extra pawn on the kingside, while his opponent's pawns on the other side of the board are doubled. As compensation, white has good piece play.

6...♘xc3 7.dxc3 ♗e7 8.♘f3 0-0

8...♘c6 was more precise; after the game move, white could have slowed the development of his opponent's queenside with 9.♘e5.

9.♗f4 ♘c6 10.0-0 ♕b6 11.b3 ♖d8 12.♖ad1 ♗d7 13.♘g5

This move in and of itself is good, but white subsequently chose the wrong plan.

13...♗e8

14.♕e4?

A mistake. Nothing comes out of the attack, and white's queenside is defenseless (the threat ♛a5 is rather unpleasant).

Black's play would have been much harder after 14.♘e4!, targeting d6 and c5.

14...g6 15.♗c1

Threatening ♛h4. Still, 15.♗e3 was more precise.

15...♖xd1 16.♖xd1 ♖d8!

17.♖e1

After 17.♖xd8 ♛xd8 with threats ♗xg5 and ♛d1+, white's position would have been very poor. However, he should have put the rook on f1.

17...♛a5 18.♛h4 h5 19.b4

A mistake. After 19.♛c4!?, white had a chance to hold the position.

19...♛xa2 20.♗f3

Not 20.g4 ♛c4 21.♗e4 ♛xc3 and then ♛h8. White still placed some ephemeral hopes on ♗xh5 or g3-g4.

20...♛xc2 21.g4 ♛xc3 22.♖f1 ♘e5

22...♗xg5   23.♗xg5   ♛xf3 24.♗xd8 ♘d4 25.♖e1 ♗c6 won as well.

23.♗e2 ♛c2

White resigned. Indeed, after

24.♖e1 black won with the simple 24...♗c6 25.♔f1 ♗f3 or 25...♖d4.

Black's central strategy was unstoppable!

No. 25. Queen's Gambit
Sorokin – Rauzer
7th Soviet Championship
Moscow 1931

This game is somewhat interesting because of its opening. The players followed the 12th game of the Alekhine – Capablanca match. However, in the transition from the opening to the middlegame, N. Sorokin played without any plan and without trying for an initiative. With 15.♗xe4, he ceded control of the center to his opponent; from the 16th move onward, he made 8 out of 9 moves with the same knight, and then, in a worse position, allowed his opponent to decide the game with an elegant combination. If, instead of 25.exf4, white had played 25.♖xc4, then black would have played 25...f3!. The same reply would have followed after 25.♘xd8. Perhaps white overlooked the timely reply 26...♛f6!, attacking the rook.

1.d4 d5 2.♘f3 ♘f6 3.c4 e6 4.♘c3 ♘bd7 5.♗g5 ♗e7 6.e3 0-0 7.♖c1 c6 8.♗d3 a6 9.a3 h6 10.♗h4 b5 11.cxd5 cxd5 12.0-0 ♗b7 13.♛e2 ♘e4 14.♗xe7 ♛xe7 15.♗xe4? dxe4 16.♘d2 f5 17.♘b3 e5 18.♘a5 exd4 19.♘xb7 dxc3 20.♖xc3 ♘e5 21.♘c5 ♘c4! 22.♘b3 ♖ad8 23.♘d4?

23...f4! 24.♘c6 ♕d7 25.exf4 ♕xc6 26.b3 ♕f6! 27.♖xc4 bxc4 28.♕xc4+

White resigned without waiting for his opponent's reply.

No. 26. Queen's Gambit
Rauzer – Zamikhovsky
7th Soviet Championship
Moscow 1931
Annotated by V. Sozin

1.d4 d5 2.c4 c6 3.♘f3 ♘f6 4.♘c3 e6 5.♗g5 ♘bd7

6.♕b3

Rauzer's novelty. Its purpose is avoiding the Cambridge Springs variation.

6...♗e7 7.e3 0-0 8.♗e2 a6

The most sensible development plan here is 8...b6 (as happened in the fragment No. 13 Rauzer – Botvinnik).

9.a4 ♖e8 10.0-0 ♘f8

10...♘e4 was worth considering.

11.♖ad1 ♘g6 12.♗d3 dxc4 13.♕xc4 ♕b6

A pointless move. It was necessary to play 13...♘d5, to ease the position via trades.

14.e4!

14...♕b4

After 14...♕xb2 15.♖b1 ♕a3 16.♖b3? b5!, black gets an advantage. However, by playing 16.♗c1!? b5, white retained the better chances.

15.♕a2 e5?

This loses a pawn.

16.♗c4! ♖f8 17.♘xe5 ♘xe5 18.dxe5 ♘g4 19.♗f4 ♕c5 20.e6!

Black probably missed this move when he gave up a pawn on the 15th move.

20...fxe6   21.♗xe6+   ♔h8 22.♗g3 ♘e5 23.♘e2 ♗f6 24.♘d4 ♖e8 25.♗xc8 ♖axc8 26.♘f5 ♖cd8 27.♕b3 ♕c4 28.♕xb7 ♖xd1

Not 28...♕xe4 due to 29.♘d6 ♕e2 30.♖de1 and 31.♘xe8.

29.♖xd1 ♕xa4

If now 29...♕xe4, then 30.♘d6 ♕e2 (30...♕xa4 31.b3) 31.♖f1 ♖f8 32.♗xe5 ♗xe5 33.♘f7+ ♔g8 34.♘xe5 ♕xe5 35.♕xc6, winning another pawn.

30.♖f1   ♖d8   31.♘d6   ♖xd6 32.♗xe5 ♖d1

32...♖d8 is somewhat better.

33.b3 ♖xf1+ 34.♔xf1 ♕a5

35.♕b8+ ♗d8?

35...♕d8 was necessary, even though the endgame was still lost. After the game move, white could win immediately with 36.♕d6! (36...♕b5+ 37.♔g1 or 36...♔g8 37.♕e6+ ♔f8 38.♗d6+).

36.b4? ♕b6?

Black should have played 36...♕b5+, because now white could again have won immediately with 37.♕d6! ♕b5+ 38.♔g1 ♔g8 39.♕e6+ ♔f8 40.♗d6+ and a quick checkmate.

37.♕xb6? ♗xb6 38.♗d6

The endgame is very simple.

38...♔g8 39.f4 ♔f7 40.♔e2 ♔e6 41.♗c5 ♗c7 42.♔e3 a5 43.bxa5 ♗xa5 44.f5+ ♔f7 45.g4 ♗c3 46.♗d4 ♗b4 47.e5 g6 48.♔e4 ♗a3 49.♔e3 ♗e7 50.e6+ ♔f6 51.g5+ ♔g7 52.♗d4+

Winning the bishop for three pawns with 52.f6+ would, of course, have only made the win harder.

52...♔f8 53.f6 ♗d6 54.♔d3 c5 55.♗e3 ♗e7 56.♔c4 h6 57.fxe7+

Black resigned.

No. 27. English Opening
Kasparyan – Rauzer
7th Soviet Championship
Moscow 1931

The outward serenity of the game hides a great internal intensity. When white tried to show some activity on the kingside, black declined to settle for passive defense. For instance, if, instead of 30.hxg4, white had played 30.♖xg4?, he would have gotten into big trouble (30...♖h1+ 31.♔g3 ♕e1+ 32.♖f2 ♕g1+ 33.♖g2 ♕e3+ 34.♔h4 ♕xh3+ with mate next move). However, everything finished peacefully in the end. Black had to calculate his finishing blow that forced the draw five moves ahead.

1.c4 e6 2.b3 d5 3.♗b2 ♘f6 4.g3 ♗e7 5.♗g2 0-0 6.♘f3 c5 7.0-0 dxc4 8.bxc4 ♘c6 9.♘e5 ♘xe5 10.♗xe5 ♘g4 11.♗c3 ♗f6 12.♗xf6 ♕xf6 13.♘c3 ♖d8 14.♘e4 ♕e7 15.♖b1 ♖b8 16.♕c2 ♗d7 17.h3 ♘e5 18.f4 ♘c6 19.♘g5 f5 20.♗xc6 ♗xc6 21.♘f3 ♗xf3 22.♖xf3 ♕f6 23.♔h2 ♖d7

24.d3 ♖bd8 25.♖g1 ♖d6 26.♖g2 ♖b6 27.♕a4 ♖b1 28.♕xa7 ♕a1 29.g4 fxg4 30.hxg4 ♖h1+ 31.♔g3 ♕e1+ 32.♖ff2 ♖xd3+!

Draw.

No. 28. Queen's Gambit
Rauzer – Yudovich
7th Soviet Championship
Moscow 1931
Annotated by M. Botvinnik

1.d4 ♘f6 2.c4 e6 3.♘c3 d5 4.♗g5 c6 5.♘f3 ♘bd7 6.♕b3

Rauzer's move. It was played in the game Rauzer – Botvinnik of the same tournament.

6...♗e7 7.e3 0-0 8.♗e2 dxc4

It seems that the most accurate defense here is to fianchetto the light-squared bishop with 8...b6, as happened in the aforementioned game.

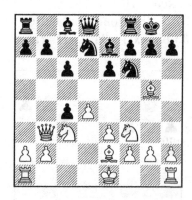

The defensive system chosen by black in this game has the following drawback:

Black follows the Capablanca system (dxc4 and ♘d5), which is appropriate for the Orthodox Defense with the move ♖ac1. In that line (1.d4 d5 2.c4 e6 3.♘c3 ♘f6 4.♗g5 ♗e7 5.♘f3 ♘bd7 6.e3 0-0 7.♖c1 c6 8.♗d3 dxc4 9.♗xc4 ♘d5), black can play the liberating break e6-e5. In this game, however, black couldn't play e6-e5 for a long time because of his opponent's various threats. And when he finally does manage to make this move, it turns out that it's not particularly useful anymore.

9.♕xc4

"Not a pretty move!" Tarrasch would have probably written. Indeed, the bishop capture looks more natural. Essentially, however, it's better to capture with the queen, because 9.♗xc4 can be met with 9...c5, and black frees up his position somewhat.

9...♘d5 10.♗xe7 ♕xe7 11.0-0

Contrary to the Rubinstein variation (the position is similar to the actual game, but with the queen on d1, rook on c1 and bishop on c4), where black can play 11...♘xc3 12.♖xc3 e5, he cannot make the same move here, because 11...♘xc3 is met with 12.♕xc3, making e6-e5 impossible. Thus, if black follows the Capablanca system, Rauzer's move is justified.

11...♖e8

Preparing e6-e5.

12.♖fd1

White again indirectly prevents e6-e5 due to the line 12...♘xc3 13.♕xc3 e5 14.dxe5 ♘xe5 15.♘xe5 ♕xe5 16.♕xe5 ♖xe5 17.♖d8+. Still, black does find an opportunity to play e6-e5.

Black could meet 14.dxe5 with 14...♔f8, regaining the e5 pawn. So, 14.♘xe5 is more precise.

12...♘5b6 13.♕b3 e5 14.a4

Black has largely solved the main problem of the Orthodox Defense – the development of the c8 bishop. But now he faces a new problem: what to do with the e5 pawn? White threatens a4-a5. Therefore, black pushes the pawn, but this is not a satisfactory solution. In this position (like in all similar positions arising from the Orthodox Defense), the correct way is 14...exd4! 15.♖xd4 ♘c5 with chances to equalize.

Pushing the pawn is a mistake for the following reasons: 1) the e4 pawn is going to be weak; 2) black gets his pieces into action much more slowly than after 14...exd4; 3) since the center remains closed, white calmly develops very strong pressure on the queenside.

14...e4 15.♘d2 ♘f6 16.a5!

The pawn move is very strong – the c6 pawn is now weakened. Black still has to take care of the e4 pawn. Not 16...♗e6 because of 17.♕c2.

16...♘bd5 17.a6 b6 18.♖dc1 ♗f5?

This move should be considered the decisive mistake. Black thought that the c6 pawn was weak, especially because it can only be defended with pieces. But he didn't take into account the fact that the c6 pawn was also holding off his opponent's pieces. Thus, it was necessary to preserve it. The correct move was 18...♗d7!, retaining both the c6 pawn and the piece outpost on d5. White immediately pounces on the chance and opens the c-file. It's all too easy to seize now because the c6 square is weak.

19.♞xd5 cxd5 20.♗b5 ♗d7 21.♗c6 ♗xc6

Black is forced to trade (otherwise ♗xd5), and this gives white a tempo to double the rooks.

22.♖xc6 ♖ec8 23.♕c3 ♕d7

Black goes for the endgame with hope to find salvation there. However, even without the queens, he has no future prospects. The c-file is fully controlled by his opponent.

24.♖c1 ♖xc6 25.♕xc6 ♕xc6 26.♖xc6 ♞e8

It's necessary to defend the c7 and d6 squares from the rook invasion.

27.♞b1 ♔f8 28.♞c3 ♖d8 29.♞b5 ♖d7 30.g4!

The white king enters the fray, and black's kingside gets blocked at the same time. 30.♖c8 ♔e7 31.♖a8 ♞c7 would give him nothing: compared with the game move, white simply wastes time.

30...♔e7 31.♖c8

Of course, the move ♔d8 should not be allowed.

The game move is actually not necessary. White can simply go forward with the king, as black cannot trade any pieces because of the weak a7 pawn, and he will have to resort to passive kingside pawn moves.

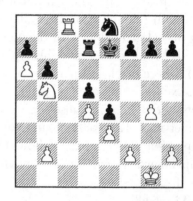

31...♞d6

Black offers to exchange the knights, probably relying on Tarrasch's profound utterance that "rook endings can never be won". Unfortunately, in this game, the rook ending is won! Material advantage in rook endings is not as important as positional ones, and this rule fits the position rather well. On the other hand, white could have forced the knight trade at any time by playing ♖a8.

The rook ending is, of course, won for white mainly because the a7 and a6 pawns limit black's mobility. White only needs to put the rook on b7 at the right moment. Right now, this doesn't give him anything, so he first brings the king closer.

32.♘xd6 ♔xd6 33.b4 ♖c7 34.♖h8 h6

Black cannot give away the kingside pawns.

Actually, he can! After 34...♔c6!, Tarrasch's "diagnosis" would have indeed been proven true – as well as the postulate above, "material advantage in rook endgames is not as important as positional ones". In this case, black could have saved the game by activating his king. However, the game move loses. White actually made a mistake on the 33rd move.

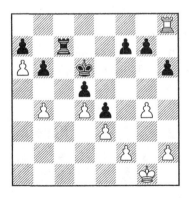

35.b5!

Just in time. The threat ♔c6 is now neutralized, and black is doomed to complete passivity.

35...♖c1+ 36.♔g2 ♔e6

The rook cannot leave the c-file because otherwise the a7 pawn falls. White also threatened ♖h7.

37.♖a8 ♖c7 38.♔g3 g6

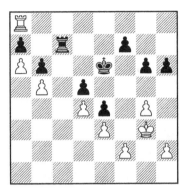

Inventive, but rather obvious. At first glance, it's simplest for white to grab the h6 pawn and win easily after 39.♖h8 ♖c2 40.♖xh6 ♖b2 41.♖h8 ♖xb5 42.♖a8 ♖a5 43.♖xa7 b5 44.h4.

However, in actuality 39.♖h8 is met with 39...♔f6!!, and the h6 pawn is taboo, because after 40.♖xh6 ♔g7 41.g5 ♖c2

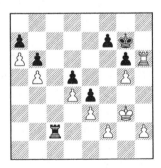

and ...♖b2 it's black, not white, who wins! Whereas, after white's calm reply, the text move simply leads to a weakening of black's position.

White still wins even in this line. Let's continue: 42.♖h3 ♖b2 43.♔f4 ♖xb5 44.♔e5 ♖a5 45.♖h4 b5 46.♔xd5, and white wins thanks to his active king.

39.h4! ♔f6 40.♖d8 ♔e6 41.g5

Fixing the f7 pawn.

41...hxg5 42.hxg5 ♖c2 43.♖a8 ♖c7 44.♖b8!

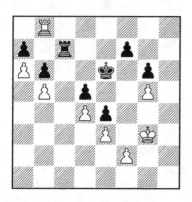

The decisive move. White threatens 45.♖b7 ♔d6 46.♔f4 ♖c2 (otherwise 47.♖xc7 and ♔e5; black also loses after 46...♖xb7 47.axb7 ♔c7 48.♔e5 ♔xb7 49.♔xd5 a5 50.bxa6+ ♔xa6 51.♔c6! etc.) 47.♖xa7 ♖xf2+ 48.♔g4 ♖g2+ 49.♔h4 ♖h2+ 50.♔g3 ♖e2 51.♖b7 ♖xe3+ 52.♔g2 ♖a3 (it's necessary to stop the pawn) 53.a7!, and there's no defense to ♖xb6+ with the subsequent ♖a6.

But white can play simpler and prettier: he threatens 45.♖b7 ♔d6 46.♔g4!! Now, 46...♖c2 is met with 47.♖xf7, 46...♖d7 with 47.♔f4!, while after 46...♖xb7 47.axb7 ♔c7 48.♔f4 ♔xb7 49.♔e5 a5 50.bxa6+ ♔xa6 51.♔xd5 ♔b5 (51...♔b7

52.♔d6!) 52.♔d6! ♔c4 53.♔c6 b5 54.d5 b4 55.d6 b3 56.d7 b2 57.d8=♕ b1=♕ 58.♕d4+ ♔b3 59.♕b6+ ♔c2 60.♕xb1+ ♔xb1 61.♔d5 white still wins. So, after 44...♔d6, white plays 45.♖b7!, too. Beautiful lines!

Black avoids them, but is still forced to give up soon.

44...♖c2 45.♖b7 ♖b2 46.♖xa7 ♖xb5 47.♖b7 ♖b1 48.a7 ♖a1 49.♖xb6+ ♔f5 50.♖f6+ ♔xg5 51.♖xf7 ♖g1+ 52.♔h2 ♖a1 53.♔g2

Black resigned.

Rauzer exploited his opponent's mistake on the 18th move with classic simplicity.

No. 29. King's Indian Defense
Rauzer – Riumin
7th Soviet Championship
Moscow 1931
Annotated by M. Botvinnik

1.d4 ♘f6 2.c4 g6 3.f3 ♗g7 4.e4 0-0 5.♗e3 c6

The normal development system here is 5...d6 with the subsequent e7-e5.

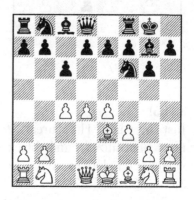

The idea of the game move is to establish a strong pawn on d5, rather than e5.

The main problem of the opening for black is placing his bishops. General considerations seem to suggest d7-d6 and e7-e5, which increases the activity of the g7 bishop. Concerning the c8 bishop, it certainly has better prospects after c7-c6 and d7-d5, because white's pawn structure gives it certain freedom of movement. Thus, black's chosen continuation is probably stronger than d7-d6 and e7-e5, even though it still cannot be considered fully correct.

There was no sense in pushing the e4 pawn, either now or earlier, because black would have attacked it with d7-d6, improving his prospects.

6.♘c3 d5 7.cxd5 cxd5 8.e5

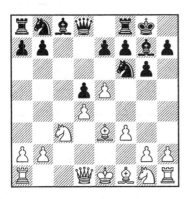

8...♘e8

In a similar position (with the c-pawns still on the board) in the 15th game of the [1929] Alekhine – Bogoljubov match, black sacrificed a pawn with ...♘fd7. It seems that

Bogoljubov had studied this line very well, because the pawn sacrifice was never refuted – neither by Alekhine nor by subsequent analysis. The correctness of the sacrifice is also proven by the match game collection published in our country. On the other hand, Riumin avoids the sacrifice, quickly gets a difficult position and is ultimately forced to give up the pawn anyway, but in a much worse situation.

9.♗d3

White didn't need to fear the light-squared bishop's development to f5. The d3 bishop will eventually be forced to retreat anyway.

Thus, the immediate 9.f4 was the correct move, winning an important tempo.

9...♘c6 10.f4 ♘c7 11.♘f3 ♗g4 12.0-0 ♘e6

Black has managed to develop his pieces fully, but still, his position cannot be considered fully satisfactory. His g7 bishop is shut out, the d5 pawn is weak (black cannot play e7-e6 because this weakens the

dark squares), and, finally, he has no strong points, either in the center or on the flanks. White's center, on the other hand, is very solid, and his pieces enjoy greater freedom.

Black is seemingly "attacking" now, but, a couple of moves later, these factors will make themselves known with great vengeance.

13.♗e2 ♗h6 14.♕d2 ♘a5 15.b3 ♖c8 16.♖ac1 ♘g7 17.h3

It's hard to find a satisfactory continuation in this position. For instance, 17...♗e6 18.g4 ♘e8 19.f5 ♗xe3+ 20.♕xe3 gxf5 21.♕h6 f6 22.♗d3 ♕d7 23.♔h2 etc., with a mating attack, or 17...♗xf3 18.♗xf3 e6 19.♘xd5! with an overwhelming advantage.

In view of that, black is forced to sacrifice a pawn to at least try and sharpen the game. However, the extra passed pawn that white gets after this sacrifice leaves no doubt as to the game's outcome.

17...♗d7 18.♘xd5

White accepts the pawn sacrifice, giving black some opportunities to

resist. However, white could win immediately with 18.g4! For instance, 18...♘e8 (there's nothing else; now the black rooks are disconnected, and white can safely take the pawn) 19.♘xd5, and white gets an overwhelming advantage, because, obviously, 19...♗xg4 20.hxg4 ♖xc1 21.♖xc1 ♕xd5 22.♖c5 leads to the loss of a piece. Still, as stated above, even the immediate acceptance of the sacrifice is winning for white.

18...♗xh3   19.♘xe7+   ♕xe7 20.♕xa5

Of course, stronger than 20.gxh3 ♘f5!, and white's kingside weakness becomes rather obvious.

20...♘f5 21.♗f2 ♗g4 22.♕d2

22...♖cd8!

Black defends with the greatest tenacity. His main goal is to stop the advance of the d-pawn. Now, for instance, white cannot play 23.d5, because the endgame after 23...♗xf3 24.♗xf3 ♕xe5 25.fxe5 ♗xd2 is roughly equal. Since the immediate 23.d5 is impossible, black has enough time to play ♖d5. The rook can only be expelled by the bishop from c4, but at the price of doubled f-pawns. Thus, white can only push his d-pawn by giving black some chances on the kingside.

And still, even this shouldn't have saved black had white found the correct move 23.♖cd1! Unfortunately, he protects the queen with the other rook. Of course, it was difficult to foresee all the subtleties of the subsequent struggle, but general positional considerations – the f1 rook is important for the kingside defense – could serve as a hint about the correct way to win for white.

It's hard to believe that Botvinnik's line leads to a "roughly equal" endgame. Despite the equal material and active positions of most black pieces, white's central pawn pair, bishop pair and control over the c-file allow us to evaluate the position as clearly better for white, which is corroborated by the computer evaluation, ±/+−.

23.♖fd1 ♖d5 24.♗c4 ♗xf3 25.gxf3 ♖dd8 26.d5 ♘g7! 27.d6 ♕d7

The position of the white king is clearly weak. Black threatens ...♘h5, ...♕f5 and ...♕h3. White's maneuver, leading to a bishop trade, cannot be approved of. It was preferable to first bolster the king's position with 28.♗f1 ♕f5 29.♗e3 etc.

28.♗h4 ♘h5!

It seems that white underestimated this counter-maneuver. He was probably counting only on 29.♗xd8 ♗xf4 30.♕e2 ♗xc1 31.♗e7 etc. In actuality, by sacrificing an exchange with 30...♕xd8!, black would get some good chances. Now, instead, white is forced to trade bishops and give back the pawn.

In this line, white has a strong Zwischenzug, 30.e6!

29.♗g5 ♗xg5 30.fxg5 ♕f5 31.♕e3

And now white's inaccuracy on the 23rd move tells! If the rook were on f1, he could have played 31.f4!, reducing black's chances to zero. Black seizes the initiative again, but even this cannot eliminate white's main asset, the d6 pawn.

31...♘f4 32.♖d4 ♕xg5+ 33.♔f1 ♕g2+ 34.♔e1

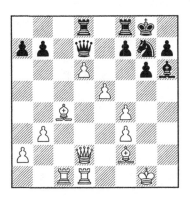

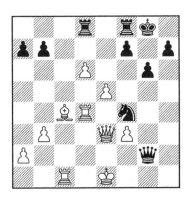

34...♕h1+

Overdoing things – the white king now finds a safe haven on the queenside. To be fair, we should point out that after 34...♘e6 35.♖g4! (not 35.♖d2 ♕h1+ 36.♗f1 f6 etc.) 35...♕xa2 36.♔d2, white should still win. After the game move, everything is essentially over, and white only needs to convert his advantage technically.

There followed:

35.♔d2 ♕h2+ 36.♔c3 ♘e6 37.♖d2 ♕h5 38.♔b2 ♕f5 39.♗xe6 ♕xe6 40.♖c7 ♖d7 41.♖xd7 ♕xd7 42.♖c2 ♕e6 43.♖c7 ♖d8 44.♕d4 ♖d7 45.♖xd7 ♕xd7 46.♕xa7 ♕b5 47.♕d4 ♕e2+ 48.♔a3

Black resigned.

Riumin fell victim to poor opening play. Rauzer, even though he committed some inaccuracies, still played the game very strongly.

No. 30. Four Knights Opening
Rauzer – Ragozin
Kiev – Leningrad team match
Leningrad 1932

1.e4 e5 2.♘f3 ♘c6 3.♘c3 ♘f6 4.♗b5

Back then, theory gave white a choice between three main lines: the Scotch (4.d4), Italian (4.♗c4) and Spanish (4.♗b5). The third option was the most popular. Rauzer chose it as well – he was quite happy with symmetrical development.

4...♗b4 5.0-0 0-0 6.d3

6...♕e7

On the other hand, V. Ragozin seemed to think that the sooner he avoided symmetry, the better. Later practice established the line 6...d6 7.♗g5 ♗xc3 8.bxc3 ♗d7 9.♖e1 ♘e7 10.♗xf6 ♗xb5, with a roughly equal position, as the most acceptable. Perhaps the move 6...♕e7 was inspired by S. Tartakower, who wrote in his famous *Hypermodern Chess Game* (part 2), "And now let's mention something completely new: 6...♕e7, for instance, 7.♗g5 ♗xc3 8.bxc3 h6 9.♗h4 ♕h8! 10.♖e1 g5 11.♘xg5 hxg5 12.♗xg5 ♖g8 13.♕d2 ♕d6! 14.♕e3 ♘h7, and white's rampage is over."

7.♗g5 ♗xc3 8.bxc3 ♘d8 9.d4 d6 10.♖e1 ♘e6

Kicking the g5 bishop away and unpinning the black king's knight is the essence of an old system developed by the German master J. Metger. However, the bishop retreats to c1, threatening to go to a3. Another source of difficulty for black is the f5 square, which needs defending (the threat is ♘f3-h4-f5). Overall, a complicated struggle ensues, as a lot of games played in this line have proved. However, Ragozin always preferred this type of game.

11.♗c1 ♖d8 12.♘h4 g6

Naturally, black didn't like the position after 12...d5 13.♘f5 .

13.g3 ♔g7

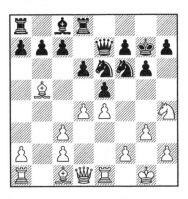

14.♗f1

An attempt to cause complications ("rampage", using Tartakower's term) with 14.♘f5+ gxf5 15.exf5 ♔h8 16.fxe6 ♗xe6 looked too risky. Thus, white simply consolidates his position by transferring the bishop to g2. On the other hand, all these motifs are well-known.

14...h6

14...♘g8 (and if 15.♗g2, then 15...♘f4) was more in the spirit of the position.

Black plays h7-h6 with the idea to transfer the knight to h7 and, if the chance arises, to g5. This plan is not good and only helps white to play f2-f4, opening the f-file.

15.♗g2 ♘h7 16.♖f1 ♗d7 17.♖b1 ♖ab8 18.♕e1!

Black cannot stop the advance of the f-pawn; from this square, the queen protects the h4 knight when needed.

18...a6

19.f4 ♘ef8

Of course, not 19...♘hf8, because the f-pawn will advance to f6.

20.♕e3 exf4

The h6 pawn was under threat.

21.♕xf4 g5 22.♘f5+ ♗xf5 23.♕xf5 ♕e6 24.♕f3 ♖d7 25.h4 ♘g6

Provoking h4-h5, after which the h6 and g5 pawns will at least be protected.

26.h5 ♘gf8

Black is again on the ropes, but it's not that simple to knock him out. First, the white bishop must get to d4.

27.d5! ♕e8 28.♗e3 ♖e7 29.♗d4+ ♔g8 30.♗f6 ♘xf6 31.♕xf6 ♘h7

31...♔h7 is no better: 32.♗h3 and then ♗f5+, taking the h6 pawn.

32.♕xh6 ♖e5 33.♗h3 ♕f8

To safeguard the king after the queen trade; however, white breaks through on the other flank. The game is already decided.

34.♕xf8+ ♘xf8 35.♗f5 b6 36.a4! ♖d8 37.a5 bxa5 38.♖b7 ♘d7 39.♖xc7 ♘c5

Black has improved the position of his knight at the cost of a pawn. But now, his kingside weaknesses are exposed again. Rauzer's play is very precise.

40.h6 ♖f8 41.♗g6! f6

Not 41...fxg6? because of a mate in two.

42.♖xf6! ♖ee8 43.♖ff7

Black resigned.

No. 31. Queen's Gambit
Lisitsin – Rauzer
Kiev – Leningrad team match
Leningrad 1932

In the next game, Rauzer proves himself as a virtuoso of positional play and endgame technique. Straight out of the opening, he devises a plan to exploit his queenside pawn advantage (the c-pawn!). And he implements this plan with inexorable consistency and logic. All this is full of internal beauty, which is no less captivating than any picturesque outward effects.

1.♘f3 d5 2.c4 e6 3.d4 ♘f6 4.e3 ♗e7 5.♗d3 0-0 6.0-0 dxc4 7.♗xc4 c5 8.♘c3 ♘c6 9.♘e5 ♕c7 10.♘xc6 ♕xc6 11.d5 exd5 12.♘xd5 ♘xd5 13.♗xd5 ♕b6 14.♕f3 ♗f6 15.♖b1 ♖d8 16.e4 ♗e6 17.♗f4 ♖d7 18.♖fe1 ♖ad8 19.g3 h6 20.♗xe6 ♕xe6 21.e5 ♗e7 22.b3 b5 23.♖ec1

23...c4 24.bxc4 bxc4 25.♕e2 ♖c8 26.♖c3 ♗c5 27.♗e3 ♗d4 28.♗xd4 ♖xd4 29.♖bc1 ♕d5 30.a3 ♖d2 31.♕f1 ♖c6 32.♕g2 ♖d1+

33.♖xd1 ♛xd1+ 34.♛f1 ♛d4 35.♛e1 ♔f8 36.♔g2 ♔e7 37.f4 ♖b6 38.♛e3 ♖b2+ 39.♔h3 ♛xe3 40.♖xe3 ♔e6

The game was adjudicated as a win for black.

No. 32. French Defense
Rauzer – Alatortsev
8th Soviet Championship
Leningrad 1933
Annotated by V. Rauzer

1.e4 e6 2.d4 d5 3.♘c3 ♗b4?

It's hard to imagine that an opening where black pawns are developed on light squares, and then the dark-squared bishop, which is supposed to defend the squares between them, is brought out to be traded, can be considered acceptable!

4.e5

Other continuations aren't attractive at all: there is nothing to say about 4.exd5 (Capablanca – Alekhine, 1st game of the 1927 world championship match), while after 4.♘ge2 dxe4 5.a3 ♗e7 6.♘xe4 ♘f6 the knight is positioned rather poorly on e2 (or g3).

4...c5 5.a3

White decided against 5.♛g4 due to 5...♘e7; for instance, 6.♛xg7 ♖g8 7.♛xh7 cxd4 8.a3 ♛a5 9.♖b1 dxc3 10.axb4 ♛a2, and black wins a rook.

5...cxd4

5...♗xc3+ with subsequent long castling was somewhat better, because this doesn't give white a

tempo while it disrupts his pawn structure and closes off the diagonals for the c1 bishop.

6.axb4 dxc3

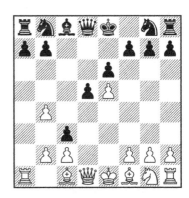

7.♘f3!

As I remembered the well-known game Em. Lasker – Maroczy from the New York 1924 tournament, where white played 7.bxc3, I noticed the lack of logic behind 7.bxc3: it's not beneficial for white to hold onto the c3 pawn at any rate; why then should he waste tempi to capture the c3 pawn? So I decided to spend that tempo on some beneficial move, specifically 7.♘f3: if black wants to get an extra pawn, he will have to gift white another tempo with 7...cxb2 8.♗xb2. However, it's clear that the weakness of all dark squares and black's lag in development cannot be compensated by the extra pawn on a7, which is placed on the white rook's open file in any case.

After 7...cxb2 8.♗xb2 f5, recommended by some analysts, white can just calmly play 9.♗d3.

In the resulting position, black's lag in development and the weakness of his dark squares is obvious. 8...f5 9.exf6 ♘xf6 (Kan – Orlov, 1934 Moscow championship) is worse for white, because it frees black from the strong pressure from the e5 pawn and gives him an opportunity to close the gap in development. After 7...cxb2 8.♗xb2 f5, there's also no necessity to play 9.♕d4, because the only purpose of this move is to force cxb2 ♗xb2 or to capture the c3 pawn with the queen, disrupting the pawn structure.

7...♕c7

Compared with 7...cxb2, this move looks preferable, because it doesn't gift white any more tempi.

8.♕d4

With this move, white tries to convince black to accept his "Greek gift", the b2 pawn, but black stubbornly (and quite reasonably) refuses.

8...♘e7 9.♗d3 ♘d7 10.0-0

It's worth pointing out how casually white is developing – even 10...♘c6, with a triple attack on the e5 pawn, cannot stop him.

10...♘c6?

Probably a simple oversight, because after 11.♕xc3 black cannot play ♘dxe5 due to b4-b5, winning a piece.

11.♕xc3 ♕b6

White threatened b4-b5.

12.b5

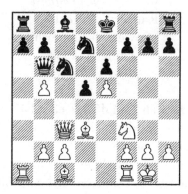

12...d4?

Black probably missed white's reply.

13.♕e1

White is consistently playing along the dark squares. The advanced d4 pawn is doomed and black's position is lost.

13...♘e7 14.♕e4 ♘g6 15.♖e1 0-0 16.b4 ♖d8

Black tries to protect the d4 pawn in vain.

17.♗b2 f5 18.exf6 ♘xf6

It seems that white has to retreat with his queen (to ♕e2), but...

19.♗xd4!

Still, this is all rather transparent. It's worth pointing out, however, that the seeming "ease" of the win in this game was achieved by difficult analytical work that allowed white to steer the game in the right direction straight from the start.

19...♕c7 20.♕e3 ♘d5

Or 20...♘g4 21.♕g5 ♖xd4 22.♗xg6! (22.♘xd4? ♕xh2+ 23.♔f1 ♘f4 24.♕d8+ ♔f7 25.♕c7+ ♔e8, and black wins) 22...♖xb4 23.c3 ♖c4 (23...♖f4 24.♘e5) 24.b6 ♕xb6 25.♕e7

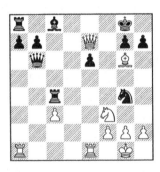

25...hxg6

a) 25...♕xf2+ 26.♔h1 hxg6 27.♕d8+ ♔h7 28.♘g5+ ♔h6 29.♘f7+ ♕xf7 30.♕h4#;

b) if 25...♗d7, then 26.♗f7+ ♔h8 27.♕xd7, and black's counter-attack is stopped easily.

26.♕e8+ ♔h7 27.♘g5+ ♔h6 28.♘f7+ ♔h5 29.♕h8+ ♘h6 30.♖e5+, and white wins.

21.♕g5 ♘xb4

This move loses in a rather curious way. However, it's already hard to find a good continuation for black.

22.♗xg6 hxg6 23.b6 ♕d7 24.♖xa7 ♘xc2 25.♖d1 ♖b8 26.♖d2 ♕e8 27.♗e5

Black resigned.

No. 33. Caro-Kann Defense
Rauzer – I. Rabinovich
8th Soviet Championship
Leningrad 1933
Annotated by V. Rauzer

1.e4 c6 2.d4 d5 3.♘c3 dxe4 4.♘xe4 ♘f6

4...♗f5 is somewhat better: there are fewer pawn defects in black's position.

5.♘xf6+!

In view of the subsequent improvement – again (like 3.♘c3) the only correct decision.

5...exf6

After looking through the game until the end, it's easy for a commentator to point out: "It was better to play 5...gxf6." But who of those who have tried to play 5...gxf6 believe that? White still plays g2-g3 and gets an advantage thanks to the opportunity to push all his queenside pawns: c4, b4, a4, then c5 and b5. The game Rauzer – Grigorenko, played at the 1933 Ukrainian Championship before the All-Union tournament, was won in a similar way.

6.g3!!

After 5...exf6, white has got an extra pawn on the queenside, while black's kingside pawns are doubled. Thus, white's plan is as follows: castle short, push the queenside pawns and convert his essentially extra d-pawn. The plan is simple and clear. To implement this plan, it's very important to put the bishop on g2 to support the pawn onslaught, which should go as follows: c4, b4, a4, then c5 and b5 or (instead of c5) d5, depending on circumstances. Further, the move g2-g3 kills the activity of black's dark-squared bishop along the d6-h2 diagonal (the ill-fated h2 square!), bolstering white's kingside and his king's position, and (which is important too!) puts another barrier on the way of the black kingside pawns on f4. If one carefully considers all the features of the move g2-g3, it becomes clear that this is the best move in this position (following Tarrasch's principles).

6...♗d6 7.♗g2 0-0 8.♘e2 ♖e8 9.0-0

9...♗f5

Up until now, black has made very natural moves (except for ♘f6). Now, however, 9...♗g4 was clearly more active. An interesting line could arise: 10.♗e3 f5 11.♕d2 ♗xe2 12.♕xe2 f4 13.gxf4 ♗xf4 14.♕f3 ♗xe3 15.fxe3±. f6-f5 instead of ♗f5 or ♗g4 also gives black nothing, because the f4 square is well protected by the c1 bishop and e2 knight.

10.c4 ♘a6 11.♘c3 ♕d7

If 11...♘b4, then 12.a3 ♘d3 13.♗e3 ♘xb2 14.♕e2 ♘d3 15.♖fd1±.

12.a3

If white plays 12.♗e3 immediately, then 12...♘b4 with the threats ♘c2 and ♗d3.

12...♗h3

The g2 bishop is of course very important for the attack, but any simplifications are also beneficial for white thanks to his "extra" pawn. Thus, ♗h3 is not as strong as it might seem at first glance.

13.♗e3 ♗xg2 14.♔xg2 ♘c7

15.♕f3!

A very important move that strengthens the king's position and prepares the eventual b2-b4-b5 breakthrough.

15...b5?

This move makes it easier for white to create a passed pawn and open lines; however, it's psychologically very hard to just sit there and quietly wait for your opponent's position to improve.

16.cxb5 cxb5 17.♖ac1 b4 18.axb4 ♗xb4 19.♖fd1

This move finishes the preparations for the d-pawn advance. However, now, after making the move ♖fd1, I would have probably chosen a different game plan (see the next note).

19...♗d6 20.d5?

Is the assault beginning? Actually, this move is bad, because the pawn can quickly go to d8 only if black plays poorly. In case of a more stubborn defense, white would have stopped this march himself, because after some trades, the black king threatened to get too close to the pawn. So, white had to either stop pushing the pawn or constantly avoid simplifications (the queen trade!), which wouldn't lead to anything good either. It was more accurate to leave the pawn on d4 and simplify the position as much as possible; for instance, 20.♗f4, then ♖e1 etc.

20...♖eb8?

A very poor move that leaves the a8 rook out of play for a very long time.

21.♘e4 ♘e8 22.♘xd6 ♘xd6 23.♗c5 ♘b5?

Not 23...♖xb2 due to 24.♕a3, but after ...♘b5, this knight gets completely stalemated – it's killed by the d6 and b2 pawns together with the c5 bishop.

24.d6 ♖e8 25.♖e1 h6 26.♖cd1

There's no need to hurry.

26...♖ac8 27.♖e7 ♖xe7 28.dxe7 ♕e8 29.♕b7 ♔h7

White threatened ♕xc8 and ♖d8+.

30.♖d8 ♖xd8 31.exd8=♕

Finally!

31...♕xd8 32.♕xb5 ♕d5+ 33.f3

Black resigned.

In addition to the opening novelty, this game is important because, thanks to white's strictly principled play (3.♘c3! instead of 3.exd5?, 5.♘xf6+ instead of 5.♘g3?, 6.g3 instead of 6.c3? or 6.♗c4?), it poses the important question of whether these moves are the only good ones for white.

No. 34. Ruy Lopez
Rauzer – Savitsky
8th Soviet Championship
Leningrad 1933

This game holds an important place in Rauzer's creative evolution. Let us remind you that he wrote, "In the 1933 Soviet Championship, I surprised my opponents by winning games that I played very consistently from the very first moves. I can point to several such games in that tournament – against I. Rabinovich, Alatortsev, and Savitsky."

The following notes by Rauzer, made back then, are complemented with analytical and historical materials by the author.

1.e4 e5 2.♘f3 ♘c6 3.♗b5 a6 4.♗a4 ♘f6 5.0-0 d6 6.♗xc6+

As Rauzer explained, "the move order was influenced by the game Rauzer – Selezniev, played at the Ukrainian championship beforehand. In the aforementioned game, there was 5...♗e7 6.♖e1 and only then 6...d6 7.♗xc6+ bxc6 8.d4 ♘d7 9.♘a3! f6 10.♘c4 ♘b6 11.♘a5 ♗d7 12.c4 exd4 13.♘xd4 c5 14.♘f5±."

I think that Rauzer also studied the first game of the first Lasker – Janowski match (1909), which he would have found in the chess column of the "Monthly Literary and Popular Scientific Appendices" of the *Niva* magazine (not a bad source from the early 20th century!). In that game, like in this one, black chose the Chigorin System, where black defends his central pawn with the maneuver ♘f6-d7.

In the world championship match, they played: 5.0-0 ♗e7 6.♖e1 d6 7.♗xc6+ bxc6 8.d4 ♘d7 9.dxe5 dxe5 10.♘bd2.

"This game can serve as a great example of how to attack and defend the weak c6 pawn – the attack on it begins with this move," wrote master Znosko-Borovsky, who took over the chess column after Chigorin's death. The game indeed continued in a fascinating way: 10...f6 11.♘c4 a5 12.♗d2 a4 13.♘a5 ♖a6 14.♕e2 ♘c5 15.♖ed1 ♗e6 16.b4 axb3 17.axb3 ♕a8 18.♗c3 ♔f7 (18...0-0? 19.b4 ♘d7 20.♘xc6! with the threat ♘xe7+) 19.♘h4 g6 20.♖f1 ♔g7 21.f4 exf4 22.♘f5+ ♗xf5 23.exf5 ♗d6 24.♘c4 ♖xa1 25.♖xa1 ♖e8 26.♕f3 ♕d8 27.♕xc6 ♘e4 28.♘xd6 ♕xd6 29.♕xd6 cxd6 30.♗d4 gxf5 31.♖a2 ♔f7 32.c3 ♔e6, and a draw was agreed after 8 more moves.

Back in 1933, Rauzer had already found a more effective way of attacking the queenside – **A. K.**

6...bxc6 7.d4 ♘d7

Another idea – a pawn exchange in the center (7...exd4 8.♘xd4 c5, putting the bishop on b7 to attack the e4 pawn) – proved to be more effective in tournament play – **A. K.**

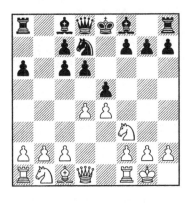

8.♘a3! f6 9.♘c4 a5 10.♖e1 ♘b6
This move drives the knight away from its formidable position on c4,

but the black knight now falls under attack: c2-c4-c5.

The doubled pawns aren't actually that weak: black should have played 10...c5! – **A. K.**

11.♘e3 ♗e7?

Another mistake. The correct move was 11...♗e6, developing the piece and hindering the threat c2-c4-c5. However, after that move white would have still prepared the c2-c4-c5 push with b2-b3. For instance, 12.b3 ♘d7 13.♗a3! (preventing c6-c5), then c2-c4-c5. The difference between this line and what happened in the actual game (without b2-b3) will be evident later.

12.c4 ♗e6 13.c5

13...♘c4?

If 13...♘c8 (♘d7), then 14.♕a4! ♕d7 15.♖d1 or 14...♗d7 15.♕c4±. Obviously, the strong move ♕a4 is only possible because of the absence of b2-b3 (see the note to move 11). Of course, 13...dxc5 is no better, because then, after 14.dxe5, white would have five pawns against three on the kingside, while the black queenside pawns would be held by just two white ones. After 13...♘c4, however, due to the unavoidable trade of black's light-squared bishop, his position immediately becomes full of holes on the light squares and thus totally hopeless.

Still, 13...♘c8 was a bit better. For instance, 14.♕a4 ♘a7 15.♘c4 (15.♕xa5 ♘b5) 15...♘b5; if now 16.d5!? (which seems very strong)

then 16...♗d7 17.dxc6 ♗xc6 18.♘xa5 (it all seems great: white has won a pawn and threatens ♘xc6, but...) 18...♘d4!! 19.♘xc6 ♖xa4 20.♘xd8 ♘c2, and black is better. (After 13...♘c8 14.♕a4 ♘a7 15.♘c4 ♘b5, white should play 16.♗e3 instead of 16.d5.)

Still, the line with 16.d5!? is not that bad, however, after 16...♗d7 17.dxc6♗xc6, instead of 18.♘xa5?, white should play 18.cxd6, and then 18...cxd6 19.♕c2 with better chances.

14.♘f5 ♗xf5

This and the next moves are forced because of the threat b2-b3.

15.exf5 dxc5 16.♕a4

16.♕e2!?♕d5 17.b3♘b6 18.dxe5 with a clear advantage for white was much stronger.

16...♕d5 17.dxe5 fxe5

If 17...♘xe5, then 18.♘xe5 fxe5 19.♖d1.

17...0-0!? was interesting; because of the white queen's awkward position, his advantage is not as great as after 16.♕e2!?

18.b3 ♘b6 19.♕g4 0-0 20.♗b2 ♗d6

20...♗f6 21.♖ad1 ♕f7 22.♘xe5 ♗xe5 23.♗xe5 ♘d5 was a bit better; still, even this continuation was not enough to prevent the loss.

21.♘xe5 ♗xe5

White threatened ♖ad1.

22.♖xe5 ♕d2 23.♖e2 ♕d7 24.♖ae1 ♖f7 25.♖e6 ♘d5

The ill-fated knight finally joins the game.

26.♕e4 ♖af8 27.g4 ♘f6 28.♕c4

The immediate 28.♗xf6 was simpler, eliminating the need to care for the g4 pawn.

28...♕d5 29.h3 a4? 30.♕xa4 ♕d3 31.♖6e3 ♕d2 32.♗c3 ♕d7

33.♗xf6 ♖xf6 34.♕c4+ ♔h8
35.♕xc5 h5 36.♖e7 ♕d2 37.♕e3
♕xa2 38.♕g5 ♖6f7 39.♖xf7

Black resigned.

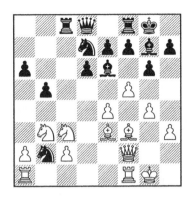

No. 35. *Sicilian Defense*
Rauzer – Chekhover
8th Soviet Championship
Leningrad 1933
Annotated by V. Rauzer

1.e4 c5 2.♘f3 ♘c6 3.d4 cxd4
4.♘xd4 ♘f6 5.♘c3 d6 6.♗e2 g6
7.♗e3 ♗g7 8.0-0 0-0 9.♘b3 ♗e6
10.f4 ♖c8 11.h3 a6 12.♕d2 b5
13.♗f3 ♘d7 14.♕f2 ♘a5

15.g4?

Consistent, but poor. The g2-g4 push completely weakens white's already disheveled position. 15.♘xa5 ♕xa5 was the lesser evil.

15...♘c4! 16.f5 ♘xb2

Black sacrifices a piece for two pawns and a significant positional advantage. 16...♘xe3 17.fxe6 ♘xf1 18.exd7 ♕xd7 19.♖xf1 ♗xc3 20.bxc3 ♖xc3 was possibly better.

17.fxe6 fxe6 18.♘d1 ♘e5
19.♘d4 ♘xf3+ 20.♘xf3 ♘c4
21.♖c1 ♘e5!

Wins a third pawn.

22.♕e2 ♖xf3 23.♖xf3 ♘xf3+
24.♕xf3 ♕a5 25.♕e2 ♕xa2
26.♕d3 ♕c4?

A mistake that misses the win. Black had to play 26...♖c4! with the subsequent ♕a4, completely tying up white's position.

27.♔f1! a5 28.♔e2 b4 29.♕xc4
♖xc4 30.♔d3 d5 31.c3!

This move saves white.

31...♖xe4 32.cxb4 ♖xb4 33.♖c7
e5 34.♖xe7 a4 35.♖e8+ ♔f7 36.♖e7+

36...♔g8?

It was better for white not to offer the rook trade, and it was better for black to accept it. After 36...♔xe7 37.♗c5+ ♔f6 38.♗xb4 ♔g5, black has some winning chances. Now, however, white manages to draw.

37.♖e8+　♔f7　38.♖a8　e4+ 39.♔e2 ♗e5

If 39...d4, then 40.♖a7+ with perpetual check (or 40...♔f6 41.g5+ winning).

40.♗d2! ♖b3 41.♖xa4 ♖xh3 42.♖a7+　♔e6　43.♖a6+　♔d7 44.♖a7+ ♔c6 45.♖a6+ ♔d7

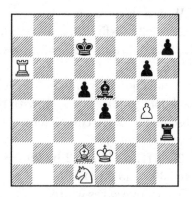

Draw.

Indeed, after 45...♔b7 46.♖a5 ♖h2+ 47.♘f2 ♗g3 48.♗e3 ♗xf2 49.♗xf2 d4 50.♖a4! e3 51.♖xd4 exf2 52.♖c4, it was a theoretical draw, while 45...♔c7 46.♖a7+ ♔b6 47.♖e7 ♗d6 48.♗e3+! ♖xe3+? 49.♘xe3 ♗xe7 50.♘xd5+ also led to a draw.

No. 36. Reti Opening
Sorokin – Rauzer
Tbilisi 1934
Annotated by V. Rauzer

1.c4 e6 2.♘f3 d5 3.g3

Fianchettoing the bishop in this position is not the strongest continuation, because white cannot use this diagonal and is forced to close it with his own pawn.

3...♘f6 4.♗g2 c5

Since d2-d3 is necessary, it was better to play it before black got to develop his pieces.

5.0-0 ♘c6 6.cxd5

After 6.d4, there could follow 6... dxc4 with an attack on d4.

6...♕xd5

A bold move that prevents d2-d4. The very fact that this move is possible and reasonable shows that white's opening play was poor.

7.b3

It was better to play 7.♘c3, forcing 7...♕d8, because 7...♕h5 does not work in this case.

7...♗e7 8.♗b2 ♕h5 9.d3

White misses the last chance to play d2-d4. After 0-0 and ♖fd8, black seizes the d4 square and gets a better position.

9...0-0　10.♘bd2　♖d8　11.♘c4 ♘d5

Preparing b7-b6 and ♗b7, which doesn't work immediately because of ♘fe5.

12.♕d2 b6 13.♘fe5 ♘xe5 14.♘xe5 ♗b7 15.h4

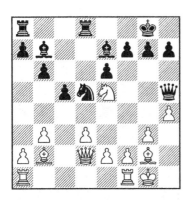

With a concrete threat ♗f3, but positionally the move is bad, because flank advances with an opened center only waste time and weaken the position.

15...f6 16.♗f3 ♕e8 17.♘c4 ♗c6 18.♘e3 ♘b4 19.♗xc6 ♘xc6 20.♖ac1 f5

To make use of his positional advantage, black needs to trade his passive e7 bishop.

21.♘c4 ♕g6 22.♕f4

Black threatened ♗xh4 – this is a consequence of the move h2-h4.

22...♗f6 23.♘e5 ♗xe5 24.♗xe5 ♖d5

Black has a clear advantage.

25.♗b2 ♖ad8 26.♔g2 e5 27.♕g5 ♕f7 28.♕e3 a5 29.a4

A poor move, since the b3 pawn is very weak.

29...♖e8 30.♖c4

White gets into zugzwang

because of this mistake. The correct move was 30.♕f3.

30...♘d4 31.♗xd4 exd4 32.♕f3 ♖de5 33.♖e1 ♕e6 34.♔f1 g6

White is slowly running out of moves. The position of the c4 rook that protects the important b3 pawn is rather troubling.

35.h5 ♔g7 36.♔g2 ♖e7

36...♖xe2 was worse due to 37.♖xe2 ♕xe2 38.♕b7+ and ♕xb6.

37.♖c2 ♕xb3 38.♖c4 ♕b2 39.h6+ ♔xh6 40.♕a8 ♖e8 41.♖h1+ ♔g7 42.♕f3 ♕xe2 43.♕b7+ ♖8e7 44.♕xb6 f4 45.♖xc5 fxg3 46.♖f1 ♖f7 47.♖xe5 ♕f3+ 48.♔g1 gxf2+ 49.♔h2 ♕f4+ 50.♔g2 ♕xe5 51.♖xf2 ♖xf2+ 52.♔xf2 ♕f6+

White resigned.

No. 37. Ruy Lopez
Rauzer – Levenfish
9th Soviet Championship
Leningrad 1934
Annotated by G. Levenfish

1.e4 e5 2.♘f3 ♘c6 3.♗b5 a6 4.♗a4 d6 5.c3 ♗d7 6.0-0 g6

The same move would have followed after 6.d4, as happened in a match game between Bogoljubov and Alekhine.

7.d4 ♗g7 8.♖e1 ♘ge7

Black can't play 8...♘f6 due to 9.♗xc6 ♗xc6 10.dxe5 dxe5 11.♕xd8+ ♖xd8 12.♘xe5 ♗xe4 13.f3, but 8...♕e7! with the subsequent 9...♘f6 was perfectly possible.

In the first line, black can sacrifice a pawn for an advantage in development and the initiative: 10...♘xe4!? 11.exd6 0-0 12.dxc7 ♕xc7.

9.♗e3 0-0 10.♘bd2 h6 11.♗b3 ♔h7 12.dxe5 dxe5 13.♗c5

The best move. After 13.a4 there's 13...b6, and then black calmly regroups: ♘g8 and ♕e7 with the subsequent f7-f5.

13...b6 14.♗a3 ♘a5 15.♗d5 c6 16.b4 ♘b7 17.♗b3 ♕c7 18.♕e2 c5

Even though this maneuver helps black to seize the d4 square, he, on the other hand, gives up

the d5 square, which leads to very complicated play. The correct continuation was 18...♖ae8 and 19...a5. 19.♕xa6 leads to the loss of a bishop after 19...♖a8.

19.♘f1 ♗b5 20.c4 ♗c6 21.♗c2 ♘c8 22.♘e3 ♘cd6

23.bxc5

Had white immediately seized the d5 square with 23.♘d5, it would have led, after 23...♗xd5 24.cxd5 c4 and the subsequent b7-b5, to black's advantage, while after 24.exd5 e4, white lost an exchange.

23...bxc5 24.♘d2

24.♘d5 ♗xd5 25.cxd5 ♘b5 26.♗b2 ♘d4 is still not advantageous for white.

24...♔g8

An unfounded attempt to play f7-f5. Black should have played 24...♖fe8 immediately.

25.♗b2 ♖ae8 26.♘d5 ♕c8 27.♖ab1 ♘d8 28.♗a1 ♘e6 29.♕g4 ♕d8 30.♗c3 ♘d4 31.♗d3 ♔h7 32.f3 ♖e6 33.♖b2 f5

After a lot of preparation, black finally pushes the f-pawn. A crisis looms. White, obviously, cannot take on f5, because after 34.exf5 gxf5 35.♕h3 ♖g6, black's attack is too strong.

34.♕g3 fxe4

34...f4 yielded nothing either: 35.♕f2 g5? 36.♗xd4 cxd4 37.♖eb1±.

35.♘xe4 ♘4f5

35...♘xc4 is deceptive: 36.♘ef6+! ♖exf6 37.♘xf6+ ♕xf6 38.♗xc4±; or 35...♘6f5 36.♕h3 ♗xd5 37.cxd5 ♕xd5 38.♘g5+, also with an advantage for white.

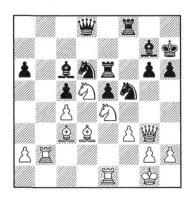

36.♕f2

This quickly defuses the tension and leads to a draw. Interesting complications could arise after 36.♘xc5 ♘xg3 37.♘xe6 ♕h4 38.♘xf8+ ♗xf8 39.hxg3 ♕xg3. Following 40.♖xe5 ♘f5 41.♘f6+!, black's position is hopeless. However, after 37...♕c8! 38.♘xf8+ ♕xf8 39.hxg3 ♗xd5 40.cxd5 e4! 41.♗xg7 ♕xg7, black wins.

36...♘xc4   37.♗xc4   ♗xd5 38.♕xc5   ♗xc4   39.♕xc4   ♕c8 40.♕xc8   ♖xc8   41.♖d1   ♖ec6 42.♖d3   ♖8c7 43.♔f2 g5 44.♗a5 ♖c2+   45.♖xc2   ♖xc2+   46.♖d2 ♖c4

Draw.

No. 38. Queen's Gambit
Chekhover – Rauzer
9th Soviet Championship
Leningrad 1934

1.d4 d5 2.c4 e6 3.♘c3 ♘f6 4.♗g5 ♘bd7 5.e3 ♗e7 6.♘f3 0-0 7.♖c1 a6

After the Capablanca – Alekhine match, this system became rather popular. Rauzer added it to his opening repertoire as well. We have already seen one such example (game 25).

8.cxd5 exd5 9.♗d3 c6 10.♕c2 ♖e8 11.0-0 ♘f8 12.♘a4

White more often plays 12.h3, because the maneuver ♘a4-c5 is not too effective.

12...♗g4 13.♘e5 ♗h5

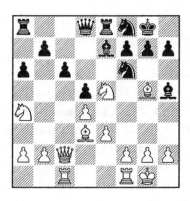

14.♘c5?

This is already a mistake, even though 14.f4 ♘g4 is good for black, too.

14...♗xc5 15.♕xc5

Or 15.g4 ♗d6 16.gxh5 ♗xe5 17.dxe5 ♖xe5 with an advantage for black.

15...♘e6 16.♕b4 ♘xg5 17.♕xb7 ♖b8 18.♕xa6 ♖xb2 19.♖xc6 ♘fe4 20.f4 f6 21.fxg5 fxe5 22.♗xe4 dxe4 23.♕c4+ ♔h8 24.♖e6 ♖xe6 25.♕xe6 exd4 26.♕xe4 dxe3 27.♕f4

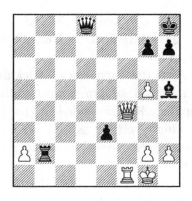

27...♕d5! 28.♕e4

V. Chekhover manages to prolong the game with tactical tricks, but the end result doesn't change.

28...♗f7 29.♕xd5 ♗xd5 30.♖f8+ ♗g8 31.♔f1 ♖xa2 32.♖e8 e2+ 33.♔e1 g6 34.♖xe2 ♖xe2+ 35.♔xe2 ♔g7 36.♔e3 ♗d5 37.g3 ♔f7 38.♔f4 ♔e6 39.h3 ♗g2 40.♔g4 ♔f7 41.♔h4 ♔g7 42.g4 h6 43.♔g3 ♗f1 44.gxh6+ ♔xh6 45.h4 ♔g7 46.♔f4 ♔f6 47.♔f3 ♔e5 48.♔g3 ♗e2 49.♔h3 ♔f4 50.h5 g5 51.h6 ♗xg4+ 52.♔h2 ♗f5

White resigned.

Perhaps this game wasn't exactly worth remembering, if not for a curious detail. Rauzer's trap was sprung again 14 years later, in the miniature Barsauskas – Konstantinopolsky played in the Soviet Team Championship (Leningrad 1948). In the position on the first diagram, there followed: 14.♘c5? (at the same place...), and then 14...♗xc5 15.♕xc5 ♘e6 16.♗xf6 (white deviated only now) 16...gxf6 17.♕c2 fxe5 18.♗xh7+ ♔h8 19.dxe5 ♘g5 20.♗f5 ♘f3+ 21.gxf3 ♕g5+, and white resigned.

"You have lost to Rauzer," I said apologetically to my opponent.

No. 39. French Defense
Rauzer – Alatortsev
9th Soviet Championship
Leningrad 1934
Annotated by V. Rauzer

1.e4 e6 2.d4 d5 3.♘c3 ♗b4 4.e5 c5 5.a3 ♗xc3+

Without a doubt, this is stronger than 5...cxd4 6.axb4 dxc3 7.♘f3, because black would have been behind in development, and it was easy for the c1 bishop to join the play.

6.bxc3 ♘e7 7.♕g4 ♕a5 8.♗d2 ♕a4

A rather dubious pawn sacrifice, especially considering that the move ♕a4 is very passive.

9.♕xg7 ♖g8 10.♕xh7 cxd4 11.♘f3

In a later round, Bogatyrchuk defeated Alatortsev with 11.♘e2. However, 11.♘f3 is much more active and also reinforces the e5 pawn and the whole kingside (see next note).

11...dxc3 12.♗xc3 ♘bc6

13.h4?

Having an extra pawn, white attempts to win the exchange as well. The calculation itself is correct, but white didn't consider the fact that to convert the material advantage, it's necessary to consolidate his own position and eliminate the positional defects and black's attack. After winning the exchange the white king is in danger, his queen is cut off, and all light squares is cut off, and all light squares

are weakened, especially the b5-f1 diagonal. All this is enough to equalize chances. Instead of chasing new material gains, white should have immediately consolidated his position and secured his king with 13.g3. For instance, 13...♗d7 14.♗g2 0-0-0 15.♕d3 (to avoid cutting off the queen), then 0-0 with the idea to bolster the kingside with h2-h4, ♘g5 and f2-f4.

13...♗d7 14.h5?

At least now, white had to stop on his wrong way and play 14.♘g5 0-0-0 15.♘xf7, even though it was harder to consolidate than in the line shown previously.

14...0-0-0 15.♖h4

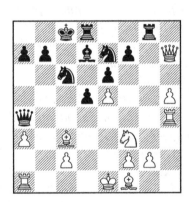

15...♖g4!

Not 15...d4 16.♘xd4 with the threat ♗b5, and if 16...♘xe5 then 17.♘f5.

16.♗b5

It's better to avoid winning *this* exchange!

16...♕xb5! 17.♖xg4 ♘f5!

Only here did white realize how difficult his position was, and he spent 50 minutes choosing between 0-0-0 and ♖d1. If 18.0-0-0, then 18...♕c5 with the subsequent ♕xf2, threatening ♘e3.

18.♖d1 ♗e8 19.♕h8 d4 20.♗d2 ♘ce7

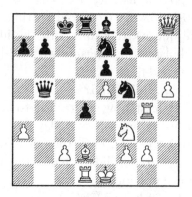

Up until now, white's play was perfectly logical, and only his subsequent poor moves allowed black to generate counterplay.

21.♗g5

White's difficulties begin with this move. The simple advance of the h-pawn quickly decided the game.

21...♕a5+   22.♖d2   ♗b5 23.♕xd8+

After 23.♕f6 ♕xa3, black's attack doesn't stop, while the white queen remains out of play. Now, white gets two rooks for the queen after great complications. However, the light squares, which weakened after winning that ill-fated exchange, remained weak until the very end of the game.

After 24.♕xf7, the position remained quite unclear.

23...♕xd8 24.♘xd4 ♕h8

The only move. If now 25.♘xb5, then 25...♕xe5+ and ♕xb5.

Computer analysis shows that the only correct continuation was 24...♕c7! This way, black retains all the threats, but deprives white of the important tempo-winning move 26.♗f6.

25.♘xf5 exf5

If 25...♕xe5+ then 26.♘e3. If 25...♘xf5 then 26.♖d8+.

26.♗f6

This move (see the note to black's 24th move) actually saves white.

26...♕xh5 27.♖h4 ♕g6 28.♗xe7 ♕xg2 29.c4

A temporary lull begins. 29...♗c6 is, of course, impossible due to 30.♖h8+ ♔c7 31.♗d8+ and 32.♗a5+. Since after 29...♗a4 white gets nothing by giving checks, black obtains some winning chances thanks to white's weak light squares.

29...♗a4   30.♖h8+   ♔c7 31.♗d8+ ♔c6 32.♖h6+

At that moment, white was already in severe time trouble, and the goal of the subsequent useless checks was to gain time. Of course, it was better to leave the king on c6, where it blocked its own bishop. But ♖h6+ is another time-trouble move!

Both this check and 32.♖d6+ were fine.

32...♔c5

33.♖h4

Or 33.♗e7+ ♔xc4 34.♖h4+ ♔b5 35.♖b4+ ♔a5; or 35.♖b2+ ♔a5 36.♗b4+ ♔a6.

33.♗e7+ was actually the saving move; however, instead of the losing rook checks on the 35th move, it was necessary to find 35.♖d7!, which is incredibly difficult for a human chess player, especially in time trouble.

33...♗c6 34.♔e2 ♗f3+

34...♕f3+!? was stronger. The game move allows white to complicate matters.

35.♔e3 ♗g4

And now, as a consequence of the previous moves, black makes a mistake, and the result becomes unclear again. The correct move was 35...♗e4!

36.♔f4 ♔xc4 37.♗c7

This protects the e5 pawn, but gives up a3.

In the irrational position that arose after the 32nd move, it's hard for either side to find correct moves. The only move was 37.♔g5! Now, however, the game ends quickly.

37...♔c3   38.♗a5+   ♔b3 39.♖d3+

White is trying to save everything in time trouble, but blunders a full rook.

39...♔a4

The h4 rook is out of play, and white cannot create any threats to the black king.

40.f3

Black threatened ♕e4+, and the a5 bishop is under attack.

40...♔xa5 41.fxg4 ♕e4+

White resigned.

A very intense game that was played strategically incorrectly by black (3...♗b4 and ♗xc3+, also giving up the g7 and h7 pawns) and tactically incorrectly by white (13. h4, 14.h5 and 15.♖h4, winning an exchange but weakening the light squares).

In this game, Rauzer continued the creative discussion around the French Defense that started in the previous national championship (game 32) and continued in the next one (game 65).

I'm afraid that I was to blame for the risky move 13.h4!?, because I successfully implemented this plan (to get the pawn to h6, then obtain an advantage with the sacrifice ♕xg8 and h6-h7) against V. Ragozin in the Ukrainian Physical Education Committee correspondence tournament. The game was never published, but Rauzer, of course, knew about it.

No. 40. Catalan Opening
Ragozin – Rauzer
9th Soviet Championship
Leningrad 1934

1.c4 e6 2.g3 d5 3.♗g2 ♘f6 4.d4 ♗e7 5.♘f3 0-0

While white was busy with tricky move transpositions, black, playing Queen's Gambit Orthodox Defense lines, solved two very simple problems: he defended the central pawn on d5 and secured his king's position. Even back then, we already knew that black could use such a system against many closed openings, such as the English, Reti, Bird (1.f4) and others. Rauzer often used that method.

6.0-0 c5

This is a position from one of the lines of the Catalan Opening. After 7.cxd5 exd5 8.♘c3 ♘c6, the game would have transposed into a Tarrasch Defense. In this game, however, Rauzer tests the line with quick development of the black queen. The same idea brought him success in the qualifying tournament (Tbilisi 1934), in the game against master N. Sorokin (see game 36). Black's goal is to put pressure on the d4 pawn. Another idea has also been tried – 6...c6 (taming the g2 bishop) 7.♘c3 ♘bd7, using the fact that it's now bad to play 8.♘e5 ♘xe5 9.dxe5 ♘g4 10.♗f4 due to 10...g5!

In the last line, white's play can be improved with 10.♕d4!?

7.cxd5 ♕xd5 8.♘c3 ♕h5 9.e4

White could unravel the central knot by continuing 9.dxc5 ♖d8 10.♕b3 ♘c6 (10...♘a6 11.c6!) 11.♗f4 ♗xc5 12.♖ad1.

9...♖d8 10.d5

10.e5 ♘d5 (10...cxd4? 11.exf6 dxc3 12.fxe7 with an extra piece) 11.♘e4 cxd4 12.♘xd4 ♕xd1 13.♖xd1 ♘b4 14.♗g5 was more promising. V. Ragozin is trying to confuse his opponent in his signature manner, but complications fly back to him like a boomerang!

10...♘c6 11.♗f4 exd5 12.e5 ♘e8! 13.♘xd5 ♗g4 14.♘xe7+ ♘xe7

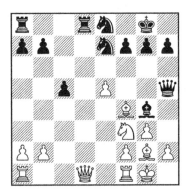

As a result, all black pieces occupy comfortable squares, the f3 knight is pinned, the white queen is forced to move to b3, but even there, it will still be harassed by a knight from c6. White somehow manages to extricate himself from these troubles by sacrificing a pawn. However, it's still too far from the safe drawing harbor.

15.♕b3 ♘c6 16.e6!? fxe6 17.h3 ♗xh3 18.♗xh3 ♕xh3 19.♘g5 ♕f5 20.♘xe6 ♘a5!

Rauzer has coolly repelled all the smart tricks by white and has won a good pawn on the queenside. There was only one question: would he

have enough time and precision to finish the game successfully?

21.♕e3 ♖d5 22.♖ad1 b6 23.♕f3 ♖xd1 24.♖xd1 ♖c8 25.♕e2 ♘f6

The position has stabilized, and white again has to come up with some small tricks to avoid losing meekly.

26.♘c7!

With this move, Ragozin temporarily defuses the e-file; the maneuver ♘c7-b5-d6 (or ♘xa7) might come in handy as well.

26...h6 27.♘b5 ♖e8 28.♕f3 ♘e4 29.♔g2 ♖e7 30.♖d8+ ♔h7 31.♕d3 ♘c6!

After the last series of moves, the situation has changed significantly: the white rook has invaded the 8th rank and the e4 knight is pinned. But with his last move, black nullifies all the tactical tricks of his opponent, trades the queens and goes for a relatively simply endgame.

32.♖d5 ♘b4 33.♖xf5 ♘xd3 34.♗b8 a6 35.♘c7 ♘xb2

The attempt to attack the white king with 35...♘e1+ 36.♔g1 (or

36.♔h1 ♘d2 and ♘ef3) 36...♘d2 37.♘d5 ♘ef3+ was repelled with the simple 38.♔g2, and after 38...♖e2 39.♘c3 ♘e1+ white would have played 40.♔h1! (not 40.♔g1? ♘df3+ and ♖xb2), and the black rook must retreat. After capturing the b2 pawn, black retained the advantage, but he still has a lot of technical challenges ahead of him.

36.♘xa6 ♘d3

Another strong continuation was 36...♖b7 37.♗e5 ♘d3, etc.

37.♗c7 ♖e6 38.a4 c4 39.♖d5 ♖c6 40.♗e5 ♘exf2 41.♗d4

41...c3(?)

As G. Levenfish pointed out in the tournament book, 41...♘g4 or 41...♘e4 was more precise. The victory slowly slips through Rauzer's fingers in time trouble.

Actually both 41...c3 and 41...♘e4 are equally strong, while 41...♘g4 is even a bit worse.

42.♖d7 ♔g6 43.♖xg7+ ♔h5?

Of course, 43...♔f5 was necessary.

44.♘b4! c2

The tournament book stated that 44...♘xb4 was the winning move.

However, even in this case, white has an interesting resource: 45.♗xf2 ♖c4 46.♗e3 c2 (46...♘d5 47.♗c1 ♖xa4 48.♔f3 with a probable draw) 47.♔h3! ♘d3 48.g4+ ♔xg4 49.♖xg4 ♘f2+ 50.♗xf2 c1=♕ 51.♖h4+ ♔g5 52.♖g4+ ♔f5 53.♖h4

with a positional fortress. At the very least, without the h6 pawn (it's unlikely that its presence on the board can change the evaluation in any way), the Lomonosov tables show that this position is drawn.

45.g4+ ♔h4

Of course, not 45...♘xg4 46.♘xd3.

46.♘xc6

Ragozin sealed this move. After a thorough analysis, this study-like position was deemed to be drawn.

The main line shown in the tournament book went as follows: 46...♘f4+ (but not 46...c1=♕? 47.♗f6+ ♕g5 48.♗xg5+ hxg5 49.♔f3, and white wins) 47.♔h2! ♘xg4+ 48.♖xg4+ ♔xg4 49.♗e3 ♔f3 50.♗xf4 ♔xf4 51.♘b4! c1=♘ 52.♘d5+, capturing the b6 pawn and forcing the draw. An elegant finish!

No. 41. Queen's Gambit
Riumin – Rauzer
9th Soviet Championship
Leningrad 1934

We have already seen how carefully and thoughtfully Rauzer studied the materials of the Alekhine – Capablanca match (1927), especially its contribution to the theory of the Queen's Gambit (games 25 and 38). Here's another example on the same topic. Of course, N. Riumin, knowing Rauzer's games, expected him to play the Swiss variation with a7-a6, which was successfully tested in the match. However, all attempts to complicate the struggle led to nothing.

1.d4 d5 2.c4 e6 3.♘c3 ♘f6 4.♘f3 ♗e7 5.♗g5 0-0 6.e3 ♘bd7 7.♖c1 a6 8.a3 dxc4 9.♗xc4 b5 10.♗a2 c5 11.0-0 ♗b7 12.♗b1 ♖c8 13.dxc5 ♘xc5 14.♕e2

14...♘ce4   15.♘xe4   ♖xc1 16.♖xc1   ♘xe4   17.♖d1   ♕c7 18.♗xe7   ♕xe7   19.♕d3   ♕f6 20.♕d4   ♕xd4   21.♖xd4   ♖c8 22.♔f1   ♘f6   23.♔e2   ♔f8   24.e4 ♔e7 25.♗d3 ♘d7 26.♗b1

Draw.

No. 42. Sicilian Defense
Rauzer – V. Makogonov
9th Soviet Championship
Leningrad 1934

1.e4 c5 2.♘f3 e6 3.d4 cxd4 4.♘xd4 ♘f6 5.♘c3 d6 6.♗g5 a6 7.♕f3

One of Rauzer's most ingenious inventions, which he fearlessly tested in early 1934 in the Kiev competition and correspondence games. Thorough joint analysis convinced us that the main factors of white's attack were: long castling; building a pawn phalanx e4-f4; and, in case of black's counter-attack with b7-b5 – the bishop sacrifice ♗xb5 for two or three pawns and the initiative. I successfully implemented Rauzer's idea in a game against A. Akshanov

(Vinnitsa Oblast championship, August 1934), and then later against E. Gerstenfeld (an exhibition tournament in Lvov, January 1940). The test of the super-new (at the time!) Rauzer Attack against the deep strategist V. Makogonov, an expert in the Sicilian, was especially valuable and principled.

7...♕c7 8.0-0-0 ♘bd7

Black follows the main lines of the Scheveningen system.

9.♕g3 b5

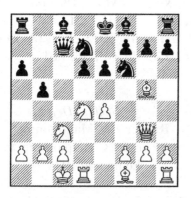

10.♗xb5!

The genius idea of Rauzer! In its time, it greatly shook the defensive structures of Sicilian Defense adherents – the bold push b7-b5 was one of black's trump cards in this structure. After black accepts the sacrifice, white has three passed pawns, but the activity of black pieces should not be underestimated. All in all, a complicated struggle with imbalanced material awaits.

10...axb5   11.♘dxb5   ♕a5 12.♘xd6+ ♗xd6 13.♖xd6

The critical position; it's hard for black to choose a plan for counterplay here. G. Levenfish recommended 13...0-0 in the tournament book, fearing neither 14.♖xd7 ♘xd7 15.♗h6 due to 15...♕e5 16.f4 ♕f6, nor 14.♗h6 because of 14...♘e8. My subsequent analysis still showed that black's position after castling was far from completely safe.

Let's look at some lines after 13...0-0.

I) 14.♗h6 ♘e8 15.♖hd1 ♔h8, and white's attack is stopped;

However, in this line 15.♖d3! is stronger, and white can try various ways to attack with ♗d2, f2-f4 or h2-h4;

II) 14.♖xd7! ♘xd7 15.♗h6 ♕e5 16.f4 ♕f6 17.♗g5 ♕g6 18.h4 h5 19.f5! exf5 20.♘d5! ♔h7 21.♘e7 ♕a6 22.♘xf5 ♖g8 23.♖d1, and it's hard for black to survive. The line 23...♕xa2 24.♖d6 ♕a1+ 25.♔d2 ♕xb2 26.♕f3! ♕b4+ 27.♔e2 is quite telling; black cannot play 27...g6 due to 28.♕xh5+! gxh5 29.♖h6#.

In the first line, the play of both white (15.♖d4!?) and black (14... ♘h5!?) can be improved, but black's chances are better.

The second line can be improved in many places. But we will point out only the mistake 25...♕xb2?. Black is fine after, for example, 25...f6!?

13...♘h5 14.♕h4 h6

Black intended to trade queens (15.♕xh5 ♕xg5+ 16.♕xg5 hxg5) and go for a safe endgame. Of course, white doesn't allow him such luxury.

15.♗e3 ♘hf6

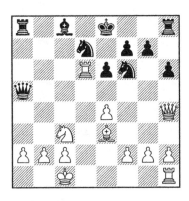

Now white could severely restrict the mobility of the black pieces with 16.♖d4!, threatening ♖a4. 16...♖b8 would be simply met with 17.♕g3 (17...♕b6 18.b3). The rook is not needed on d6 anymore.

16.f3 ♖b8 17.♖d4 ♕b6

After 17...♕c7(?) 18.♕g3 e5 19.♖xd7! ♘xd7 20.♕xg7, white's pressure increased.

The outcome depends on the order of moves: 19.♕xg7!, and if 19...♖h7 then 20.♖xd7!

18.♘a4 ♕b5 19.b3 e5

Even though it was advisable to kick the rook away from d4, ceding the key d5 square was rather dangerous.

20.♖c4 ♕a5 21.♕e1! ♕a8

After the queen exchange, black has no way to stop the advancing "three musketeers".

22.♕g3

Too slow. 22.♕c3! piled on even more pressure.

22...♗a6 23.♖c7 ♗b5

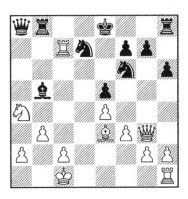

24.♘c3

24.♘b6!? looked tempting. After 24...♕xa2 25.♘xd7 ♕a1+ 26.♔d2 ♕a5+ 27.♖c3, everything seemed rather good for white. Still, there was a complicated line in this combination: 27...♖d8 28.♕xe5+ ♔xd7 29.♖d1 ♘d5!? 30.♔e1 ♗c6 31.♔f2 ♖he8 32.♕f5+ ♔c7 33.♖xc6+ ♔xc6 34.exd5+ ♔b7 35.c4, and, skillfully maneuvering "between Scylla and Charybdis", white would have achieved his aim (a bishop and three pawns for the rook). However, it's hard to calculate such a line, so Rauzer chooses a simpler route.

It's probably impossible to see all the subtleties of the complications above over the board. Of course, computer analysis allows us to find the shortcomings in the analysis of the pre-computer era. Even the first improvement for black (27...♘xd7) still allows white to attack. Despite the overall evaluation being in black's favor, white retained practical chances.

24...♕a5   25.♘xb5   ♕xb5 26.♖d1 ♕a5 27.♖a7 ♕c3

V. Makogonov defends resourcefully. The position is unclear.

28.♖d3 ♕a1+ 29.♔d2 ♖c8

With an unpleasant threat ♕b2.

30.c4 g5(?)

After 30...♕b2+ 31.♔e1, the problem of blockading the white pawns was still unsolved. However, black missed the following king maneuver that led to a queen exchange.

31.♔c2! ♕f1

Still hoping for 32.♖d1 ♕e2+ 33.♗d2 0-0, but Rauzer chooses a simpler solution.

32.♕f2! ♕xf2+ 33.♗xf2 ♘b8

It's impossible to stop the three pawns, even though black defends with all his forces.

34.♔c3 0-0

Castling didn't help the defense, and black could have played 34...♘bd7, then h6-h5 and ♖h6 or 34...♘h5, ♘g7 and ♘e6.

35.♖d6 ♔g7 36.b4 ♘e8 37.♖b6 ♘c6 38.♖d7 ♘b8 39.♖db7 ♘c6

This looks similar to the checkers-type game "ugolki" – white has completely seized the left corner, and the pawn trio advances inexorably.

40.♗c5 ♖g8 41.a4 ♘d8 42.♖b8 ♖xb8 43.♖xb8 ♘e6 44.♗e7 f6 45.c5 ♔f7 46.♖b7 ♔g6

Black is invincible in the e5-e8-h8-h5 square, but what can he do about white's a-pawn?

47.♗d6 ♘8g7 48.♔c4 ♖a8 49.a5 ♘d4 50.♖b8 ♖a7 51.♖b6 ♘ge6 52.a6 g4 53.fxg4 ♔g5 54.b5 ♔f4 55.♖b7 ♖a8 56.♖f7 ♔xe4 57.♖xf6

Black resigned.

The great Philidor would have been proud of this game!

No. 43. Caro-Kann Defense
Rauzer – Goldberg
Tournament of 12
Leningrad 1935

The introductory article mentions Rauzer's "sacrifices to the altar of Theory". This game is one of the most telling examples of that.

1.e4 c6 2.d4 d5 3.♘c3 dxe4 4.♘xe4 ♗f5 5.♕f3

Even though this move occurred in some games by P. Leonhardt and R. Spielmann, we should recognize that Rauzer was its most ardent advocate and developer. The idea behind this queen sortie is logical: to strengthen the knight's position in the center while preventing the subsequent liberating moves c6-c5 and e6-e5.

5...♗xe4

Black immediately cuts the "Gordian knot". We can't deny the consistency of this plan.

6.♕xe4 ♘f6

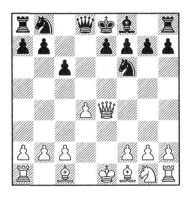

7.♕e3

Later analysis and practical outings showed that the stronger move here was 7.♕h4! with the subsequent structure ♘f3 and ♗g5 or ♗f4. This lesson benefited me when I played a correspondence game as white with V. Simagin (1969–1970): 5...e6 6.c3 ♗xe4 7.♕xe4 ♘f6 8.♕h4 ♘bd7 9.♘f3 ♗d6 10.♗f4 ♕c7 11.♗xd6 ♕xd6 12.♗c4 b5 13.♗e2 b4 14.c4 c5 15.0-0 0-0 with a complicated strategic struggle.

7...e6 8.♘f3 ♘bd7 9.g3 c5(?)

This was "a double sacrifice on the altar of the idea 5.♕f3!?", because I also quickly lost in the same line to B. Ratner in the 1935 Kiev Championship: 9...♗d6 10.♗g2 0-0 11.0-0 ♖e8 12.b3 e5! 13.♗b2 e4 14.♘d2 ♘d5 with a great position for black. However, I was consoled by the fact that I managed to "exact my revenge" the following year, easily defeating G. Stepanov in the VTsSPS (All-Union Central Soviet of Trade Unions) Championship after 5...e6 6.c3 ♘f6? (black should have played 6...♘d7 and only then ♘gf6) 7.♘xf6+ gxf6 (after 7...♕xf6, there's an unpleasant reply 8.♕g3!, threatening ♕c7 and ♗g5) 8.♗c4 ♘d7 9.♗f4 ♘b6 10.♗b3 ♘d5 11.♗d2! etc.

Alas, Rauzer's reaction to the poor move 9...c5 was even more clumsy.

10.♕b3?

"The rest is not interesting," Rauzer confessed to me in a letter written at the time. "The correct move was 10.♗g2. For example, 10...cxd4 11.♘xd4 ♗c5 12.♕d2! (the necessity of this move scared me over the board) 12...♕c7 (or 12...♕b6 13.♘b3±) 13.0-0 0-0 14.♘b5 ♕b6 15.♕e2, then b2-b3 and ♗b2. 'Just' five moves with the white queen, and his advantage crystallizes."

Since that moment, Rauzer indeed completely lost interest in the game. Unfortunately, such things happened with him when he got upset with the game's course. In such a mood, he could lose without any resistance, like in this case...

10...cxd4 11.♗g2 ♗c5 12.♕xb7 0-0 13.0-0 ♖c8 14.♕a6

Black threatened ♗b6 and ♘c5 (or ♖xc2).

14...♗b6 15.♕d3 e5 16.♘g5 h6 17.♘e4 ♘xe4 18.♕xe4 f5 19.♕d5+ ♔h8 20.♗h3 ♖xc2 21.♗xf5 ♖xf5 22.♕e4 ♖xc1

White resigned without waiting for the obvious 23.♖xc1 ♕g5.

No. 44. Ruy Lopez
Rauzer/Belakovsky –
E. Polyak/Zhukhovitsky
Korostyshevo 1935[16]
Annotated by V. Rauzer

1.e4 e5 2.♘f3 ♘c6 3.♗b5 a6 4.♗a4 ♗e7 5.0-0 ♘f6 6.♖e1 b5 7.♗b3 d6 8.c3 ♘a5 9.♗c2 c5 10.d3

This is the Carlsbad Variation of the Ruy Lopez (Carlsbad 1911), where white doesn't make committal moves such as 10.a4 or 10.h3 and then 11.d4.

10...0-0 11.♘bd2 ♖e8

With this move, the black players prepare a well-known bishop transfer from e7 to g7.

12.♘f1 h6? 13.h3 ♗f8 14.g4 g6 15.♘g3 ♗g7 16.♔h2 ♕d7

The black players prepare an unfounded counter-attack that gives

16 In summer 1935, the Korostyshevo health resort in the Zhitomir Oblast hosted the USSR's first dedicated chess school. Almost all regions of Ukraine were represented. The participants included master F. Bogatyrchuk (Kiev) and V. Kirillov (Kharkov), future masters A. Zamikhovsky, I. Pogrebyssky, B. Ratner, E. Polyak (all Kiev) and Odessa's S. Zhukhovitsky. V. Rauzer, who had moved to Leningrad a short time before, was invited as a coach and read a course of lectures on open and semi-open games. To consolidate the theoretical knowledge, the first-ever teaching tournament of consultation games was held. One of those games, annotated by Rauzer, was published in the newly-founded chess newspaper *64*.

them a material advantage, but at the price of weakening the kingside even further.

The immediate 16...♘xg4+ 17.hxg4 ♗xg4 with the threat of f7-f5 and f5-f4 was worth considering. – A. K.

17.♖g1 h5

Consistent, but makes the execution of white's planned attack easier.

18.♘f5

White has no other defense. The attack that arises after this well-known piece sacrifice is so dangerous that black probably shouldn't accept it.

18...hxg4

Or 18...gxf5 19.gxf5 ♔f8 (19...♔h8 20.♘h4 and 21.♗g5) 20.♕d2 ♗h8 21.♕h6+ ♔e7 22.♗g5 ♗b7 23.d4, opening lines in the center and pinning an enemy piece.

19.♘3h4

A continuation that would be hard to find without an analysis board. The obvious 19.hxg4 gave nothing except perpetual check:

19...♘xg4+ 20.♖xg4 gxf5 21.♖xg7+ (otherwise f5-f4 with the threat ♕h3+) 21...♔xg7 22.♕g1+ ♔f8 23.♗h6+ ♔e7 24.♗g5+ f6 25.♗xf6+ ♔xf6 26.♕g5+.

Computer analysis shows that after 22...♔h7!? black had good chances to stop white's attack and keep the advantage.

19...gxf5

If 19...gxh3 then 20.♘xg6.

20.♘xf5 ♕c7 21.hxg4

White does not fear closing off the g-file; using the g4 pawn as a battering ram is probably the best chance.

21...♘h7 22.g5 ♘c6

Or 22...♘f8 23.♕h5 ♘g6 24.♖h1 and ♔g2.

23.♗b3

The immediate 23.♕h5 ♘e7 was weaker: white doesn't have time to do anything because of the weakness on f5.

23...c4

24.g6 was a threat. If 23...♗e6 then 24.g6 fxg6 25.♖xg6, and white wins.

24.dxc4 ♘a5 25.c5?

Due to the lack of time (the result of "intensified" consultation, i.e. arguments), white is tempted with winning a third pawn for the sacrificed piece, and the attack (involving ♕h5) develops too slowly. The correct move was 25.♗c2! bxc4 26.♕h5, and, thanks to the lack of a d3 pawn (i.e. the c2 bishop has a better range) as well as the black a5 knight's departure from the kingside, white's attack becomes even stronger.

For instance, 26...d5 27.♘xg7 ♔xg7 28.♕h6+ ♔g8 29.exd5 e4+ 30.d6 etc.

25...♘xb3 26.cxd6 ♕b7

The best move was 26...♕c5!? with unclear play.

27.axb3

27...♕xe4?

In time trouble, black returns the sacrificed piece, hoping to exploit the exposed position of the white king. Black should have played 27...♗e6 with the threat ♕xe4. White still has three pawns for the piece, but the white attack disappears without a trace.

This statement is questionable. After 28.g6 fxg6 29.♖xg6, white retained a dangerous initiative. – **A. K.**

28.d7 ♗xd7 29.♕xd7 ♖ad8 30.♘h6+ ♗xh6 31.gxh6+ ♔h8 32.♕h3

It was simpler to go into a won endgame after 32.♕g4 ♕xg4 33.♖xg4, with an extra pawn and a weakness on a6 for black.

Too optimistic – it's more like an "endgame with winning chances". The game move was probably the best.

32...♖g8 33.♗e3 f5 34.♖xg8+ ♖xg8 35.♖g1 ♖xg1 36.♔xg1 ♘f6 37.♕g2 ♕b1+

Time trouble had now ended.

38.♔h2 ♘g4+ 39.♔h3 e4

The only defense against white's threat 40.♕a8+ ♔h7 41.♕b7+ and ♕g7#.

40.♔h4!

Threatening 41.♕g3 ♕h1+ 42.♔g5 ♕xh6+ 43.♔xf5 etc.

40...♕d1

If 40...♕xb2 then 41.♗d4+ ♔h7 42.♕g3 ♔xh6 43.♕c7 and ♕g7#.

41.♕g3 ♕d8+

41...♕h1+ was no better: 42.♔g5 ♕xh6+ 43.♔xf5 ♘xe3+ 44.fxe3 with an extra pawn, and the second pawn (e4) falls soon.

42.♗g5 ♕b6 43.♔h5 ♔h7 44.♕f4 ♕g6+ 45.♔h4 ♕f7

If 45...♘xh6, then 46.♗xh6 ♕xh6+ 47.♕xh6+ ♔xh6 48.c4 ♔g6 (or 48...bxc4 49.bxc4 first)

49.c5 ♔f6 50.c6 ♔e6 51.♔g5, and white wins.

46.c4 bxc4 47.bxc4 ♔g6

Black can do nothing.

48.♕d6+ ♔h7 49.c5 ♕e8?

A blunder, which, however, changes nothing.

50.♕c7+

Black resigned.

No. 45. Caro-Kann Defense
Rauzer – Goldberg
Leningrad Championship, 1936

1.e4 c6 2.d4 d5 3.exd5 cxd5 4.♗d3 ♘c6 5.c3 ♘f6 6.♘f3

Many (including Bobby Fischer) preferred 6.♗f4. The key to this position is whether black manages to find some rational play for his light-squared bishop. In this game, its travels along the path of c8-g4-h5-g6 did weaken black's kingside somewhat.

6...♗g4 7.h3 ♗h5

7...♗xf3! 8.♕xf3 e6 was safer – in a closed position, white's bishop pair is not that dangerous.

8.♕b3 ♕c8

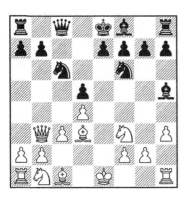

9.♘e5 e6

Avoiding 9...♘xd4? 10.♕a4+ ♘c6 11.♗b5 ♕e6 12.♗xc6+ bxc6 13.♕xc6+ ♕xc6 14.♘xc6 e6 15.♗e3, and black still has some concerns on the queenside, even though nothing is lost yet.

This line is fine for black. His play can be improved, for instance, with 11...a6!? or even continuing the line with 15...a6!? Thus, white's 9th move should be considered poor.

10.♗f4 ♗e7 11.♘d2 ♘xe5 12.♗xe5 0-0 13.0-0 ♗g6

Perhaps the plan with 13...♕d7 and then ♗d6, ♖fb8 and b7-b5 with queenside play was more prudent. After the trade on g6, black must be very careful.

14.♗xg6 hxg6 15.♖ae1 ♕c6

This move connects the rooks, but as preparation for the maneuver ♘f6-e4, it was poor.

16.♘f3 ♘e4?

16...♘d7 was better – not to trade the e5 bishop, but to prevent the white knight from reaching e5.

17.♗f4 ♗d6 18.♗xd6 ♕xd6

19.♕d1!

Now white is targeting the seemingly well-defended position of the black king. Of course, black goes for a pawn minority attack with the b5-b4 break, but his king is a more important target!

19...b5 20.♘e5 ♖ab8 21.a3 ♖fc8 22.h4 ♘f6 23.g4! a5

Both opponents are ready for attacks on their respective flanks. White is the first to strike telling blows, however.

24.h5 gxh5 25.g5 ♘g4 26.♘xg4 hxg4 27.♕xg4 g6 28.♔g2 ♔g7 29.♖h1 ♖h8

Black has seemingly parried the threats along the menacing file and can catch his breath. However, the second attack of white's major pieces is more formidable, now that it's joined by the f2 pawn.

30.♕f3 ♕d8 31.♕f4! ♖h5

In view of the threat ♕e5+, this is the only reply that prolongs the struggle.

32.♕e5+ ♔h7 33.f4 ♕h8

Otherwise there would follow 34.♖xh5+ gxh5 35.♖h1 ♔g6 36.♕e2 ♕h8 37.♕d3+ ♔g7 38.f5. But even now, the f-pawn is up to the task.

White's threat only works in certain conditions. One can ascertain that by looking, for instance, at the line with a typical pawn minority attack: 33...b4 34.♖xh5+ gxh5 35.♖h1 ♔g6 36.cxb4! with the subsequent ♖c1 and the rook threatening to join the attack from the side. Black's position looks dangerous, but computer analysis shows that white has nothing concrete. After the game move, however, the breakthrough is indeed decisive.

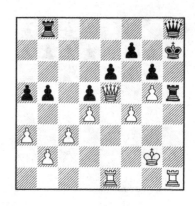

**34.♕c7   ♕e8   35.f5!   ♔g8
36.♖xh5 gxh5 37.g6 ♔g7**

White threatened 38.♖xe6 fxe6
39.♕h7+ ♔f8 40.f6. And still:

38.♖xe6 ♖c8 39.♕e5+

Black resigned.

Rauzer played this attack with
classical simplicity and clarity!

No. 46. Queen's Gambit Accepted
Levenfish – Rauzer
Leningrad Championship, 1936

**1.d4 d5 2.c4 dxc4 3.♘f3 ♘f6
4.e3 c5 5.♗xc4 cxd4 6.exd4 e6
7.0-0 ♗e7 8.♘c3 0-0**

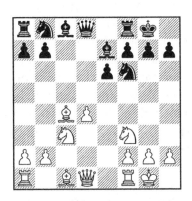

The well-known Steinitz position
in the Queen's Gambit Accepted.
Rauzer tested it numerous times
(see a detailed discussion in game 61,
Kan – Rauzer). G. Levenfish, being
a subtle psychologist, of course took
his opponent's tastes into account
and placed his pieces in such a way
as to prevent the blockade on d5 and
prepare the d4-d5 break himself.

**9.♕e2 a6 10.♗g5 b5 11.♗b3
♗b7 12.♖fd1**

12...♘bd7

12...b4? was risky due to 13.d5!
bxc3 14.dxe6 ♕c7 15.exf7+ ♔h8
with a strong attack for white.
The dangers that await black can
be illustrated by the following
approximate lines:

a) 16.bxc3, and white has three
pawns for the knight and an attack;

b) 16.♘d4 (threatening ♘e6
and ♘f5) is probably even stronger:
16...♗c8 17.♖ac1 ♗b4 18.♕f3 ♗b7
19.♕xf6!, and black's position is
poor. Therefore, after 12...b4 the
13.d5! break opens a way for white
to win.

The game move doesn't prevent
d4-d5, however, the consequences
are much different.

**13.d5   exd5   14.♘xd5   ♗xd5
15.♗xd5   ♘xd5   16.♖xd5   ♗xg5
17.♘xg5**

If 17.♖ad1 then black has the
defense 17...♕e7!, but not 17...
♖a7? 18.♘xg5 ♕f6 19.♘xh7! (19.
♘e4 ♕e6 is insufficient), and white
emerges a pawn up.

**17...h6 18.♕d2 hxg5 19.♖xd7
♕f6 20.♖d1 ♖ae8 21.h3**

White has seized the d-file, while black controls the neighboring e-file and both kings are safe. The drawing beacon can already be seen ahead... The opponents continued to maneuver even after the queen trade that soon took place, but probably only for psychological reasons.

21...♖e6 22.♕d4 ♕xd4 23.♖7xd4 ♖e2 24.♖4d2 ♖xd2 25.♖xd2 ♖e8

Black has fully equalized, and white's symbolic attempts to gain some small advantage are easily repelled.

26.♔f1 ♖e6 27.♖e2 ♖d6 28.♔e1 ♔f8 29.♖e4 f6 30.♔e2 ♔f7 31.♖e3 f5 32.♖d3 ♔e6 33.♖c3 ♔f6 34.♖c7 g6 35.♖c3 ♔e5 36.♖g3 ♔f6 37.♖a3 ♔e5 38.♖e3+ ♔f6 39.♖g3 ♖d4 40.♖a3 ♖d6

Time control has been reached, but the leader of the white army is still testing the fortitude of the "newcomer" who was contending the leadership of the tournament from the start. The game was played in the sixth round and both Rauzer and Levenfish had three wins and two draws.

41.♔e3 ♔e5 42.g3 ♖c6 43.f4+ gxf4+ 44.gxf4+ ♔e6 45.♔d4 ♖c4+ Draw.

The game between the same opponents in the 10th Soviet Championship (Tbilisi 1937 – game 70) was very important for further development of the creative discussion in this system: 12.♖fe1! – a move prepared by Levenfish that created the threat ♗xe6!. Against the plan 12...♘bd7 13.♖ad1 ♘b6, recommended by some analysts – it occurred in the game Stolberg – Rauzer (12th Soviet Championship semi-final, Kiev 1940) – Rauzer showed a very strong reply 14.d5!! in the post-mortem, with an advantage for white in all lines. The boomerang came back – it became harder for black to defend in this system. As we can see, Steinitz's idea of blockading the d4 pawn requires extraordinary care and using tempi sparingly.

No. 47. Latvian Gambit
Rauzer – Ilyin-Zhenevsky
Leningrad Championship, 1936
Annotated by A. Ilyin-Zhenevsky

1.e4 e5 2.♘f3 f5

One can hardly believe that such a long-forgotten and "obviously unsound" opening as this gambit for black can occur in a serious modern competition. However, as I think, this opening is much better than its reputation suggests, and the resulting sharp play creates great conditions for chess players with a combinational style.

3.♘xe5

This move is considered one of the strongest.

3...♕f6 4.d4 d6 5.♘c4 fxe4 6.♘c3 ♕g6

The queen on g6 prevents the normal development of the opponent's kingside and, together with the advanced e-pawn, puts pressure on his entire position.

7.h3

Theory recommends 7.f3 exf3 8.♕xf3 ♘f6 9.♗d3 ♕g4 etc., which, I think, gives black satisfactory play. White's plan of attacking the e4 pawn is refuted by black with some energetic play.

Modern practice shows that after 9.♘e3! (instead of 9.♗d3), the black queen's poor position far away from the c7 square tells. White has won 100% of the games in the database in this line.

7...♘f6 8.g4 ♗e7 9.♗g2 0-0

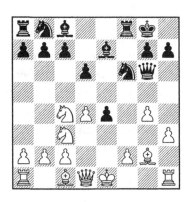

10.♗e3

The direct attempt to win the e4 pawn gave white nothing. After 10.g5,

black could simply play 10...♗f5, ignoring the attack on the knight. 10.♕e2 was met with 10...d5 11.♘e5 ♕e8 12.g5 ♘fd7 13.♘xd5 ♘xe5 14.dxe5.♗c5 15.0-0 (if white took the c7 pawn, he would have come under a crushing attack after 15...♕f7) 15...♕xe5 16.♕xe4 (of course, not 16.♗xe4 due to 16...♕g3+) 16...♕xe4 17.♗xe4 with a good game for black.

In the case of 10.♕e2, it's better for black not to weaken the e5 square since he's a pawn down. Instead of 10...d5, it's better to play 10...♘c6.

10...c6

If black does manage to play d6-d5, his position would clearly be better, and so white prevents it.

11.d5 b5

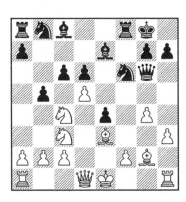

12.♘a5!

The only move, since 12.♘d2 is met with 12...b4 13.♘e2 ♘xd5 14.♗xe4 ♘xe3 15.♗xg6 (if 15.fxe3, then, of course, 15...♗h4+) 15...♘xd1, and black wins a piece.

Instead of 13.♘e2, there's a better move, 13.♘cxe4, but even here, black is better after 13...♘xd5.

12...b4 13.♘e2

Now black can't play 13...♘xd5 due to 14.♘xc6 ♘xe3 15.♘xe7+ ♔f7 16.♘xg6 ♘xd1 17.♖xd1 hxg6 18.♗xe4, and white wins.

13...c5 14.♕d2

There's nothing better. If, for instance, 14.♘f4, then 14...♕f7 15.g5 ♘e8 16.♗xe4 ♗xg5 with strong pressure along the f-file.

The move 14.♘f4!? is actually worth considering. However, instead of the weak 16.♗xe4, white should play 16.h4!? with black suffering from a cramped position and a weak c6 square.

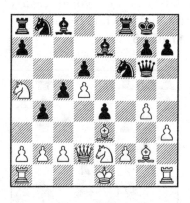

14...♕e8!

An unexpected transfer to the queenside. Now white cannot win a pawn with 15.g5 ♘fd7 16.♗xe4 due to 16...♗d8, and two white pieces are under attack at the same time. Meanwhile, black threatens 15...♕b5 16.♘b3 c4, and the d5 pawn is in serious danger.

15.♘c4 ♗a6 16.b3 ♘fd7

Now white cannot take the e4 pawn due to 17...♗f6. Black, on the other

hand, is threatening 17...♗xc4 18.bxc4 ♘b6, winning the c4 pawn. What can white do now? 17.♘g3 or 17.♘f4 are simply impossible due to 17...♗f6. 17.♘b2 ♗f6 is also better for black.

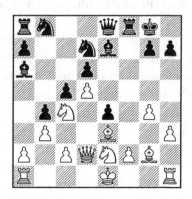

17.0-0!

Without a doubt, this is best. White simply gives away the c4 pawn, planning to win the e4 pawn instead.

17...♗xc4 18.bxc4 ♗f6 19.♖ae1

Seemingly an oversight. The correct move was 19.♖ad1 with the possible continuation 19... ♘b6 20.♘g3 ♘xc4 21.♕e2 ♘xe3 22.♕xe3 ♘d7 23.♘xe4 ♗d4 24.♕g5 ♕e5 with double-edged play.

The game move is not bad – it might be that Rauzer deliberately sacrificed an exchange, getting enough compensation in the process.

19...♘b6 20.♘g3

If white doesn't give away the exchange, he simply gets a lost position, being a pawn down.

20...♗c3 21.♕c1

With 21.♕e2, white could keep the pawn, losing only an exchange, but his attacking chances would have suffered, for instance, 21...♗xe1 22.♖xe1 ♘8d7 23.♘xe4 ♕e5.

21...♗xe1 22.♖xe1 ♘xc4 23.♗f4

This bishop plays a very important role in white's plans, so he must not trade it.

23...e3

Trying to force white to either trade the bishop or close off the f-file.

24.♘f5

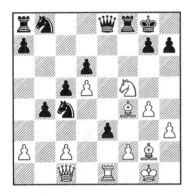

24...♘d7

24...♖xf5!? was also worth considering

25.♗xe3 ♕f7?

A horrible blunder that loses the game. Black still had some winning chances after 25...♖xf5!?

26.♗h6! ♖fe8 27.♗xg7 ♕g6

Otherwise 28.♘h6+.

28.♖e7 ♘f8

Planning to meet 29.♘h6+ with 29...♕xh6 and 30...♖xe7, getting two rooks for the queen.

White still wins here: 30.♗xh6 ♖xe7 31.♕g5+ ♘g6 32.f4.

29.♕f4

29.♖c7 won even more quickly: there's no stopping 30.♘h6+.

29...♘e5 30.♗xe5 dxe5 31.♕xe5 ♘d7 32.♕e6+! ♕xe6 33.dxe6 ♖xe7

If 33...♖ad8 then 34.♖g7+ with the subsequent 35.exd7.

34.♘xe7+ ♔f8 35.♗xa8 ♘b6 36.♘d5!

After other moves, black could still resist.

36...♘xa8 37.f4 a5 38.♔f2 a4 39.♔e3 ♘c7 40.♘xc7 c4 41.e7+ ♔xe7 42.♘d5+ ♔d6 43.♘xb4

Black resigned.

No. 48. Ruy Lopez
Rauzer – Ragozin
Leningrad Championship, 1936
Annotated by V. Rauzer

1.e4 e5 2.♘f3 ♘c6 3.♗b5 a6 4.♗a4 ♘f6 5.0-0 ♗c5

The Moller Defense, highly recommended by Alekhine in his book *On the Ways to the Highest Chess Achievements*. In the Leningrad championship, however, its performance was 3/3 in white's favor.

6.c3 ♗a7 7.d4 ♘xe4

Of course, it's not easy to find the correct reply in practice, however, rich experience in the Ruy Lopez shows that it's never good for black to open up the position by taking the e4 pawn.

8.♕e2 f5 9.♘bd2 0-0 10.♘xe4 fxe4 11.♕xe4

11...d5

Black is forced to sharpen the play: his kingside is too weakened, and he has no time to play e5xd4. For instance, 11...exd4 12.♘g5 g6 13.♕h4 ♕e7 14.♗b3+ ♔h8 15.♗d2 followed by ♖ae1 with a strong attack.

12.♗b3 ♗e6 13.♕e3

Not 13.♕e2 because of 13...♗g4.

13...♖f5

This awkward maneuver is forced, because 13...♕f6 is met with 14.dxe5! ♕f5 (or 14...♕g6 15.♕g5) 15.♘d4, and white is better.

14.♘g5 ♕e8

If 14...♕f6, then 15.♕h3 ♖xg5 (15...h6 16.♘xe6 ♕xe6 17.♗xd5) 16.♗xg5, winning an exchange. After the game move, 15.♕h3? does not work due to 15...♖xg5, and the black queen is not under attack.

15.♗c2 e4

Now the a7 bishop and the c6 knight will be out of play.

16.f3?

Too hasty. By weakening the a7-g1 diagonal, white allows some activity for the a7 bishop and c6 knight, basically losing almost all his advantage. The correct plan was to put the bishop on e3, ensuring the inactivity of black pieces, and only then play the f2-f3 break: 16.♕g3 h6 17.♘xe6 ♕xe6 18.♗e3 ♖af8 19.♖ae1, and now f2-f3.

16...h6 17.♘xe6 ♕xe6 18.♗d2

Not 18.fxe4 ♖xf1+ 19.♔xf1 ♖f8+ 20.♔g1 ♕f6 with an attack for black.

18...♕f6 19.♔h1

If 19.fxe4 then 19...♘xd4!

19...♖f8 20.♖fe1 ♖h5?

Black overestimates his position. It's better to play 20...♘e5, and if 21.dxe5 then 21...♗xe3 22.exf6 ♗xd2 23.♖ed1 ♗g5 24.fxg7, and, even though white is a pawn up, the draw is more or less unavoidable because of the opposite-colored bishops.

21.fxe4

21...♘xd4?

This is probably a miscalculation. Still, black couldn't save the game even after 21...♘e5 22.♕g3 ♘c4 23.e5 ♕f2 24.♕xf2 ♖xf2 25.♗g6, and white wins. Or 22...♕f2 23.♕xf2 ♖xf2 24.♗d1 ♖h4 25.♗e3 ♖xb2 26.♗b3 etc.

22.cxd4 ♗xd4 23.♕d3

Black will have to spend time on defending from ♕h7+, so it's now easy for white to convert his extra piece.

23...♗e5 24.h3 ♕f2 25.exd5 ♖ff5 26.♖xe5 ♖xe5 27.♖f1

Black resigned.

No. 49. French Defense

Rauzer – I. Rabinovich

Leningrad Championship, 1936

Annotated by V. Rauzer

1.e4 e6 2.d4 d5 3.♘c3 ♗b4 4.e5 c5 5.a3 ♗xc3+ 6.bxc3 ♘c6

Probably planning to pose insurmountable problems for white with his 10th move (♕c7).

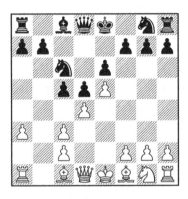

7.♕g4

I'm never deterred by the banality of some attacks or moves. In keeping with the adage "perfect is the enemy of the good", I think that a good banal move is better than a poor "modern" one.

7...♘ge7

This gives white a new chance thanks to the passed h-pawn and a foothold on f6 (a dark square!). It wouldn't be easy for white to break through after 7...g6 8.h4 h5 9.♕f4, even though the dark squares in black's position are very weak. After the fashionable sacrifice of the g7 and h7 pawns, white's play is much more comfortable.

8.♕xg7 ♖g8 9.♕xh7 cxd4 10.♘f3 ♕c7

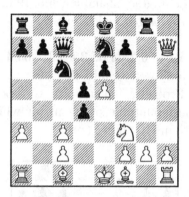

A very tempting move. It seems now that the e5 pawn cannot be properly defended: 11.cxd4 is met with 11...♘xd4 and ♕c3+. If 11.♗b5 (as played in the game Kotov – Chekhover, VTsSPS Championship semi-final, 1935), then 11...♖xg2!, depriving the white king of a safe haven and weakening white's light squares (f3), which is especially important in view of the intended b5 bishop trade. But it's all an illusion!

The last recommendation is not good. After 12.♔f1! ♖g6 13.♖g1 ♖xg1+ 14.♔xg1, the surviving h-pawn, as often happens in similar lines, should decide the game.

11.♗f4

The point! Now, after 11...♘xe5? the simplest winning line is 12.♗b5+ ♔d8 13.♘xe5 ♕xc3+ 14.♔e2, threatening 15.♘xf7#!

11...♗d7

Black prudently prepares to castle long.

12.♗d3 0-0-0

Not 12...♖xg2 13.♗g3, winning an exchange.

13.♗g3!

A very important move that prepares castling. If white simply plays 13.0-0, then black has 13...f5!, depriving the white queen of a safe haven on f6 and threatening ♖h8. Moreover, continuing 14.exf6 ♕xf4 15.fxe7 is bad:

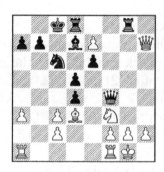

if black doesn't want to play for a win, he can force perpetual check with 15...♖xg2+ 16.♔h1 (16.♔xg2 ♕g4+ with an immediate perpetual) 16...♕xf3

17.exd8=♕+ ♘xd8 18.♗e2 ♕xe2
19.♔xg2 ♕g4+ 20.♔h1 ♕f3+ etc.

If we check both of white's proposed 16ᵗʰ moves here, we see that in fact they end in decisive material losses for white.

However, the recommended 13... f5 is also too hasty, because after 14.♘xd4 white eliminates the threats to his queen and even gets some advantage. Only the immediate 13... ♖h8 maintains equality.

13...♖df8 14.0-0 dxc3

It's hard for black to come up with a good plan.

15.♖fe1

Freeing the g3 bishop from defense of the e5 pawn and threatening to put it on f6.

15...♘g6 16.h4 ♖h8

After 16...♗e8, white could sacrifice the queen: 17.h5 ♖h8 18.hxg6 ♖xh7 19.gxh7, for instance: 19...♘e7 20.♗h4 ♘g6 21.♗f6 ♘h8 (otherwise 22.♗xg6 and h8=♕) 22.♗g7! with an advantage for white.

17.♕g7 ♘ce7 18.♕f6 ♖h5

Defending from 19.♕g5 and the subsequent h4-h5.

19.♘g5(?)

An inaccurate, albeit very natural move. To continue the attack, it's necessary for white to drive away the h5 rook and play h4-h5. Thus, he needs to clear the d1-h5 diagonal by moving the knight away, and then play ♗e2 and ♕f3.

White gave the wrong answer to the question of where to put the knight, since after ♘g5 and ♗e2 black can complicate the game with an interesting combination. This combination is based on the fact that, after ♗e2, the f5 square is now available for the black pieces. Still, it was difficult to foresee this combination. As will become obvious several moves later, the correct move was 19.♘d4!, targeting the f5 square with the knight and freeing the bishop from defending it, for instance: 19...♕c5 20.♖ed1 ♗e8 21.♗e2 ♖h6 22.h5 ♖fh8 23.♕g5, intending ♕e3 and f2-f4. Black couldn't do much against that.

Rauzer's annotations show that he was highly critical of his own play. Actually, the game move is the best, and 19.♘d4 is met with 19...♖fh8, intending to sacrifice an exchange on h4 and put up stiff resistance.

19...♗e8

20.♗e2

The consequences of 20.♕f3 ♖fh8 21.♘xf7 ♗xf7 22.♕xf7 ♘xh4! 23.♕xe6+ ♔b8 were quite unclear. Due to threats to his king, it's hard for white to exploit his passed pawns, for instance: 24.♕d6 ♘hf5 25.♕xc7+ ♔xc7 26.♔f1 ♘xg3+ 27.fxg3, and it would be very hard to win. Or 24.♕g4 ♘hf5 25.♔f1 ♕b6−+. Or 24.♔f1 ♘hf5 with the threats ♘xg3+, ♖h1+ and ♘d4+.

As white played 20.♗e2, he missed black's subsequent combination that complicated the game enormously.

20.♖ab1!? was worth considering, to meet 20...♖fh8 with 21.♗b4, neutralizing the threats along the h-file.

20...♖h6 21.h5 ♘f5!

The point! Now 22.hxg6 is bad, not due to 22...♖xg6, because then white wins with 23.♘xe6!, but in view of 22...♘xg3! (threatening ♖h1#) 23.♘h3! (not 23.fxg3 ♕c5+ 24.♕f2 ♖h1+ 25.♔xh1 ♕xf2, and black wins) 23...♖xg6, and black eliminates the h-pawn and the white dark-squared bishop.

In this difficult position, white finds the best chance.

22.♗h2!

Withdrawing the bishop from the f5 knight's attack and threatening 23.hxg6 ♖xg6 24.♘xe6! again.

Actually, the text move is not the best one, and were black to find the right continuation white would be in serious difficulties. 22.♗g4!? was more resilient with chances to survive.

22...♖fh8?

This was the highest point of intensity in the game, and black had to keep up the pressure. The correct move was 22...♕c6! (but not 22...♘f4? 23.♘xe6!), getting the queen out of the g5 knight's range. After that, a forced line followed: 23.hxg6 ♖xg6 24.♘xe6 ♕xe6∓. After the erroneous game move, black loses an exchange, and the tensions in the position defuse.

23.hxg6 ♖xh2 24.♘h7!

Black probably overlooked that.

24...♖2xh7 25.gxh7 ♖xh7 26.♗d3 ♖h6 27.♕g5 ♕e7

There's no other defense from ♗xf5.

28.♕xe7 ♘xe7 29.f4 ♗c6 30.♔f2 ♖h4

To distract white from calmly seizing the h-file.

31.g3 ♖h2+ 32.♔e3 ♗a4 33.♖h1 ♖d2 34.♖ad1 ♘f5+

The last trick.

35.♗xf5 d4+ 36.♔f3

It wasn't too late to get checkmated: 36.♔e4 ♗c6#!

36...exf5 37.♖xd2 cxd2 38.♔e2 ♗xc2 39.♔xd2 ♗b3 40.♔d3 b6 41.♔xd4 ♗e6 42.♖h5 ♔c7 43.g4 fxg4 44.f5 ♗b3 45.♖g5 a5 46.♖xg4 ♔c6 47.♖h4 ♗a2 48.♖h6+ ♔c7 49.♖h7 ♔c6 50.a4 ♗b3 51.e6!

The quickest way to win.

51...fxe6 52.f6 ♔d6 53.♖b7 e5+ 54.♔c3 ♗g8 55.f7 ♗xf7 56.♖xf7

Black resigned.

No. 50. Queen's Gambit
Freymann – Rauzer
Masters qualifying tournament
Leningrad 1936

1.d4 d5 2.♘f3 ♘f6 3.c4 e6 4.♘c3 ♗e7 5.♗g5 0-0 6.e3 ♘bd7 7.♖c1 a6

This defensive system in the dangerous Queen's Gambit was constantly revised and re-evaluated. After the Alekhine – Capablanca match, Rauzer thoroughly refined it and played it with great skill. Here's another example in addition to those we have already seen (Nos. 25, 38 and 41).

8.cxd5 exd5 9.♗d3 c6 10.0-0 ♖e8

A standard position in this system, where white players have tested various plans. Master Sergei Nikolaevich Freymann chooses an original plan, albeit not entirely appropriate for this structure. He puts the rook on c2 (it can quickly get to the kingside from there), the queen on b1 (with the subsequent b2-b4), the knight goes to e5, and the f-pawn to f4. Rauzer counters this system with calm, simple play. In addition, 11.♖c2 was already tested in the game between the same opponents in the 9th Soviet Championship (1934): there followed 11.♖c2 ♘f8 12.♘e5 ♗e6 13.f4 ♘6d7 14.♗xe7 ♖xe7 15.♘g4? ♗xg4 16.♕xg4 ♖xe3, and white went on to lose.

11.♖c2 ♘f8 12.♕b1 ♗g4 13.♘e5 ♗h5 14.b4 ♘g4

A simplifying operation to open the way to the kingside for the black pieces.

15.♗xe7 ♕xe7

If white now avoids the trade (16. ♘f3), then 16...♕d6! 17.♖e1 ♖ac8 18.h3 ♘f6 with roughly equal play. The trade on g4, initiated by white, allows black to actively maneuver on "his" flank.

16.♘xg4 ♗xg4 17.a4

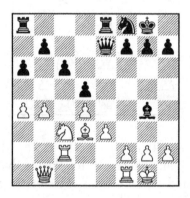

17...♕h4

Planning to transfer the e8 rook to h6.

18.♕e1 ♕g5

Avoiding 18...♖e6 19.f3! ♕xe1 20.♖xe1 ♗h5 21.♔f2 ♗g6, which, however, maintained the balance.

19.♔h1 ♖e6 20.h3 ♖h6

The naive threats ♗xh3 and ♖xh3+ force white to play f2-f4, weakening the e3 pawn. On the other hand, the c2 rook now protects the king.

21.f4 ♕h5

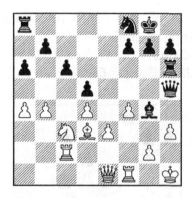

The threat ♗xh3 etc. forces white to go in full defense mode. 22.♕g3 ♖e8 was useless: black subsequently plays ♗f5 and ♖he6, increasing the pressure on e3.

22.♗e2 ♕f5!

Much better than 22...♗xe2 23.♖xe2. Freymann, a strong tactician, still tries to liven up play.

23.e4 dxe4 24.♗xg4 ♕xg4 25.♕xe4 ♕d7

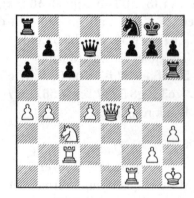

It seems that at this point in time (for instance, after 26.f5, restricting the activity of the f8 knight and h6 rook), the opponents' resources are approximately equal. However, white's next move opens up the position, which is more beneficial for his opponent. The c3 knight does reach the central square d5, and the c2 rook is freed up, but it's obvious that time-trouble excitement (and perhaps tiredness) has started to affect play.

26.d5 ♖e8 27.♕f3

**27...cxd5   28.♘xd5   ♕xa4
29.♖c7**

After 29.♖d2, the end result was far from clear. Anything could happen in such an open position, even though black's pieces are placed somewhat more solidly.

29...♖d6

The battle scene has changed considerably, and black should be on guard. No wonder that some "miracles" happen in time trouble.

30.♘c3?

White could capture the b7 pawn (either immediately or after the preliminary check 30.♘e7+), but Freymann seemingly hoped to invade the seventh rank with his second rook as well.

30...♕xb4 31.♖b1

31.♕xb7 was still good. But when time control is near, you can make all sorts of moves...

31...♕d4

To win the queen after 32.♖bxb7? ♖e1+ 33.♔h2 ♕g1+ 34.♔g3 ♖e3. Still, white's game move is no better.

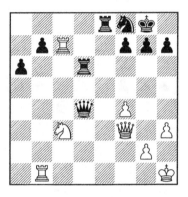

32.♕xb7 ♕xf4 33.♘d5 ♖xd5

White resigned in view of 34.♕xd5 ♕xc7.

No. 51. French Defense
Rauzer – Konstantinopolsky
Masters qualifying tournament
Leningrad 1936

1.e4 e6 2.d4 d5 3.♘c3 dxe4

A difficult system where black intends to develop his light-squared bishop on the long diagonal (through b7 or with ♗c8-d7-c6).

4.♘xe4 ♘d7

Preparing ♘gf6, which is not safe immediately, because after the trade on f6 black either has to double his pawns (gxf6) or put the queen on the poorly-defended f6 square.

5.♘f3 ♘gf6

5...♗e7 seems more solid, to recapture with the bishop in the case of a trade on f6, controlling the e5 square. However, after 6.♗d3 ♘gf6 7.♕e2 0-0 8.♗g5 c5 9.dxc5 ♘xc5 10.♘xc5 ♕a5+ 11.c3 ♕xc5, white retains the initiative.

6.♘xf6+ ♘xf6 7.♗g5 ♗e7

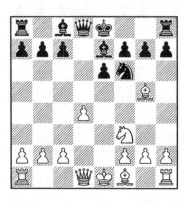

8.♗d3

White also sometimes played 8.♗c4. Black intended to meet this with 8...0-0 9.♕e2 b6 10.0-0-0 ♗b7, and if 11.♘e5, then 11...♘d5!, simplifying the game somewhat and getting a solid position.

The structure with ♗d3 and ♕e2 prevents black from putting his bishop on b7; white also intends to play the aggressive 0-0-0, increasing the pressure in the center. On the kingside, white is ready to launch the standard h2-h4 attack at any moment. It's clear that black should play c7-c5, trading the d4 pawn and opening a way for his queen.

8...0-0 9.♕e2 c5

There's no other way (9...b6? 10.♗xf6 and 11.♕e4).

10.dxc5 ♕a5+ 11.c3 ♕xc5 12.0-0-0!

The quiet 12.0-0 ♖d8 13.♖fe1! ♗d7 14.♘e5 ♗e8 15.c4 gave white the better chances.

12...h6!

There's no other way to develop the "infantile" c8 bishop. For instance, 12...♗d7? 13.♗xf6 with the subsequent 14.♗xh7+ and 15.♖xd7.

13.h4! ♗d7

Obviously, taking on g5 spells doom for black.

14.♘e5 ♗c6!

14...♗a4 was pointless due to 15.♖d2! (not 15.♗xf6 ♗xf6 16.♕e4 ♖fc8!).

The reply 14...♗c6 forces a trade and opens the b-file for black – white needs to support the g2-g4-g5 attack. Even though this looks unpleasant for black, he nevertheless gets a foothold on d5, and the battle continues.

15.♘xc6

15...bxc6!

The endgame after 15...♕xc6 16.♗xf6 ♗xf6 17.♕e4!

was considered better for white by both opponents, despite the opposite-colored bishops. For instance, 17...♖fd8 (17...♕xe4 18.♗xe4 ♖ab8 19.♖d7 is even worse) 18.♕xc6 bxc6 19.♗e4 ♖xd1+ 20.♖xd1 ♗xh4 21.g3 ♗f6 22.♗xc6 ♖c8 23.♗e4 ♖c7 24.♔c2, and white can still activate his queenside pawns.

In the bracketed line, black can hold after 19.♖d7 thanks to the attack on the c3 pawn with 19...b5.

16.♗f4 ♖fd8 17.g4 ♘d5

The centralized knight easily repels the flank attack, but black still has to negotiate many obstacles.

18.♗e5 ♗d6 19.♗d4

The white bishops look formidable (19...♕a5 20.♕e4 g6 21.h5), but the knight does complete his mission.

19...♘f4!

The ensuing series of tactical blows defuses the tension.

20.♗h7+ ♔h8 21.♕f3!

In the line 21.♕a6!? ♕b5 22.♕xb5 cxb5 23.♗e4 white has some practical winning chances.

21...♕b5! 22.♗e4 ♘e2+ 23.♔b1 ♖ab8

I didn't like 23...♗a3 24.♖d2 ♘xd4 25.cxd4 ♖xd4 26.♗xc6 ♖xd2 27.♗xb5 ♖xb2+ 28.♔a1 ♖b8 29.♕xa3, and white wins.

Instead of the outwardly spectacular, yet straightforward 25...♖xd4, black could maintain the tension with 25...♕b4.

24.b3 c5 25.c4 ♘xd4 26.♖xd4 ♕e8 27.♖dd1 ♗e5 28.♗c2 ♖xd1+ 29.♖xd1 g6

The position with opposite-colored bishops is still better for white (h4-h5 and ♕e4), and so black still has a lot of work to do to repel the attack.

30.h5 ♗g7 31.hxg6 fxg6 32.♕e4 ♚h7

The black king and his pawn cover look quite suspect, but counterplay along the long dark-squared diagonal has to be worth something. White tries to re-ignite the fading initiative.

33.g5! hxg5

But definitely not 33...h5 34.♖h1!

34.♕g4 ♕f7 35.♕xg5 ♕f6 36.♕xf6 ♗xf6 37.♖d7+ ♚h6 38.♖xa7 ♗d4 39.f3

White has managed to win a pawn. His pre-control move is inaccurate, but 39.♖a6 ♖e8

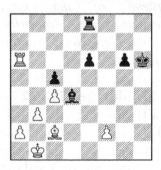

40.f4 ♚g7 and then ♚f6 led to a draw, because the black rook will soon invade the opponent's camp through h8. White prevented it in the actual game, but the king became active instead.

This alternative line deserves consideration. Instead of 40.f4, white can try to play for a win with 40.a4, since the g1-a7 diagonal is closed for the black bishop by its own c5 pawn, and black needs to defend along the 6th rank.

39...♚g5 40.♖h7 ♚f4 41.♗e4 g5

An equal position arose – for example 42.♚c2 ♚e3 (or 42...g4 43.♖h4) 43.♗b7 ♖f8 (threatening g5-g4) 44.♖h2 ♗e5 45.♖g2 ♖h8. Therefore, the opponents agreed to a draw.

No. 52. Caro-Kann Defense
Rauzer – Sozin
Masters qualifying tournament
Leningrad 1936
Annotated by G. Lisitsin

1.e4 c6 2.♘f3 d5 3.♘c3 ♗g4

Black chooses a weak continuation that allows white to retain the initiative. The simplest continuation was 3...dxe4 4.♘xe4 ♘d7 5.♗c4 ♘gf6.

4.h3 ♗h5?

This natural bishop retreat may be the decisive mistake, because now white's attack develops with ever-increasing strength. He should have played 4...♗xf3 5.♕xf3 e6! with a worse but solid position.

White's plan now includes exploiting the bishop's poor position on h5.

Let's not forget that the evaluation of opening lines was based on the state of chess theory of the 1930s.

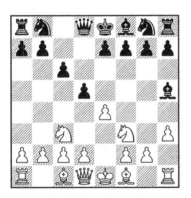

5.exd5! cxd5 6.♗b5+ ♘c6 7.g4 ♗g6 8.♘e5 ♖c8

Black had to try and go for a sharp, double-edged struggle with 8...♕d6 9.d4 (threatening 10.♗f4) 9...f6 10.♘xg6 hxg6 11.♕d3 ♔f7. Passive defense, as a rule, only helps the attacking side to implement his plan.

9.d4 e6 10.h4!

White threatens to win the g6 bishop with 11.h5 ♗e4 12.f3 and forces his opponent to weaken his position further by moving the f-pawn.

10...f5

Again, this move is not the best. 10...f6 was stronger, for instance, 11.♘xg6 hxg6 12.♕d3 ♔f7 13.h5 ♘ge7, and black has better chances than in the game.

11.♕e2

The e6 square is weakened, and white now threatens to win a pawn with ♘xg6 and ♕xe6.

The continuation 11.h5 ♗f7 12.♕f3 looks stronger, but Rauzer's plan also leads to a clear advantage for white.

11...♕e7

A sad necessity, but there's nothing better.

12.h5 ♗f7 13.g5!

White has managed to paralyze black's pieces. With his last move, he closes off the kingside to cramp his opponent's position even further. White delivers the final blow on the queenside.

13...♕d8 14.♗xc6! bxc6 15.♕a6 ♗e8 16.♗f4 ♕b4

The last attempt to extricate himself.

17.♕xa7! ♖c7

To make the development of the dark-squared bishop possible.

17...♕xb2 is bad: 18.♕a5+! ♖c7 (18...♔e7 19.♖b1) 19.♖b1 ♕a3 20.♖b8+ ♔e7 21.♕xc7+ ♗d7 22.♕xd7#.

18.♕a8+ ♖c8 19.♕a6 ♗d6

19...♕xd4 20.♕a5+ ♔e7 (20...♖c7 21.♘xc6+) 21.♘e2 ♕xb2 22.0-0 loses quickly – black is helpless against white's onslaught.

20.♘d3 ♕b8 21.♗xd6 ♕xd6

After the dark-squared bishop is traded away, the white knights seize the weak c5 and e5 squares.

22.♘a4 ♖c7

Necessary, because after 23.♘c5, there was a threat 24.♘b7+.

23.♘ac5 ♔e7 24.0-0-0

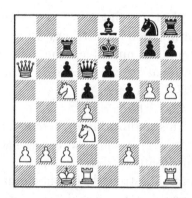

Now, due to the threat ♖de1, material losses are unavoidable.

24...♗d7   25.♘xd7   ♕xd7 26.♘c5   ♖a7   27.♕b6   ♕c7 28.♕xc7+   ♖xc7   29.♖de1   ♔f7 30.g6+ ♔f6

Obviously, the g6 pawn cannot be captured.

31.♖xe6+   ♔g5   32.♘d3   ♘f6 33.f4+ ♔g4 34.♖ee1 ♘e4 35.♖eg1+ ♘g3

Or 35...♔f3 36.♖h3+ ♔e2 37.♖e1#.

36.♘e5+

Black resigned.

The g3 knight is doomed: 36...♔xf4 37.♖h4+ ♔g5 38.♘f3+ etc.

Rauzer exploited black's opening mistake very well for the entire course of the game.

No. 53. Alekhine Defense
Rauzer – Mazel
Masters qualifying tournament
Leningrad 1936

Rauzer played the game against I. Mazel in the same way. An early opening mistake (6...g6?) irrevocably compromised black's position. Several energetic blows allowed white to corner his opponent.

1.e4 ♘f6 2.e5 ♘d5 3.d4 d6 4.c4 ♘b6 5.exd6 exd6 6.♘c3

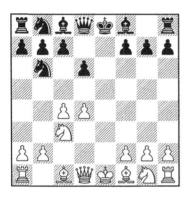

6...g6?

A mistake that gives black a poor position. Black should have played 6...♗f5.

7.♘f3 ♗g7 8.♗g5 f6 9.♗e3 0-0 10.c5! dxc5 11.dxc5 ♘6d7

Not 11...♕xd1+ 12.♖xd1 ♘6d7 13.♘d5! ♘a6 14.♘e7+ ♔f7 15.♘xc8, and white wins a piece.

12.♕d5+ ♔h8 13.0-0-0 ♘c6

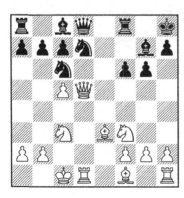

14.h4!

Threatening to push the pawn further: h4-h5.

14...♘de5 15.♘xe5 fxe5 16.♕xd8 ♘xd8 17.h5 gxh5 18.♘d5 ♗f5 19.♘e7! ♗e6 20.♖xh5 ♗g4

This move, made in an already hopeless position, gave white an opportunity to conclude the game with a rook sacrifice.

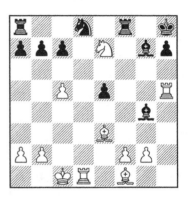

21.♖xh7+! ♔xh7 22.♗d3+ ♗f5 23.♖h1+ ♗h6 24.♗xh6

Black resigned.

No. 54. French Defense
Rauzer – Konstantinopolsky
All-Union Young Masters
Tournament
Leningrad 1936
Annotated by V. Panov

1.e4 e6 2.d4 d5 3.♘c3 dxe4 4.♘xe4 ♘d7 5.♘f3 ♗e7 6.c3

In my opinion, this move, as well as his whole system of play, doesn't give white any advantage. 6.♗d3 ♘gf6 7.♕e2 is stronger, with the subsequent ♗g5 and 0-0-0 and good attacking prospects.

6...♘gf6 7.♘xf6+ ♘xf6

Here, 7...♗xf6 with the eventual e6-e5 equalizes quickly.

8.♗d3 0-0 9.♘e5

Preventing the common move b6 because of the threat ♘c6 and ♕f3.

9...c5 10.♗e3 cxd4

The preliminary 10...♕c7 was stronger, preparing b6 and ♗b7 or ♖fd8. 10...♘d5 is dangerous due to 11.♕h5 with an attack.

11.♗xd4 ♕c7 12.♘g4

After 12.0-0 or 12.♕c2, black could trade the dangerous bishop with 12...♗c5!, liquidating white's attack.

12...♘xg4?

Only after this trade is black forced to weaken his position considerably. He should have played 12...♘d5, after which white, for instance, cannot play 13.♘h6+ gxh6 14.♕g4+ due to 14...♗g5 15.h4 ♕f4. It seems that after 12...♘d5 white would have had to play 13.0-0 with subsequent double-edged play. If 13.♕c2 then 13...f5 14.♘e5 ♗d6!

In the first line, after 15...♕f4?

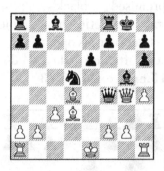

black is crushed by 16.♗xh7+! ♔xh7 17.hxg5!!, and now 17...♕xg4 is met with a mate in two: 18.♖xh6+ ♔g8 19.♖h8#.

13.♕xg4 g6

13...e5 is of course bad due to 14.♕e4 etc.

14.♕e2 ♗d6 15.♗f6! ♗e7

And now 15...e5 is bad because of 16.h4!, and black has no defensive counter-strike f5.

However, black now can seize the initiative with a pawn sacrifice 16...e4!?

16.♗e5 ♗d6

Silently proposing a draw by threefold repetition.

17.f4! ♗d7

VTsSPS Championship, Moscow 1936. Konstantinopolsky versus Tolush.

After 17...f6 18.♗xd6 ♕xd6 19.g3 and 20.0-0-0, white gets a big positional advantage.

18.0-0-0 ♗c6 19.h4

The tempting-looking 19.♗xg6 ♗xe5! 20.♗xh7+ ♔xh7 21.♕h5+ ♔g8 22.fxe5 ♖fd8 led only to a draw.

The bishop sacrifice 19.♗xg6 is incorrect, because after 22...f5! black defends, retaining the extra piece.

19...♗xe5 20.fxe5 h5

If black waited passively, he would have still lost, for example, 20...♖ad8 21.h5 ♖d7 22.hxg6 fxg6 23.♖h3 ♖df7 24.♗xg6! hxg6 25.♖dh1 etc.

Black has some chances here as well; instead of the weak 23...♖df7, he has to play 23...♕b6!?, going on the counter-offensive.

21.♖hg1 ♖ad8

Black has no satisfactory antidote to white's pawn break.

22.g4 hxg4 23.♖xg4

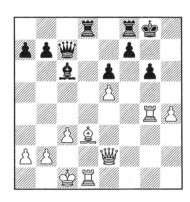

Now white, in addition to 24.h5, also threatens 24.♗xg6 ♖xd1+ 25.♕xd1 fxg6 26.♖xg6+ ♔f7 (26... ♔h8 27.♕h5+ ♕h7 28.♖h6)

27.♕h5, quickly crushing black. Thus, the subsequent exchange sacrifice is forced, even though it still doesn't save the game.

23...♖xd3 24.♖xd3

After 24.♕xd3 ♕xe5 25.♖dg1 ♕f5!, black could still defend.

24...♗b5

25.c4!

This unexpected move quickly decides matters.

25...♗xc4

After 25...♗e8 26.h5, white's material advantage would have eventually led to a win.

26.♕c2 b5

If 26...♖c8, then 27.♖xc4! ♕xc4 28.♖d8+, and white wins.

27.b3 ♕xe5 28.bxc4 bxc4 29.♖xc4 ♔h7 30.♕c3 ♕e2 31.♕d2 ♕e5 32.♕c3 ♕e2 33.♖d2 ♕e1+ 34.♖d1 ♕e2 35.♖d2 ♕e1+

White repeats moves to gain time.

36.♔b2 a5

If 36...♖b8+ then 37.♖b4.

37.♖d7 ♕f1 38.♔a3 e5 39.♖cc7 e4 40.h5! g5 41.♕e3 ♕b1 42.♖c4

♕b5 43.♕xe4+ ♔g8 44.♖d5 ♕b8 45.♖xg5+ ♔h8 46.♖c6

Black resigned.

No. 55. Queen's Gambit
Konstantinopolsky – Rauzer
All-Union Young Masters
Tournament
Leningrad 1936

1.♘f3 d5 2.c4 e6 3.d4 ♘f6 4.♘c3 ♗e7 5.e3

White avoids the well-trodden theoretical paths, but doesn't get any advantage out of the opening.

5...0-0 6.b3 ♗b4

At the cost of a tempo, black prevents the common structure in this position: ♗b2, ♗d3, etc., due to the threat of ♘e4, c5 and ♕a5 with an advantage.

7.♗d2 ♕e7 8.♗d3 b6 9.0-0 ♗b7 10.♕c2

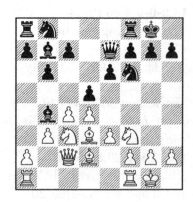

10...dxc4

If black plays 10...c5 immediately, then 11.cxd5, and black is forced to recapture with the pawn, closing off his bishop's diagonal.

11.bxc4 c5 12.♘e4

Tempting, but ultimately leads to premature simplifications. 12.dxc5 and 12.♘e5 were worthy of consideration.

12...♗xd2

After 12...♘xe4 13.♗xb4, white gets an advantage in all lines.

13.♘xf6+ ♕xf6 14.♗xh7+ ♔h8

15.♗e4!

Retaining the extra pawn.

15...♘c6!   16.♕xd2   ♖ad8 17.♕e2   cxd4   18.♘xd4   ♘xd4 19.♕h5+   ♕h6   20.♕xh6+   gxh6 21.♗xb7 ♘e2+ 22.♔h1 ♖d2

Draw agreed.

Even though white has an extra pawn, the active position of the black pieces serves as good compensation.

No. 56. Reti Opening
Chekhover – Rauzer
All-Union Young Masters
Tournament
Leningrad 1936
Annotated by V. Rauzer

1.♘f3 d5 2.b3 ♗g4

This defensive system after 2.c4 c6 3.b3 was first used by Bogoljubov and then by Capablanca against Reti in the 1st Moscow International Tournament.

3.♗b2 ♘d7

This move order seems to be the most correct for black, since it's harder for white to put his knight on e5 this way. Black's play in the 12th round (Alatortsev – Rauzer) was weaker: 2...♘f6 3.♗b2 ♗g4 4.♘e5 ♗h5 5.d4 e6 6.♕d3 with the threats ♕b5+ and ♕h3 followed by g2-g4.

4.g3 e6 5.♗g2 ♘gf6 6.0-0 ♗d6 7.c4 c6

Tournament practice showed that it's not beneficial for black to be always ready to meet c4xd5 with both c6xd5 and e6xd5, depending on circumstances. For instance, after 8.h3 ♗h5 9.cxd5 exd5 10.♘d4 ♗g6 11.d3, there's an unpleasant threat f2-f4-f5 and g3-g4, trapping the bishop.

8.♘c3 0-0 9.d3

The oldest interpretation of the Reti Opening. White prepares e2-

e4, and black should be ready to play d5xe4 and e6-e5. Thanks to the bishop on g4, black doesn't need to waste tempi on h7-h6 or withdrawing the bishop after e2-e4. White has a more active continuation, 8.d4 0-0 9.♘bd2, also preparing e2-e4.

9...♕e7 10.♕c2

10.a3 was better, preventing ♗a3 and preparing the eventual b3-b4.

10...♗a3 11.♖ad1

Since white played c4xd5 just two moves later, it was better to play 11.♖ac1. In the post-mortem analysis, it turned out that white played 11.♖ad1 with the naive hope to continue 12.♗a1.

11...♗xb2 12.♕xb2 e5 13.cxd5

Opening the c-file is probably more beneficial for black (the c3 square); on the other hand, white's g2 bishop gets into play.

13...cxd5 14.h3 ♗h5 15.♘h4

15.g4 (threatening g4-g5 and ♘xd5) is not good for white: 15...d4 16.gxh5 dxc3 17.♕xc3 ♖fc8! and 18...♘xh5, following which white's kingside is too weakened.

15...d4

Rauzer. Friendly cartoon by Yu. Yu.

16.♘b1?

After this knight retreat, white of course gets a worse position. The correct move was 16.♘d5. As Chekhover explained later, the move ♘b1 was caused by the popular but erroneous belief that "as soon as the g2 bishop comes alive in the Reti Opening, white gets better play." This leads to overestimating one's position and avoidance of the knight trade. My evaluation of Reti's teaching was always negative. I thought and still think that as soon as black gets his rook away from a8 and plays b7-b6 or b7-b5, the g2 bishop will be out of play. In addition, it's not beneficial to trade it because this would weaken the light squares.

16...♘b6

Black transfers the knight to d5 to exploit the weakness of the c3 square. I found this idea in the Reti Opening back in 1926, in the game Kallioti – Rauzer from the Odessa – Ukraine team match.

17.♖c1 ♖ac8 18.♘f3

Preparing to trade both rooks, which is impossible immediately due to the loss of the e2 pawn. This shows that the black bishop, with its simple and "old-fashioned" development, is more dangerous than the white "hypermodern" one on g2.

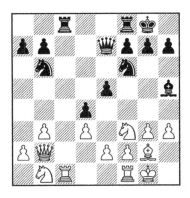

18...♘fd5

18...♘bd5 with the threat b7-b5-b4 and ♘c3 was no better. For instance, 19.♖xc8 ♖xc8 20.♖c1 ♖c7 21.♖xc7 ♕xc7 22.g4 ♗g6 23.g5 ♘d7 24.♘xd4 exd4 25.♗xd5. Therefore, black prepares f7-f6 and ♗f7, strengthening the d5 knight's position.

In Rauzer's line, black has enough compensation for the pawn – he controls the c-file and the c3 square, and the white pieces are positioned

rather awkwardly. In addition, black's play can be improved with 24...♘f4! 25.♘f3 ♕c1+! 26.♕xc1 ♘xe2+, with an advantage for black.

19.♖xc8 ♖xc8 20.♖c1

The correct tactic: ease the tension with trades in a worse position.

20...♖c7 21.♔f1

Getting the king to the queenside and freeing the knight from defending the e2 pawn (♗h5!).

21...f6 22.♘fd2 ♗f7 23.♔e1 ♘c8

Opening the way for the b7 pawn.

24.♔d1 b5

25.♗xd5

White cannot delay this trade anymore, because otherwise there follows ♘cb6, b5-b4 and ♘c3 with strong pressure. Now, however, the black bishop gets especially strong, since the moves g2-g3 (fianchettoing the white bishop!) and h2-h3 make it easier for black to create a passed pawn. (See the note to move 29.)

25...♗xd5   26.♖xc7   ♕xc7 27.♕c2 ♕xc2+

Otherwise ♕c5, with enough counterplay for white.

Rauzer means ceding the c-file to white, for instance, 27...♕b7. Black can, of course, play 27...♕c6, which still leads to a queen trade, and the bishop does look better on d5.

28.♔xc2 ♘d6

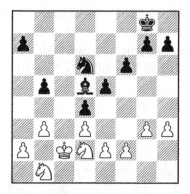

The endgame starts. I often see a lot there, but I don't know what to choose.

There have been lots of articles written about the play of Soviet masters, but I would say that my play was not described thoughtfully enough. For instance, G. Y. Levenfish, in his article "The Ways of the Soviet Masters" (*64*, 5th November 1936), expressing the opinion of the majority, wrote the following, "In Rauzer's play, opening system analysis has suppressed the main essence of chess art, and so the talented master has turned into a dry dogmatist." The All-Union Young Masters Tournament clearly showed me that my weakest side is endgame play (the four games

against Chekhover and Alatortsev, a draw with Ragozin and a win against Kan which was not too "clean"), and I play most precisely in the middlegame, where I ruined my chances only in one game, with white against Chekhover (16. ♖h1-h2?). The opening is not even my strongest side, which is proved by my games against Kan, Alatortsev (lost), Goglidze (with white) and Konstantinopolsky (with black).

Thus, I showed my best play in this tournament in the middlegames: against Riumin, Ragozin and Kan (wins), draws with Chekhover (this game) and Konstantinopolsky (with white), while my middlegame play was good even in the loss against Alatortsev. The reason for my partial success in the middlegame, in my view, is that I have internalized the middlegame principles as described by Tarrasch in his book *Die Moderne Schachpartie* and firmly believe in them. I also think that, in the middlegame, you can develop and widely use positional intuition that can extend even to tactics (for instance, using intuition to determine the strength and tempo of the attack or the strength of a certain threat). For example, thanks to this intuition, I quickly preferred 18...♘fd5 to 18...♘bd5. At this moment, during the transition into the endgame, it was perhaps better, instead of 28...♘d6, to play 28...g5 with the threat ♗g2. Then 29.♘e4! ♔g7(f7) and, finally, ♗e6, provoking g3-g4 or h3-h4 with an obvious weakening of the kingside pawns (after g3-g4, the break h7-h5 and maneuver ♘c8-e7-g6-f4 are possible). With 28...♘d6, black prevents the defense ♘e4 and threatens g7-g5 with even greater strength. White precludes that with 29.h4.

29.h4 ♔f7

Bringing the king closer out of general considerations. Nevertheless, 29...h5! was very strong, threatening to create a passed h-pawn with g7-g5. White cannot allow g5xh4, since he simply loses a pawn after ♘f5.

30.a4

White intends to create counterplay on the queenside. Now, however, the a4 pawn is weak. On the other hand, completely passive defense (for instance, 30.♔d1 – what else can white do?) looks dreary.

30...bxa4 31.bxa4 ♔e6

Now black wants to deflect the white pieces, bring his king as close to the a4 pawn as possible, and only then execute the threat h7-h5 and g7-g5.

32.♘a3 ♔d7

33.♔b2

White had to play 33.♘b3, which prevented ♗c6 because of ♘c5+.

33...♗c6

Wins a pawn by force.

34.♘b3

If 34.♔b3, then 34...♘b7 35.♔b4 (otherwise ♘c5+) 35...a5+ 36.♔b3 ♘c5+ etc.

34...♘b7 35.a5 ♗d5

35...♗a4? lost a piece to 36.a6!.

36.a6 ♘d6 37.♘a1

White cannot save the a6 pawn, so it's hard to give him any good advice.

37...♔c6 38.♘1c2 ♔c5

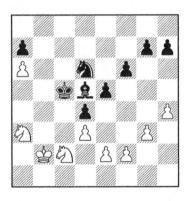

39.e4!

With the idea to deprive the e5 pawn of protection with f2-f4 and f4xe5.

39...♗e6 40.f4 ♗c8 41.♘e1 ♗xa6 42.♔c2 ♔b4

The immediate 42...♗c8 is bad: 43.fxe5 fxe5 44.♘f3 ♘f7 45.♘c4, winning the e5 pawn.

43.♘b1 ♗c8 44.♘d2 ♗g4 45.♘ef3 ♘f7?

Missing the move 47.♘g5! because of time trouble (control was on the 48th move). I should say that thanks to marking my game sheets in a certain way (15 minutes per 4 moves, solely for convenience), I never get into desperate time trouble, though. It would be interesting to test this method in the Moscow Championship, where participants suffer from chronic time trouble.

The correct move was 45...♗xf3 46.♘xf3, and only then 46...♘xf7–+.

46.fxe5 fxe5

47.♘g5! ♘xg5?

The second, decisive mistake that spoils the win. The correct move was 47...♘d6 48.♘xh7 a5, and, thanks to the bishop's good position on g4, white cannot quickly exploit his g- and h-pawns, while black's passed a-pawn ensures that his king gets to c3.

Computer analysis shows that white can save the game: 49.♘f8 a4 50.♘g6 ♘f7 51.♘c4, and he holds.

48.hxg5 a5

There's no way to save the e5 pawn now.

49.♘c4   ♗e6   50.♘xe5   a4 51.♘c6+ ♚c5 52.♘e7 ♚d6

Black could get better, albeit problematic, chances after 52...g6 53.♚b2 ♚d6 54.♘d5 ♗xd5 55.exd5 ♚xd5   56.♚a3   ♚e5   57.♚xa4 ♚f5 58.♚b4 ♚xg5 59.♚c4 ♚g4 60.♚xd4 ♚xg3 61.♚c5!

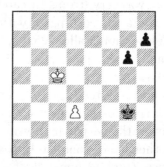

reaching a queen endgame with an extra pawn for black, which is most likely drawn.

Yes, it's a draw, and endgame tables prove that.

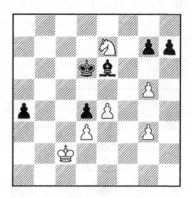

53.♘f5+ ♚e5

After 53...♗xf5 54.exf5 ♚e5 55.g4, only white would have had chances.

White would easily win this pawn endgame.

54.♘xg7 ♗b3+ 55.♔c1!

If 55.♔b2, then 55...♗d1 with the subsequent ♗e2, winning the d3 and e4 pawns for the a4 pawn.

55...a3 56.♘h5 ♗c4! 57.♘f4

57.dxc4 d3 loses: one of the pawns promotes.

57...♗xd3

Black cannot improve his position with any maneuvers.

58.♘xd3+ ♔xe4 59.♘b4 ♔f5 60.♘c2

Draw.

No. 57. Simagin-Larsen Opening
Ragozin – Rauzer
All-Union Young Masters
Tournament
Leningrad 1936
Annotated by V. Rauzer

1.b3

There's a popular opinion among players that the most correct method to play against a "theoretician" (I, for one, have such a reputation) is to make a "non-theoretical" opening move as soon as possible to deviate from the lines he knows best (or, should we say, are crammed into his head!), which would render the theoretician completely helpless. Evidently, V. V. Ragozin decided to test this method in practice.

1...e5

If black had a desire to transpose into more familiar variations, it was enough to play 1...d5, and white would have had to play either the Bird Opening (f2-f4) or the Nimzowitsch system (♘f3). But both of these options are worse than 1...e5 because they cede the e5 square and justify white's opening experiment.

2.♗b2 ♘c6 3.e3 ♘f6

Another possible move was 3...d5 4.♗b5 ♗d6 5.f4! ♕e7 6.♘f3 (6.fxe5 ♗xe5 7.♗xe5 ♕xe5 8.♘c3 with the subsequent ♘f3 was also good)

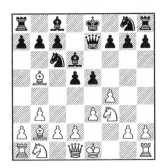

6...♗g4 (6...f6? loses the e5 pawn) 7.h3 ♗xf3 8.♕xf3 ♘f6 (threatening exf4) 9.g3 with unclear, roughly equal play. 9.0-0 (instead of 9.g3) is worse: 9...exf4 10.exf4 0-0 11.♗xc6 bxc6 12.♘c3 ♖fe8 is better for black.

After 6...f6 7.fxe5 fxe5 8.♗xc6+ bxc6 9.♘xe5, white does indeed win the pawn, but in modern practice this pawn sacrifice is considered promising. After 9...♕h4+, black gets a strong initiative as compensation.

4.♘f3

What's psychologically interesting here is that white falls into the same trap that he prepared for his opponent:

in a mutually unknown opening, he started to make mistakes earlier than his opponent!.. Immediately after the game, I showed the best move 4.♗b5, later also analyzed by P. A. Romanovsky in *Shakhmaty v SSSR* (No. 1, 1937). After that move, white threatens 5.♗xc6 and 6.♗xe5. If 4...e4 (4...d6 5.d4 ♗d7! is not bad either) 5.♘e2 d5 6.♘d4 ♗d7 7.0-0 ♗d6, then 8.f4! Because of this line, P. A. Romanovsky considers the 1.b3 opening worthy of consideration. However, it doesn't even give white full equality: 8...exf3

9.♕xf3 ♘xd4 10.♗xd7+ ♕xd7 11.♗xd4 ♘g4 12.g3 (12.h3 ♘h2) 12...h5 with an attack for black.

Or 9.♗xc6 bxc6 10.♕xf3 0-0 11.♘f5 (11.♘c3 ♘g4 12.g3 ♘e5∓) 11...♗xf5 12.♕xf5 ♘e4 with the threat of ♕h4 and a better position for black, for instance, 13.♕g4 g6 and ...f5; 13.♕h5 f5! 14.♖xf5 ♖xf5 15.♕xf5 ♕h4; or 13.d3 ♕h4 14.♗e5 ♖ae8 15.♗xd6 ♘xd6 etc.

Therefore, after 8.f4 exf3, it's best for white to play defensively 9.♘xf3! ♕e7, then 0-0-0 with somewhat freer play for black (the e4 square). The

game move, 4.♘f3, is much weaker than 4.♗b5.

4...e4 5.♘d4 ♘xd4

6.exd4?

This move is perplexing – if not for the opponent, then at least for the commentator!

6...d5 7.c4

The e4 pawn is the most unpleasant piece for white. So, he had to undermine it as soon as possible with 7.d3. The line that was shown by Blumenfeld and Kots in the tournament bulletin, 7...♗b4+ 8.c3 ♕e7 9.dxe4 (9.cxb4? exd3+ 10.♔d2 ♘e4+ 11.♔c1 ♘xf2 and ♘xh1) 9...♘xe4 is not dangerous for white because of 10.♕e2, for instance, 10...♗d6 11.f3 ♕h4+ 12.g3 (12.♔d1? 0-0!) 12...♗xg3+ 13.hxg3 ♕xh1 14.fxe4 etc. The move 7.c4, preparing ♕c2 and 0-0-0, only makes it harder to play the d2-d3 break (a chance for ♗b4+).

Instead of 10...♗d6, 10...0-0!? is worth considering. If, for instance, 11.cxb4, then 11...♖e8! 12.♘d2 ♗g4 with a very strong attack.

7...c6 8.♗e2

If 8.d3, then 8...♗b4+ 9.♗c3 ♗d6 10.♘d2 ♗f5 11.dxe4 ♘xe4 12.♘xe4 ♗xe4 with better play for black.

8...♗d6 9.♘c3 0-0 10.♕c2

Or 10.0-0 ♖e8 11.d3 ♕c7 12.g3 (h3) e3 etc.

10...♗f5 11.♘d1

Intending to play ♘e3, close the diagonal for the f5 bishop and prepare 0-0-0. But this plan is refuted by black thanks to the f-pawn push.

11...♘d7!

Preparing ♗e6 and f7-f5. The move ♘d7 only became possible after ♘d1, removing the second attack from the d5 pawn. After 11...♘d7, it becomes obvious that ♘c3-d1 was simply a waste of time.

12.♘e3

Even though this move is now not good for white, it's still necessary, allowing 0-0-0.

12...♗e6 13.0-0-0

Trying to prevent f7-f5 with 13.g4 is bad due to 13...♕h4.

13...f5 14.♖de1

If 14.g3, then still 14...f4 15.gxf4 (15.♘g4? f3) 15...♖xf4.

14...♘f6

To keep the white knight off g4 after f5-f4. Another solution is also possible here: 14...f4 15.♘g4 ♕g5 16.h3 h5 17.h4 ♕g6 18.♘e5 ♗xe5 19.dxe5 ♕xg2 with great complications in black's favor.

15.d3

This move is played far too late – black has already bolstered the e4 pawn very well. It was better to play 15.h3, protecting the g4 square for the knight.

15...f4 16.♘d1

White's game is positionally lost.

16...♗f5 17.♘c3

Not 17.dxe4 ♗xe4 18.♗d3 ♗xg2 19.♖hg1 f3 and ♗xh2.

17...♕a5

Preparing ♖ae8 with full consolidation and moving the queen to a great square where it puts pressure on both a2 and e1.

18.c5

A rather cunning move; white intends, after the natural 18...♗c7, to play 19.a3! (threatening 20.b4 ♕a6 21.dxe4) and force black to close off his own rook with 19...♗b8, since the trade e4xd3 is even less interesting for black.

"The natural 18...♗c7" would indeed be a poor decision due to 19.dxe4! ♘xe4 20.♗d3, and white is all right. However, the threat 19.a3 doesn't work because of the same reply as in the actual game: 19...f3! 20.b4 ♕a6 21.dxe4 ♗f4+ 22.♔b1 ♘xe4! 23.♗xa6 ♘d2+ 24.♔a1 ♗xc2 25.♗xb7 fxg2–+.

18...f3!

This allows black not to deviate from his intended consolidation plan – ♖ae8. The resulting "extra" pawn on d3 for white proves to be extraneous, because it only hinders the movement of white's own pieces.

19.gxf3

Or 19.dxe4 ♗f4+ 20.♔b1 ♘xe4 21.♗d3 (21.♘xe4? fxe2) 21...fxg2 22.♖hg1 ♘d2+ (22...♗d2 is also possible) 23.♔a1 ♗xd3 24.♕xd3 ♘xb3+ 25.♔b1 ♘d2+ 26.♔a1 (26. ♔c2 ♗h6 27.♖xg2 ♖f3 28.♕e2 ♖xc3+) 26...♖ae8 27.♖d1 ♘c4 28.♖xg2 b6 with both a material and a positional advantage.

19...♗f4+ 20.♔b1 exf3 21.♗xf3 ♖ae8

With this "sacrifice", black has got the most threatening positions for his pieces and has created new weaknesses in his opponent's camp: the h2 and f2 pawns.

22.♘e2

Loses a pawn. However, in view of the four weaknesses (h2, f2, d3 and d4) as well as his passive position, white would otherwise only make his position even more cramped. The sadness of his position is exemplified in the line 22.♖xe8 ♖xe8 23.♘e2 ♕c7 24.h3 (24.♘xf4 ♕xf4 25.♕d1 ♗g4 26.♗xg4 ♘xg4 27.♖e1 (27. ♗c1 ♕f5) 27...♖xe1 28.♕xe1 ♔f7 29.♕e2 h5) 24...♗e3! 25.♘g3 (or 25.♘c1; if 25.fxe3 then 25...♖xe3, winning) 25...♕f4 with material gains.

22...♗xh2 23.♗c3 ♕b5 24.♖d1 ♗c7 25.♔b2 b6

Winning the doubled pawn will enliven the c3 bishop, so the immediate 25...a5 was probably better.

26.♕d2 a5 27.a4 ♕a6 28.♘c1

White cannot make any active moves, so he protects his weaknesses.

28...b5 29.axb5 ♕xb5 30.♖de1

Black's queenside pressure forces white to go for trades.

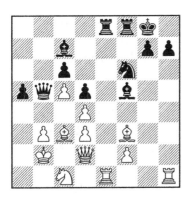

30...♘d7!

Of course, declining the trade altogether is bad: 30...♖b8? 31.♖e7 ♗d8 32.♖a7. With the game move, black prepares the maneuver ♗c7-d8-f6, and also ♘d7-f8-e6, which occurred in the actual game.

31.♖xe8 ♖xe8 32.♖e1

This is excessive simplification that leads to an endgame and is therefore beneficial for his opponent. It was better to play 32.♕g5 ♗g6 33.♗g4 ♘f8 and then wait again, avoiding trades.

32...♖xe1 33.♕xe1 ♘f8 34.♗d2

If 34.♕e8 (threatening ♗xd5+), then 34...♗d7. If 34.♕e7, then 34...♕b8 and ♕d8.

34...♘e6

34...♗xd3 was weaker. Black doesn't need this pawn at all.

35.♕e2

White has created the threat 36.♗g4 ♗xg4 37.♕xg4 ♘f8 38.♗h6 etc.

35...♕b8 36.♗c3 ♘f4 37.♕e7 ♕d8

38.♕xd8+

This doesn't affect the result, but it's completely illogical. 38.♕e3 was more resilient. The endgame is completely hopeless because of black's passed h-pawn and doesn't need much explanation. Still, the way to win is somewhat instructive.

38...♗xd8 39.♔c2 ♔f7 40.♗d2 ♗c7 41.♗xf4 ♗xf4 42.♘e2 ♗c7 43.♔d2 g6 44.♘g1 ♗h2 45.♘e2 h5 46.♔e3 ♔f6 47.♗g2 g5 48.♗f1 g4 49.♗g2 h4 50.♗f1 h3 51.♘g3

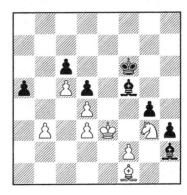

51...♗xg3!

The simplest way to win. In the ensuing endgame, the white king should constantly protect the d3 square (not even the pawn!), because after any king move (except ♔f2), there follows ♗xd3!, ♗xd3 h2, and the pawn promotes. Black wins with a king march to the queenside. Without the b3 and a5 pawns, the way to win would be the same: a king march to the queenside, then along the a-file to a2, ♔c3 is met with ♔b1, and so on.

52.fxg3 ♔e7 53.♔d2 ♔d8 54.♔e3 ♔c7 55.♔f2 ♔b7 56.♔e3 ♔a7

56...♔a6 was also possible, for instance, 57.♔f4 h2 58.♗g2 ♗xd3 59.♔xg4 ♗e4 60.♔h3 h1=♕+ 61.♗xh1 ♗xh1, and black wins.

57.♔e2 ♔a6 58.♔d2 ♔b5 59.♔c3 ♗g6

White is now in zugzwang. If, for instance, 60.♔c2 then 60...♔b4, and white can't play 61.♔b2 due to 61...♗xd3 62.♗xd3 h2.

60.b4 a4

White resigned.

Remarkably, the d3 pawn stayed in place until the very end of the game as a living reproach. If not for this pawn, the black king would have been checkmated in this position!

The game may also serve as a warning to those who forget that a good position is more important in a game between masters than a familiar or unfamiliar opening.

No. 58. Ruy Lopez
Rauzer – Riumin
All-Union Young Masters
Tournament
Leningrad 1936
Annotated by M. Botvinnik

1.e4 e5 2.♘f3 ♘c6 3.♗b5 a6 4.♗a4 ♘f6 5.0-0 ♗e7 6.♖e1 d6 7.c3 b5 8.♗b3 ♘a5 9.♗c2 c5 10.d4 ♕c7 11.♘bd2

11...♘c6

Too premature. It was better to play 11...0-0 or 11...♗g4. After the game move, white gets an opportunity to seize the a-file.

12.a4 ♖b8

And now we see the dark side of the move 11...♘c6; black cannot play 12...b4, because the white knight gets to c4. However, the strongest move was probably 12...♗b7, still controlling the a-file.

13.axb5 axb5 14.dxc5 dxc5

Rauzer's opening play was very consistent. It will be very hard for black to defend the d5 square.

15.♘f1 ♗e6

Neither 15...0-0 16.♘e3 ♖d8 17.♘d5 ♕b7 (17...♘xd5 18.exd5 g6 19.♘g5!) 18.♗g5! nor 17...♕d6 18.♕e2 ♘xd5 19.exd5 ♕xd5 20.♘g5 with a strong attack for white are any better.

16.♘e3 0-0 17.♘g5

The simplest. White can always simply trade on e6, and black will have to recapture on e6 with the pawn, weakening the pawn structure; otherwise, the d5 and f5 squares would be too weak.

17...♖fd8 18.♕f3 ♖d6

18...h6 is met with 19.♘xe6 fxe6 20.♘g4 ♖f8 21.♘xf6+ ♖xf6 22.♕g4, and there are a lot of weaknesses in black's position.

19.♘f5!

A splendid idea. The trade on f5 is unavoidable, and afterwards, the c2 bishop moves to the very strong e4 square by force. In addition, the pawn move from e4 to f5 prepares the pawn storm of black's kingside..

19...♗xf5 20.exf5 h6 21.♘e4 ♘xe4 22.♗xe4 ♗f6

If 22...c4 then 23.♗e3, and black's position is hopeless.

23.♗e3 ♘e7 24.b4 c4 25.g3

White pieces control the entire board. Black is defenseless against the mounting attack.

25...♖d7 26.♖a7 ♕d8 27.♖xd7 ♕xd7

28.h4! ♔h8 29.g4! ♘g8

The attack plays itself.

30.g5 ♗e7 31.♖d1 ♕c7 32.f6 ♗xf6 33.gxf6 ♘xf6 34.♗c2 ♖d8 35.♗xh6 ♖xd1+ 36.♗xd1 e4 37.♗f4 ♕d8 38.♕e2 ♘d5

Black resigned without waiting for his opponent's reply.

Rauzer played this game like a true grandmaster.

No. 59. Reti Opening
Riumin – Rauzer
All-Union Young Masters
Tournament
Leningrad 1936

**1.c4 e6 2.♘f3 d5 3.b3 ♘f6
4.♗b2 ♗e7 5.g3 0-0 6.♗g2 c5 7.0-0
♘c6 8.d3**

8.cxd5 ♘xd5 9.♘c3 is more
popular.

**8...b6 9.e3 ♗b7 10.♕e2 ♕c7
11.♘c3 dxc4**

12.bxc4?

By avoiding simplifications,
Riumin only weakens his position.

**12...♖ad8 13.♖ad1 ♖d7 14.♘g5
♖fd8 15.f4 ♘b4 16.♘b5 ♕c8
17.♗xb7**

If 17.♘xa7 then 17...♕a8
18.♗xb7 ♕xb7 19.♘b5 ♘xd3 etc.

17...♕xb7 18.f5 exf5 19.e4

Or, for instance, 19.♖xf5 ♘xd3.

**19...♖xd3 20.a3 ♕d7 21.♘c3
♘c6 22.♘d5 ♖xd1 23.♖xd1 ♘d4
24.♗xd4 cxd4**

White resigned.

No. 60. Sicilian Defense
Rauzer – Chekhover
All-Union Young Masters
Tournament
Leningrad 1936

This tournament was momentous
for opening theory: it was here that
the famous Rauzer Attack first
saw the light of day. It became the
foremost weapon for white against
the Sicilian Dragon, and it still
retains this reputation, even more
than half a century later. Incredible
longevity!

Of course, there were some
small inaccuracies during these first
outings. They naturally accompany
any search for the optimal ways to
develop the attack. For instance,
of the two flank pawns, the g-pawn
should have been moved first (12.g4)
to prevent 12...♘h5; and if 12...♘e8,
then 13.h4 with the subsequent h4-
h5. (Of course, 12.♗xa7 is risky
– it simply opens the a-file for
the opponent's attack.) Instead of
16.♖h2, 16.♖h3 ♘xf1 17.♖xf1 was
more promising, and if 17...e5 18.dxe6
fxe6, then 19.h5 with a rather strong
attack. In the actual game, the h4-
h5 break only gave white a better
endgame, which black managed
to hold with very inventive play.
The rook maneuvers are especially
noteworthy: black correctly
surmised that the opportunity to
create a passed pawn on the kingside
guaranteed a draw, but while the
rooks were on the board white's

passer on the queenside was much stronger.

1.e4 c5 2.♘f3 d6 3.d4 cxd4 4.♘xd4 ♘f6 5.♘c3 g6 6.f3 ♗g7 7.♗e3 0-0 8.♕d2 ♘c6 9.0-0-0 ♘xd4 10.♗xd4 ♗e6 11.♔b1 ♖c8

12.h4 ♘h5 13.♗xg7 ♔xg7 14.♘d5 ♗xd5 15.exd5 ♘g3 16.♖h2 e5 17.dxe6 fxe6 18.h5 ♘xh5 19.♕xd6 ♕xd6 20.♖xd6 ♖fd8 21.♖xd8 ♖xd8 22.♔c1 ♘g3 23.♗d3 ♖d4 24.♖h3 ♘h5 25.g3 b6 26.♔d2 ♖d5 27.♔e3 ♖g5 28.♔f2 ♖a5 29.a3 ♘f6 30.♖h4 ♖c5 31.♖d4 ♖d5 32.♖c4 ♖c5 33.♖xc5 bxc5 34.b4 cxb4 35.axb4 ♘d5 36.b5 ♘c3 37.♔e3 e5 38.♗c4 h5 39.♔d3 ♘a4 40.♗d5 g5 41.♗c6 h4 42.gxh4 gxh4 43.f4

Draw.

No. 61. Queen's Gambit Accepted
Kan – Rauzer
All-Union Young Masters
Tournament
Leningrad 1936
Annotated by V. Rauzer

1.d4 d5 2.c4 dxc4

The Queen's Gambit Accepted is usually played in a critical tournament situation, because it usually leads to sharper lines than the Orthodox or Czech Defense (this opening is now known as the Slav Defense – **A. K.**).

3.♘f3 c5 4.e3

The game Capablanca – Zubarev (Moscow 1925) convincingly proved that 4.d5 with the subsequent isolation of the d5 pawn gives white nothing. 4.e4 was used to "fight for the win" in Tbilisi 1937. For instance, V. Makogonov – Konstantinopolsky: 4.e4 cxd4 5.♕xd4 ♕xd4 6.♘xd4 ♗d7 7.♗xc4 ♘c6 8.♗e3 ♘f6 9.f3 e6 10.♘d2 ♗c5 11.♘2b3 ♘xd4!, and they could have agreed to a draw already – of course, if the tournament committee allowed it!

4...cxd4

The Steinitz System. Even though after 5.exd4 the freed c1 bishop and open e-file do compensate the isolated pawn for white, other continuations, without exd4, are also somewhat difficult for black.

5.♗xc4 e6

Of course, not 5...dxe3 due to 6.♗xf7+. If 5...e5 then 6.♕b3, and if 6...♕c7 then 7.♘xe5; or if 6...♘h6, then 7.exd4 with the threat 8.♗xh6.

6.exd4

Necessary. After 6.♘xd4 or 6.♕xd4, the position is equal. White's isolated queen's pawn on d4 adds sharpness to the game.

Now white has to avoid simplifications, because it's easier for black to exploit the isolation of the d4 pawn in the endgame.

6...♘f6 7.0-0 ♗e7

7...♘c6 was also worth considering, tying the white queen to the d4 pawn and forcing ♗e3.

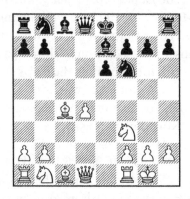

8.♕e2

There's a subtlety here: if 8.♘c3 0-0 9.♗e3, then the system with a7-a6 and b7-b5 used in this game doesn't work. For instance, 9...a6 10.♘e5 (I. Rabinovich – Rauzer, Leningrad tournament featuring Fine), and now 10...b5 is bad due to 11.♕f3. On the other hand, the e3 bishop gets attacked by the d5 knight, depriving white of chances along the e-file and weakening his prospects of attacking the h7 square (there's no threat of ♗xf6); so it's unclear whether it's better to develop the bishop to g5 or e3.

8...0-0 9.♘c3 a6

It's better to make this move before ♘bd7 (the move order

seems unimportant only at first glance): in case of a2-a4, the knight can reach b4 in two moves (♘b8-c6-b4) rather than four (♘b8-d7-b6-d5-b4).

10.♗f4 b5 11.♗b3 ♗b7 12.♖ad1 ♘d5

This move should be interpreted not only as an attack on the f4 bishop with a tempo, but also as a fork on the c3 knight and f4 bishop. Now white cannot avoid a trade and simplifications, which, of course, is better for black.

13.♗e5

N. N. Riumin often attacked black's kingside by putting his bishop on e5 instead of the knight (as white usually does). But you should do that only after the b8 knight is already developed, and the black knights are already on f6 and d5 (or b4), as happened, for instance, in the game Riumin – Kasparyan (Moscow 1931). Otherwise, black develops his knight with a tempo and threatens to simplify the game.

13...♘xc3

The simplification is more important for black than the fact that the d4 pawn is now protected – the c3 pawn itself can serve as a target for attack. This is known from old Steinitz games (against Blackburne and Pillsbury, I think).

14.bxc3 ♘d7 15.♗f4

Even though it seems that 15.♗g3 is better, because it doesn't lose a tempo after the black knight's transfer to d5, 15.♗f4 is still principled, because white retains the opportunity to play ♖d1-d3-h3 (see the note to black's 15th move).

15...♘f6

15...♘b6 made c3-c4 harder, but black feared 16.♖d3 with the subsequent ♘e5 and the transfer of the rook to the kingside. 16...♘d5 would have been met with 17.♗d2.

16.♘e5

Now 16.♖d3 was met with 16...♗e4 17.♖e3 ♗f5, threatening ♘g4 or ♘d5 (18.♘h4 ♗g4 19.f3 ♗h5 20.♘f5 ♗a3).

16...♘d5 17.♗d2

This excessive mobility does not fit the elephant's character!

The bishop is known as "slon", literally an elephant, in Russian.

17...♖c8 18.c4 bxc4 19.♗xc4 a5

The a5 pawn is not weak, because white cannot prevent ♗b4, which either seizes the c3 square or leads to new piece trades.

20.♖b1

Intending to transfer the rook to the kingside through b3 with a tempo. This is also a trap: if 20...♗b4, which seems natural, then 21.a3 ♗xd2 22.♖xb7, with some progress for white.

The evaluation was based on general considerations (the white rook is on the seventh rank, white also wins a tempo because the bishop is en prise); however, as often happens, it's refuted with a tactic: 22...♘f4! 23.♕xd2 ♕g5, and material losses for white are unavoidable because of the mating threat on g2 and the knight jumping to h3 with a check, winning the queen. If 23.♕e4, then 23...f5 24.♕c2 ♕xd4 with better chances for black.

20...♗a8 21.♖b3 ♗b4

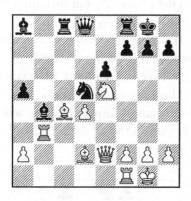

22.♗c1?

Leads to a lost position by force. 22.♖g3 or 22.♖h3 were better, with the following possible continuations: 22.♖g3 ♗xd2 23.♕xd2 ♘e7 24.♗d3 (preventing ♘f5) 24...♕d5, and if 25.♕g5 or 25.♕h6, then 25...♘g6 26.♘xg6 hxg6; or 22.♖h3 ♗xd2 23.♕xd2 ♘e7 24.♗d3 ♘g6 etc. Even though white is able to concentrate four pieces on the kingside, the knight on g6 seems enough to defend everything on its own. These lines show that while white didn't have an advantage, he could still maintain the initiative for some time.

Further, in the last line after 22.♖h3 ♗xd2 23.♕xd2

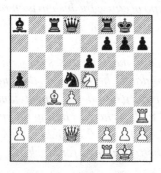

the tempting 23...f6 doesn't work due to 24.♗d3! fxe5 25.♗xh7+ ♔f7 26.dxe5 ♔e8 27.♗g6+ ♔d7 28.♖h7, and white has winning chances: 28...♖g8 29.♗f7 or 28...♕e7 29.♕xa5.

In theory, the lines shown by Rauzer are enough to scare a player who's sitting at the board away from the "tempting 23...f6", but objective computer analysis shows that after 26...g5!? black has a decisive advantage. In modern chess, players often go for such continuations because with the current level of defensive play, it's hard to achieve success with quiet moves.

22...♘c3!

Only this move finally allows black to seize the initiative. The whole previous play was defensive, trying to negate white's chances with trades. I think that only such play can lead you to success with black (especially in the Queen's Gambit) against an equally strong opponent, rather than trying to "confuse" him (and often yourself!). Thanks to the mistake 22.♗c1, the move 22...♘c3 turns out to be decisive.

23.♕g4

At first it seems that white's position is good; he threatens 24.♗g5 ♕c7 25.♗f6; or 24.♗h6 ♕f6 25.♗g5; or, finally, 24.a3. The c3 knight and b4 bishop are hanging. 23...♘xa2 is impossible due to 24.♖g3 and 25.♗xa2. But white missed a clever retort from black. At any rate, white's position was already poor.

If, for instance, 23.♕d3, then 23...♘xa2 24.♗e3 (24.♗b2 a4) 24...♗d5 with an extra pawn.

If 23.♕e3, then 23...♖xc4 24.♘xc4 ♕d5 with a double attack.

If 23.♕d2, then 23...♗d5 24.♗xd5 ♕xd5 25.♘f3 (black threatened ♕xd4) 25...♖fd8 with the threat ♘b5 and a clear advantage for black.

It's weaker to meet 23.♕d2 with 23...♖xc4 24.♘xc4 ♗d5 (24...♕d5 25.♘e3) 25.♕d3 ♕c7 26.♖xc3 ♗xc3 27.♕xc3 ♕xc4 with opposite-colored bishops. 23...♘b5 is also bad, not because of 24.♖xb4? axb4 25.♗xb5 ♕d5 and black wins, but due to 24.♗b2, and the d4 pawn is untouchable, for instance, 24...♕xd4 25.♗xb5 ♕d5 26.♖g3 ♕xb5 27.♗h6 g6 28.♘xg6, and white wins. Or 24...♘xd4 25.♖d3 ♖xc4 (25...♗c5 26.♗e3) 26.♘xc4 ♕d5 27.f3 (27.♘e3 ♘f3+)

27...♕xc4 28.♖xd4 ♗c5 29.♗e3 ♗xd4 30.♗xd4 f6 31.♖c1, and thanks to the opposite-colored bishops, white achieves a draw. It seems that this unexpected retreat onto the diagonal X-rayed by the black bishop, 23.♕d2!, gave white

an opportunity to put up the most resistance.

With 23.♕g4, white still played to win.

In the last line, instead of 27...♕xc4, black could sacrifice an exchange with 27...e5!, obtaining a great advantage. So, 23.♕d2 was bad for white as well.

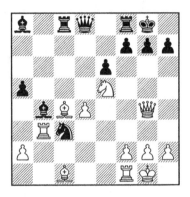

23...♖xc4!

One piece fewer means one more step towards winning the d4 pawn.

24.♘xc4

If 24.♗h6, then 24...♕f6 25.♗g5 ♕xe5!

24...♗d5

Black doesn't lose his advantage with the game move, but Zwischenzugs such as 24...f5!?, possible in this position, strengthen his play greatly.

25.♗h6

White doesn't panic and finds the best chance: he gives away the d4 pawn but saves the a2 pawn. The point of white's defense is his 30th move and its consequences.

25...♕f6   26.♗g5   ♕xd4!
27.♕xd4 ♘e2+ 28.♔h1 ♘xd4
29.♖xb4 axb4

30.♘b6!

If now 30...♗xa2, then 31.♗e7
♖b8 (31...b3 32.♗xf8 ♔xf8 33.♘c4)
32.♗xb4! ♖xb6 33.♗c5 – with a
draw.

30...♖b8

It was also possible to play 30...
f6 (preventing ♗e7) 31.♗f4! (both
31.♗d2 ♘c6 32.♖c1 ♖d8! and
31.♗e3 ♘c2 are worse) 31...♗xa2
(if 31...♖d8 then 32.♗c7, if 31...♘c6
then 32.♖c1) 32.♗d6 ♖d8 33.♗xb4,
and playing for a win would be quite
difficult, because all the pawns are on
the same flank. With 30...♖b8, black
creates a remote passed pawn and
forces the trade of opposite-colored
bishops.

31.♘xd5

If 31.♗e3, then, of course, not
31...♖xb6 32.♗xd4, but rather 31...
♘c2. If 31.♗e7, then 31...♘c6
32.♗c5 ♗xa2.

*Computer analysis shows that,
after 31...♘c2, black gets an endgame
with an extra pawn, but it's a rook
endgame, with all the trappings of
the famous chess aphorism. However,
in two other lines – in the first, after
31...♖xb6 32.♗xd4 ♖c6, and in the
third, we're getting an endgame with
two extra pawns for black, but with
opposite-colored bishops, where black
has much better winning chances.*

31...exd5 32.♖d1

32...♘e6?

A mistake that squanders
everything achieved by black with
his previous play. Black does retain
his extra pawn, but without any real
winning chances. The correct move
was 32...♘e2 33.♖xd5 ♖a8! (if 33...
♘c3, then 34.♖a5; after 33...♖a8,
there are threats ...♘c3 and b4-b3)
34.♖b5 h6 (34...f6 is also possible)
35.♗e3! (35.♗e7 ♘d4! 36.♖b7
♖xa2 37.h3 b3 etc. is worse, as well
as 36.♖xb4? ♘c6 and then ♖e8,
winning a piece) 35...♖xa2 36.g3
♖b2, and the fight continues; white
still retained some drawing chances
thanks to the active position of his
rook.

33.♖xd5 ♖a8

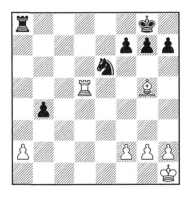

34.♗e7?

Naturally, the white player, who was under the impression that he was losing for the last ten moves, misses his opponent's mistake. 34.h3 almost guaranteed a draw; for instance, 34...♖xa2 35.♗e7 (but not 35.♖b5 f6 36.♗e3 ♖b2), and, in view of 36.♖b5, black has nothing better than 35...♖xf2 36.♗xb4, and he only has some practical chances after that. It's important in this line that 36...♖xg2? doesn't work due to 37.♖b5(a5), and white wins the rook, because the saving move ♖d2 is impossible. After the game move, however, black wins immediately.

34...b3 35.a3 b2 36.♖b5 ♖c8

The same move would have followed after 36.♖d1.

White resigned. An exceptionally interesting game.

Rauzer's annotations are complemented by a historical addition written by A. Konstantinopolsky.

Rauzer mentioned "old games" on the same opening topic. This is a pleasant sign that shows the depth of his historical chess knowledge, which enriched his over-the-board creativity. In our days, youngsters have lost a lot of this tradition. To help them, let's bring out two examples from the chess annals pointed out by Rauzer himself.

A small correction is necessary: in the game played by J. Blackburne, his opponent was J. Showalter; however, W. Steinitz was indeed the author of this opening idea.

No. 61a. Queen's Gambit Accepted
H. Pillsbury – W. Steinitz
St. Petersburg 1895/96

1.d4 d5 2.c4 e6 3.♘c3 ♘f6 4.♘f3 dxc4 5.e3 c5 6.♗xc4 ♘c6 7.0-0 cxd4 8.exd4 ♗e7 9.♗f4 0-0 10.♖c1 ♕b6 11.♕d2 ♖d8 12.♖fd1 ♗d7 13.♕e2 ♗e8

14.♗d3

14.d5 led to simplifications.
14...♖ac8
14...♘xd4? 15.♘xd4 ♖xd4 16.♗e3±.
**15.h3　♘b4　16.♗b1　♘bd5
17.♗e5 ♗c6 18.♘g5 h6! 19.♘ge4**
19.♘xe6 is very nebulous.
19...♘xc3

Now we get the "hanging pawns"
(Steinitz's term). I prefer to call
them "mysterious pawns": their
"intentions" aren't particularly clear.
**20.bxc3 ♘xe4 21.♗xe4 ♗xe4
22.♕xe4 ♕c6! 23.♕g4.**
Both here and later, white avoids
the queen trade that would have
given black a better endgame.
**23...♗f8 24.c4 f5 25.♕g6 ♕e8
26.♕g3 b6**
Decades later, A. Nimzowitsch
called the pawn structure with e6 and
b6 the "blockading ring" that limits
the activity of the "hanging pawns".
As we might see, Steinitz had already
anticipated the subtleties of modern
strategy.
27.♕b3 ♕c6 28.a4 a5!
White threatened a4-a5
29.♖c3 ♗d6! 30.d5 ♕c7.

After 30...exd5 31.cxd5 the d5
pawn becomes stronger, while the b6
pawn gets weakened.
31.♗xd6 ♕xd6 32.♖e3 e5
Black has a significant advantage.
33.♖b1 e4! 34.♖c3
34.♕xb6?? ♖b8−+.
**34...♕e5 35.♖c2 ♖d6 36.♖bc1
f4! 37.c5**
37.♖e1 was somewhat better.
**37...bxc5　38.♖xc5　♖xc5
39.♖xc5 f3!**
Now this pawn cannot be captured
because of 40.gxf3 ♕a1+ and ♖g6.
40.♕d1
40.♕b8+ ♔h7 41.♖c8 also lost.
**40...♖g6 41.g4 e3 42.♕e1 e2
43.♖c1 ♕xd5 44.♕c3 ♖c6!**
White resigned.
The annotations are based on
H. Kmoch's commentary.

No. 61b. Queen's Gambit Accepted
J. Showalter − J. Blackburne
Nuremberg 1896

**1.d4 d5 2.c4 dxc4 3.♘f3 ♘f6
4.e3 c5 5.♗xc4 e6 6.♘c3 ♘c6 7.0-0
cxd4 8.exd4 ♗e7.**

W. Steinitz's idea, first tested in the world championship match against J. Zukertort in 1886.

9.♖e1 0-0 10.a3 a6 11.♗a2? **♕c7 12.♗g5 ♖d8.**

White plays poorly in the opening; his central pawn gradually weakens and ultimately collapses.

13.♘e2 ♘d5 14.♕d3 ♗xg5 15.♘xg5 ♘f6 16.♖ad1 ♘e7 17.♖c1 ♕b6 18.b4 ♗d7 19.♖c5 ♗b5.

Black constantly provokes piece trades – the more of them, the fewer attacking chances his opponent has and the weaker the queen's pawn becomes.

20.♕c2 ♘g6

20...♗xe2 21.♖xe2 ♖xd4? 22.♘xe6 fxe6 23.♖xe6.

21.♖d1 ♗xe2 22.♕xe2 ♖d6 23.♘e4 ♘xe4 24.♕xe4 ♖ad8 25.h4 ♘f8 26.♖d3 ♘d7 27.♗b1 ♘f6 28.♕f4 ♘d5 29.♕g5 h6 30.♕d2 ♘e7 31.♕f4

The decisive mistake that Blackburne exploits brilliantly.

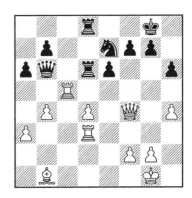

31...e5!!

From here until the end, the notes are by S. Tarrasch:

32.♕xe5

32.♖xe5 ♘g6.

32...♖e6 33.♖c7 ♖e1+ 34.♔h2 ♕xc7+ 35.♖xc7 ♘d5 36.♖xb7 ♖xb1

That's the point! The game is already decided, but the endgame is still very interesting.

37.♖a7 ♖d6 38.♖f3 ♘f6 39.g3 ♖d1 40.♖c3 ♖d2 41.♖c8+ ♔h7 42.♔g2 ♖e6 43.♖xf7 ♖ee2 44.♖cc7 ♖xf2+ 45.♔g1 ♖g2+ 46.♔f1 ♖df2+

The immediate 46...♘h5 was simpler.

47.♔e1 ♖a2 48.♔f1 ♖h2 49.♔g1 ♘h5 50.♖c3 ♖hg2+

White resigned.

No. 62. Sicilian Defense
Rauzer – Goglidze
All-Union Young Masters
Tournament
Leningrad 1936

In the next "white" game, Rauzer again got to test his opening invention against the Sicilian Dragon. This time, black deviated from the plan we know from Rauzer – Chekhover (game 60) and went for the central counter-attack, 8... d5. White reacted correctly, 9.e5 ♞e8, but then played too slowly, delaying the immediate 10.f4. This delay allowed his opponent to make a tempting pawn sacrifice with 12... ♞f5 13.♞xf5 ♝xf5. Now 14.♛xd5 is bad due to 14...♛b6, while if 14.♞xd5, then simply 14...♝xc2, returning the pawn with great play, because in case of 15.♞xe7+ ♛xe7 16.♛xc2, black's positional advantage gives him more than enough compensation for the pawn. After the game move 15...♛b6! (in the same energetic style), white's best defense is 16.♞xd5, although, by playing 16...♛d4, black later regains the d3 pawn with freer play. In the actual game, however, after 16.♛f2? d4 17.♞e4, Rauzer could have faced big trouble had black played 17...♞b4. This threatened to capture the d3 pawn or to play ♜c8, as well as the killing knight transfer to e3 through d5. The move 17... ♛b4+ allowed white to avoid the worst.

1.e4 c5 2.♞f3 d6 3.d4 cxd4 4.♞xd4 ♞f6 5.♞c3 g6 6.f3 ♝g7 7.♝e3 0-0 8.♛d2 d5 9.e5 ♞e8

10.♝h6 ♞c6 11.♝xg7 ♞xg7 12.f4 ♞f5 13.♞xf5 ♝xf5 14.♝d3 ♝xd3 15.cxd3 ♛b6 16.♛f2 d4 17.♞e4

17...♛b4+ 18.♛d2 ♜ac8 19.♚e2 f5 20.♞g5 ♛b5 21.♜hc1 ♛d5 22.♞f3 g5 23.♚f1 g4 24.♞g1 ♜c7 25.♜c4 b5 26.♜c2 ♜fc8 27.b3 ♞d8 28.♜ac1 ♜xc2 29.♜xc2 ♜xc2 30.♛xc2 ♛c6 31.♛xc6 ♞xc6 32.♞e2 ♚f7 33.♚f2 ♚e6 34.♚e1 ♚d5 35.♚d2 ♚c5 36.a3 b4 37.a4 e6 38.♞g3 ♞e7 39.♞f1 ♞d5 40.g3 h5 41.♚e2
Draw.

No. 63. Sicilian Defense
Rauzer – Ragozin
All-Union Young Masters
Tournament
Leningrad 1936

The next day, Rauzer again faced a Dragon. The draw had given him two white games in a row. Maybe he was unhappy with the previous experience, and there was not enough time to find an improvement on the fly. Whatever the reason, Rauzer eschewed the f2-f3 method in favor of another. Similarly to the system 5.♘c3 e6 6.♗g5!, which also bears his name, he plans to mobilize the pieces with ♕d2 and 0-0-0, combined with threats in the center and on the kingside. However, Ragozin's tactical blow soon changed the course of the struggle.

1.e4 c5 2.♘f3 d6 3.d4 cxd4 4.♘xd4 ♘f6 5.♘c3 g6 6.♗g5 ♗g7 7.♕d2 ♘c6 8.0-0-0 ♘xe4!?

After this move, such a multitude of lines arises that it was probably impossible to anticipate them all. After a "semi-open" start to the game, white is forced into swashbuckling with the visors raised. The main motivation behind this move was probably "surely the theoretician couldn't have foreseen *that*?" However, it was not exactly so. Or, rather, not at all so.

9.♘xe4
With this move, Rauzer avoided a number of complicated variations. For instance, 9.♘xc6 ♗xc3!? 10.♕e3! bxc6 11.♕xe4 ♗e5 12.♕xc6+ ♗d7.

9...♘xd4!
After 9...♗xd4? 10.♗b5! ♗g7 11.♗xc6+ bxc6 12.♘xd6+! ♕xd6 13.♕a5 ♗d4 14.♖xd4 ♕xd4 15.♖d1 ♕b6 16.♕e5 0-0 17.♗h6 f6 18.♕xe7, white would have won immediately. (This combination was proposed in the tournament bulletin by Moscow players B. Varshaver and F. Fogelevich.)

This combination is refuted by 16... f6! 17.♗xf6 0-0-+.

10.♘f6+!?
It's possible that this beautiful exchange tactic was anticipated by Rauzer when he developed the 6.♗g5 attack. It's seemingly good for white to double his opponent's pawns and isolate the d6 pawn at the same time. In the game, the plan succeeded; the secrets of the Dragon were only revealed later, after the talented Dnepropetrovsk candidate master I. Konstantinovsky discovered the gambit line 6.f3 ♗g7

7.♗e3 ♘c6 8.♕d2 0-0 9.0-0-0 d5!?
It turned out that, in such positions, opening the files and diagonals (with opposite-sides castling) gives black serious attacking chances. Similar complications could have erupted in this game, too.

10...exf6 11.♕xd4 0-0 12.♗f4

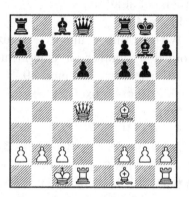

The position has become even more enigmatic. Black was thinking what he should do: get the queenside pieces into play (♗f5, ♖c8) or open the diagonal for the g7 bishop, give away the d6 pawn and go for an equal endgame.

After 12...♗f5! 13.♗xd6 ♖e8, black has great attacking chances.

**12...f5(?)   13.♕xd6   ♗e6
14.♕xd8 ♖fxd8 15.♖xd8+ ♖xd8
16.a3 ♗d4**

The passions have subsided, but black's f-pawns might need extra care in a quiet endgame.

**17.f3 f6 18.♗d3 g5 19.♗d2 h5
20.♖e1 ♔f7 21.f4 g4 22.♗e3 h4
23.♗xd4 ♖xd4 24.g3**

White's advantage slowly becomes apparent. He has a mobile extra pawn on the queenside and more active pieces. Black's only chances for counterplay involve transferring the rook to h8 and, after trading pawns on g3, penetrating to h2 or h3. Black requires great precision in implementing this plan.

24...♖d8! 25.♗f1 h3?

The defensive rhythm is immediately disrupted. The correct move was 25...hxg3 26.hxg3 ♖h8 27.♗g2 b6 28.♖h1 ♖xh1+ 29.♗xh1 ♔e7 30.b4 ♔d6 31.♔d2, and black can fight back, if only barely.

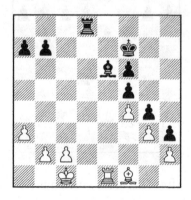

Now Rauzer energetically attacks on the queenside.

26.♖d1 ♖c8 27.♖d4 ♖c5(?) 28.♔d2 ♔g6 29.b4 ♖c7 30.c4 b6 31.♔c3 ♗c8 32.♖d6 ♗b7 33.a4

White agreed to a draw here. It's hard to say what prompted this sudden decision. Maybe he got tired, maybe he got into time trouble. After 33...♔f7 34.c5 bxc5 35.♗c4+ ♔e7 (35...♔g6 36.b5) 36.♖e6+ ♔d8 37.b5, white's advantage is obvious.

No. 64. Alekhine Defense
Rauzer – Fine
Leningrad 1937

Rauzer's first (and, unfortunately, last) meeting with the American grandmaster, who soon, after the 1938 AVRO tournament, became one of the prime candidates for the world championship match. At the same time, it was an encounter between two prominent theoreticians of the time. Fine had already played quite a few games that proved to be valuable for the development of opening theory, and also published a number of small, but informative articles on popular openings (albeit somewhat compiled from various sources).

In reply to Rauzer's principled 1.e2-e4!, the American guest played the hypermodern knight lunge, as though challenging the defender of the classical principles of the Steinitz – Tarrasch school. On the other hand, even Tarrasch himself tested the opening that got Alekhine's name

attached to it with black (for instance, in a well-known game against Em. Lasker at the Ostrava 1923 tournament), albeit unsuccessfully.

Like the ex-world champion, Rauzer chose the line that was considered one of the most promising at the time – the Four Pawns Attack, used by white to seize the initiative.

1.e4 ♘f6 2.e5 ♘d5 3.d4 d6 4.c4 ♘b6 5.f4 dxe5 6.fxe5 ♘c6 7.♗e3 ♗f5 8.♘c3 e6 9.♗e2 ♗e7 10.♘f3 0-0 11.0-0 f6

Without trading the central pawns, black cannot liberate his position, and this cannot be delayed further. The main question is who will position their pieces better for the "first middlegame".

12.exf6 ♗xf6 13.♕d2 ♕e7 14.♖ad1 ♖ad8 15.♕e1

It would be harder for black to get counterplay after 15.♕c1!

15...♘b4 16.a3 ♘c2 17.♕f2 ♘xe3 18.♕xe3 ♘d7

Theory recommends 18...c6 19.b4 ♗c2 20.♖c1 ♗g6 etc. Still, even in this line, white's chances are preferable.

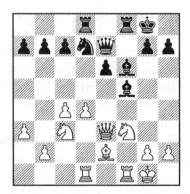

19.c5!

Splendid. A similar bishop's pawn push was successfully used by Em. Lasker. White creates a seemingly weak point on d4, but gets ample compensation for that: pawn superiority on the queenside, control over the d6 square, and a space advantage. Rauzer, of course, remembered the famous move f4-f5 played by Lasker in the decisive game against Capablanca at the St. Petersburg 1914 grandmaster tournament.

19...♞b8!

A worthy reply. The strategic battle is rife with various tactical subtleties.

A seemingly quiet walk of two chess scholars has led them into the "Valley of Mists"... Indeed, how can white increase his pressure? Commentators proposed 20.h3 here, threatening the dangerous g-pawn push. Another tempting plan involved activity on another flank – 20.b4, then b4-b5 and ♗c4 together with ♖fe1.

Instead of that, Rauzer chose a plan that involved centralization

of the queen's knight, but this maneuver allowed the "incredibly slippery Reuben" (as M. Euwe called Fine) to find "his chance".

20.♗c4 ♔h8! 21.♞e4 ♗xe4! 22.♕xe4 ♞c6

23.b4!

Strengthening the pawn chain and parrying potential attacks against the d4 and c5 pawns.

23...a5 24.♗b5 axb4 25.♗xc6 bxc6 26.axb4 ♖d5 27.♖fe1

Draw.

A short but profound duel!

No. 65. French Defense
Rauzer – Alatortsev
10th Soviet Championship
Tbilisi 1937
Annotated by V. Rauzer

1.e4 e6 2.d4 d5 3.♞c3 ♗b4

This is the third Soviet championship where Alatortsev and I played this line of the French Defense, which had become quite principled for us.

4.e5

Only this move can give white an advantage. The trade of the central pawn, 4.exd5, or its sacrifice, 4.a3, only escalates tensions in the center.

4...c5 5.a3

The idea of this move is to keep the pawn chain and force the trade of the dark-squared bishop that protects the important d6 and g7 squares.

5...&xc3+

In the 1933 championship (see game 32 – **A. K.**), Alatortsev played 5...cxd4 6.axb4 dxc3 7.♘f3 ♕c7 and got a worse position.

6.bxc3 ♕c7

Rovner's move; its tactical idea is to meet 7.♕g4 with 7...f5, protecting the g7 pawn with a tempo. In the 1934 championship, Alatortsev played 6...♘e7 7.♕g4 ♕a5 8.&d2 ♕a4 9.♕xg7 ♖g8 10.♕xh7 cxd4 11.♘f3 and also got a worse position (see game 39 – **A. K.**). Bogatyrchuk played 11.♘e2 in this line against Alatortsev, which many consider even stronger.

7.♘f3

This move was made both out of conviction that it was the best and out of practical considerations: a short while ago, in my match with Rovner (see game 73 below – **A. K.**), I played 7.♕g4 and thus thought that Alatortsev was better prepared for it.

7...♘c6 8.&d3

The most logical developing move that also contains a trap: if 8...cxd4, then 9.cxd4 ♘xd4 10.♘xd4 ♕c3+ 11.♕d2 ♕xa1 12.c3 with the subsequent ♘b3, winning the queen for a rook.

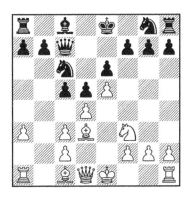

8...c4

A most debatable move – white now doesn't have to protect the d4 square, but, on the other hand, his pieces are rather cramped.

9.&e2

A debatable move as well. 9.&f1 with the subsequent g2-g3 was worth considering, and in case of f7-f6, white transfers the bishop to h3 to put pressure on the e6 square. White's center is so well-fortified that he can probably even afford to lose two tempi to implement this plan.

9...&d7 10.0-0

Perhaps the immediate 10.a4 f6 11.&f4 h6! (defending from e5xf6 and preparing g7-g5 and f6-f5) 12.h4 was stronger, intending ♔d2 or g2-g3 and then ♔e1-f1-g2. After the game move, the important reply h2-h4 in this line doesn't work anymore because the rook has left the h-file.

10...0-0-0

The game is similar to Kurkletis – Golovko, but instead of f7-f5?, black prepares the important central break f7-f6. (That game, played in the All-

Union Spartak championship, was published with joint analysis by K. Kurkletis and V. Rauzer himself, in *64*, 15th April 1937. The latter was in charge of preparing the Leningrad Spartak team for this tournament. After 7.♘f3 ♘e7 8.♗d3 c4 9.♗e2 ♘bc6 10.0-0 ♗d7 11.a4 0-0-0 12.♗a3 f5

white continued 13.a5!, creating perfectly decent threats (above all ♗d6 trapping the queen), against which black failed to find an acceptable defense – **A. K.**.)

11.a4 f6 12.♗a3

If 12.♗f4, then not 12...f5 13.♘g5 ♘h6 14.♗c1! and ♗a3 with strong pressure, but 12...h6!, threatening g7-g5 and f6-f5.

12...♘h6

Black avoids the small trap 12...fxe5 13.dxe5 ♘xe5 14.♕d4 ♘xf3+ 15.♗xf3 ♘f6 16.♕xa7. With the game move, black prepares the defense of the d6 square.

13.♗d6 ♕a5 14.exf6

Forced – black threatens ♘f7.

14...gxf6 15.♕d2 ♘f5

If 15...♘f7, then 16.♗g3 e5 17.dxe5 fxe5 18.♖fe1.

16.♗f4 ♘ce7

The position is double-edged. The other plan, 16...♖de8 17.h3 e5, had a flaw – black's central pawns are weakened.

17.h3 h5 18.♗h2 ♘g6 19.♖fb1

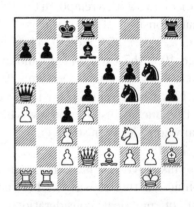

19...♗xa4

Until now, black's play has been consistent, but now he makes a gross blunder, and the outcome of the game is decided. The correct move was 19...♗c6.

20.♕e1

White threatens 21.♗xc4 and ♕xe6+. At the same time, he prepares ♘d2 with the subsequent ♘b3 or ♘xc4 (♗xc4).

20...♕a6
Protecting e6.
21.♘d2 ♘f8
Black defends from the threat 22.♖b4 b5 23.♘b3, which is met with 23...♘d7, but another threat now looms.
22.♖b4 b5

23.♘xc4! dxc4 24.♖axa4 ♕xa4
If 24...bxa4, then 25.♖xc4+.
25.♖xa4 bxa4 26.♗xc4 ♔d7
In view of the imminent time trouble, both opponents played the next stage of the game quite quickly. The black king is exposed, and it's impossible to defend it when facing the strong bishop pair.
27.d5 exd5
27...e5 could be met with 28.♗xe5 fxe5 29.♕xe5 ♘d6 30.♕g7+ ♔e8 31.♕xh8 ♘xc4 32.♕xh5+, winning the c4 knight.
28.♗xd5 ♘e7 29.c4 ♘xd5 30.cxd5 ♖h7 31.♕a5 ♔e8 32.d6
An inaccuracy: to facilitate the push of the c- and d-pawns, it was necessary to keep the pawn on d5.
32...♖c8 33.c4 ♖b7 34.♕xh5+

♔d8 35.♕a5+ ♔e8 36.♕xa4+ ♔f7 37.♗f4 ♘e6 38.♗e3 ♘d8 39.c5 ♘c6
This loses immediately, but black's position is already hopeless.
40.♕c4+
Black resigned.
This game cannot be viewed as the final answer to the question of 3...♗b4, it's only another test.

No. 66. Ruy Lopez
Rauzer – I. Rabinovich
10th Soviet Championship
Tbilisi 1937

1.e4 e5 2.♘f3 ♘c6 3.♗b5 ♘f6
A good way to transpose to the Steinitz Defense. After the immediate 3...d6 and the quick e5xd4, white can actively attack the center by castling long – the rooks' positions on d1 and h1 give him good activity. The game Alekhine – Brinckmann from the 1927 Kecskemet tournament serves as a good example.
After 3...♘f6 4.0-0 d6, the choice of active system for white is severely limited.
4.0-0 d6
Since times of the "chess revolution" of 1913–1924, opening evaluations based on S. Tarrasch's principles ("black gets a cramped, but solid position", etc.) have been annulled. By contrast, both J. R. Capablanca and A. Nimzowitsch (who were preceded in this by both world champions and, of course, M. Chigorin) eagerly went for "cramped" positions, finding quite a

few promising ideas in them. Many masters followed their lead.

I. Rabinovich, using the "difficult" Steinitz Defense against a formidable theoretician, doubtlessly remembered how he managed to get an easy draw against an even more experienced Ruy Lopez player, the ex-world champion Em. Lasker (Moscow 1925). Let me remind readers of this short game that made a big impression at the time.

No. 66a. Ruy Lopez
Em. Lasker – I. Rabinovich
Moscow 1925

1.e4 e5 2.♘f3 ♘c6 3.♗b5 ♘f6 4.0-0 ♗e7 5.♘c3 d6 6.d4 ♗d7 7.♗xc6 ♗xc6 8.♕d3 ♘d7 9.♗e3 exd4 10.♗xd4 0-0 11.♖ad1 ♗f6 12.♗xf6 ♕xf6 13.♕d4 ♖fe8 14.♖fe1 ♘e5 15.♘d2 ♘g4 16.♕xf6 ♘xf6 17.f3 d5! 18.exd5 ♘xd5 19.♘xd5 ♗xd5 20.♔f2 ♔f8 21.a3 ♖xe1 22.♖xe1 ♖d8 23.♖e3 ♗e6 24.♖d3 ♖e8 25.♖c3 ♖e7 26.♘f1 ♖d7 27.♘e3, and a draw was agreed.

5.d4 ♗d7 6.♘c3 ♗e7 7.♖e1

7...exd4!

This trade was once labeled as "ceding the center". Now, however, we know that the black e7 bishop comes alive, and black creates counterplay by attacking the e4 pawn with the e8 rook, while in case of a trade on c6, he also inserts ♖b8 and the "centrifugal" move c6-c5.

8.♘xd4 0-0 9.♗xc6 bxc6 10.♗f4

Rauzer thought that he would be able to play e4-e5 and thus break the defensive "triumvirate" c7-c6-d6. That's the purpose of the early trade of the proud "Spanish" b5 bishop.

10...♖e8 11.h3 h6 12.♕f3 c5 13.♘b3 ♖b8

The maneuver 13...♗c6 14.♘a5 ♕d7 (intending ♖ab8 and ♗a8) was also possible; 15.♘xc6 ♕xc6 16.e5 ♕xf3 17.gxf3 ♘d7 18.exd6 ♗xd6 19.♗xd6 cxd6 etc. is not dangerous for black.

Actually, this continuation is dangerous for black because of 18.♘d5!

14.e5 ♘h7 15.♘d5 ♗f8

16.c4

White's position looks imposing, but he cannot get anything real out of it – the defensive power of the black bishops is quite solid, black dominates the b-file, and he also has flank lunges ♞g5 and a7-a5 (the b2 pawn is weak) available to him.

16...a5 17.exd6 cxd6 18.♖xe8 ♝xe8 19.♖b1

Of course, such a modest move is not too attractive. However, tactical gambles such as 19.♖e1? a4 20.♞d2 ♖xb2 21.♞e4 ♖xa2 22.♝xh6 ♝c6! gave white nothing good. Black's defense is solid, and tactical swoops are easily repelled.

This line can be improved both for black and white: 21...♝c6!? as well as 22.♞xd6!?, but, of course, white should indeed avoid it altogether.

19...♞g5 20.♛g3 ♖b7 21.h4 ♞e4 22.♛e3 f5

Now black also has a centralized knight, while his other pieces work very well from the eighth rank.

23.f3 a4 24.♞c1

After 24.fxe4 axb3 25.a3 ♝c6, the balance wouldn't have been upset.

So white should have gone for this line. After the game move, however, black has an advantage.

24...♞f6 25.♞xf6+ ♛xf6 26.♛xe8 ♖e7 27.♛xa4 ♛d4+

This is black's main trump card – now the white king will be completely exposed, whereas the black king is nicely guarded by the "bad" bishop on f8.

This only leads to perpetual check. 27...♖e1+!, on the other hand, gave black a decisive attack: 28.♚f2 ♛xh4+ 29.♝g3 ♛h1+ etc.

28.♚f1

After 28.♚h1?, white got checkmated.

28...♛xf4 29.♞d3 ♛xh4 30.♖e1 ♛h1+ 31.♚f2 ♛h4+ 32.♚f1 ♛h1+ 33.♚f2

Draw.

A well-played and theoretically valuable game.

No. 67. Ruy Lopez
Rauzer – Panov
10th Soviet Championship
Tbilisi 1937

1.e4 e5 2.♞f3 ♞c6 3.♝b5 a6 4.♝a4 ♞f6 5.0-0 ♝e7 6.♖e1 b5 7.♝b3 d6 8.c3 ♞a5

Reviewing years of experience with this well-known tabiya, we can say that 8...0-0 (to meet 9.h3 with 9...♝e6, and 9.d4 with 9...♝g4) is more in accordance with M. Chigorin's ideas that came to him during the development of the closed system (5...♗e7). Nevertheless, both variations contain a lot of deep strategic and tactical problems.

9.♗c2 c5

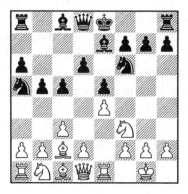

10.d4

In previous years, Rauzer preferred a quiet structure with d2-d3. Consider, for instance, his game against H. Kmoch, played in the 1934 Tbilisi Masters Tournament featuring the Austrian guest. "Rauzer considers this the best continuation," Kmoch wrote in his annotations, "and probably not without reason." Rauzer himself, however, abandoned these evaluations – possibly after analyzing my game against Panov (white) from the masters qualifying tournament (Leningrad 1936). In this game, black sacrificed the e5 pawn and seized the initiative: 10.d3 ♘c6 11.♘bd2 0-0 12.♘f1 d5 13.exd5 ♕xd5 14.♕e2 ♗b7 15.♗b3 ♕d7 16.♘xe5 ♘xe5 17.♕xe5 ♖ae8.

10...♕c7 11.♘bd2 0-0

We have seen black's plan involving 11...♘c6 12.a4 ♖b8 in game 58, Rauzer – Riumin.

12.♘f1 ♗d7

The pin 12...♗g4 was discredited shortly before this game was played, in Alekhine – Fine (Hastings 1936/37), won by white in brilliant style with a d4 pawn sacrifice: 13.♘e3! ♗xf3 14.♕xf3 cxd4 15.♘f5 dxc3 16.♕xc3 etc.

13.♘e3

13...♖ad8

This move was criticized by all commentators, who proposed creating pressure along the c-file instead (13...♖fc8 or 13...cxd4 14.cxd4 ♖fc8). Perhaps they were right, even though Master V. Panov's move was not too bad.

While the second recommendation is more or less acceptable, the first one is dubious – after 14.dxe5 dxe5 15.♘d5, black's position is unpleasant.

14.a4 c4 15.axb5 axb5 16.♕e2 ♖a8

It's important not to persevere with your mistakes and promptly correct them instead.

17.♘f5(?) ♗c6(?)

Black trades the wrong bishop. Had he played 17...♗xf5 18.exf5, he could have gained some good counterplay. It seems that the maneuver 17.♘f5 was premature. A preliminary trade was necessary. Despite the tempo loss with ♖a8-d8-a8, black has a lot of hidden resources in his position.

18.♘xe7+ ♕xe7 19.♗g5 h6

Alas! Now the pinned knight causes a lot of trouble, while white has another strong knight at his disposal.

20.♗h4 ♖fe8 21.♘d2 ♗d7 22.♘f1 ♕e6 23.dxe5 dxe5 24.♘e3 ♗c6

This bishop proved fatal for black. Its four moves turned out to be a waste of time, the f5 square is still weak, and the white knight's arrival there is most unpleasant. Rauzer executes the final attack nicely.

25.♘f5 ♔h7 26.♖ed1 ♘b7 27.♕e3! ♘d7(?)

After 27...♘g8 (protecting the h6 pawn and preparing g7-g6), it would be more difficult for white to attack.

28.♖xa8 ♖xa8 29.♗e7!

A clever transfer of the bishop to a more important diagonal (a3-f8).

White is targeting the g7 pawn.

29...♖a6 30.♗b4 ♘f6 31.h4 ♘g8 32.h5

Even though black managed to correct his mistake made on the 27th move and now protects the h6 pawn, it was already possible to play 32.♗f8 g6 33.♘xh6 ♘f6 34.♘f5! ♘g8 35.♘e7!, and white should win. Still, 32.h5 was strong enough, too.

32...♘f6

33.g4! ♘g8

Of course, not 33...♘xg4 34.♕g3 g6 35.♕xg4 gxf5 36.exf5 with the threat of ♗e7! followed by f5-f6+.

34.f3 ♕f6 35.♗f8 g6

Or 35...g5 36.♔h2 ♕e6 37.♗xh6!, and black suffers.

Computer analysis shows that instead of 36.♔h2, it's much stronger to open the h-file with 36.hxg6+, threatening ♔f2 and ♖h1.

36.♘xh6

As in the previous note, it still made sense to open the h-file with 36.hxg6+.

36...gxh5 37.♘f5 ♗e8 38.♔g2 ♕b6 39.♕g5 ♕g6 40.♕d2 f6 41.♕d5! ♖b6

Black is defenseless.

42.♔f2 ♕g5 43.gxh5 ♕xh5 44.♖g1 ♗f7 45.♖g7+ ♔h8 46.♕xf7 ♕xf7 47.♖xf7 ♖a6 48.♘h4

Black resigned.

No. 68. Caro-Kann Defense
Rauzer – Budo
10th Soviet Championship
Tbilisi 1937

1.e4 c6 2.♘c3 d5 3.♘f3 dxe4 4.♘xe4 ♘f6 5.♘xf6+ gxf6

The players repeat the opening that they played in a recent tournament featuring grandmaster R. Fine (Leningrad, March 1937) – this shows that their evaluation of this structure hasn't changed. Both opponents start out with the attitude, "Have at thee!"

6.g3 ♗f5 7.♗g2 ♕d7 8.0-0 ♗h3

The g2 bishop is not too threatening, and black's light-squared bishop is already in play. In my game against Rauzer in the same championship, I managed to get more active piece play with black.

9.b3 ♘a6 10.♗b2 ♗xg2 11.♔xg2 0-0-0 12.♖e1!

Rauzer's long-range pieces (♗b2, ♖e1) work exceptionally well. White's primary task now is to neutralize the attacking attempts h7-h5-h4, and he clearly has better prospects in the center and on the queenside. 12.d3 h5 13.a3, as played in the Leningrad encounter, is weaker: after 13...♗h6 14.♖e1 ♘c7 15.♖e4 ♘e6 16.♘h4 ♘g5 17.♖b4 ♕d5+, black got a position rich in tactical resources and won after a complicated struggle.

12...h5 13.♕e2 ♘c7(?)

If you said "A", you should have said "B" too (13...h4). The opened h-file, without a doubt, would have given black's counterplay a decent boost.

14.♕c4! ♘e6

14...♘d5 almost begged to be played. After 15.♕a4 ♔b8 16.c4 ♘f4+ and then ♘d3 or 16.♗d4 b6 (but not 16...♘f4+ 17.♔g1), preparing c6-c5 or ♘f4+, black still had some chances.

15.♖e4!

Gradual centralization increasingly cramps black's position – now he can only rely on some lucky blow on the kingside. Nevertheless, he still had 15...♕d5 available.

15...♗h6 16.♖ae1 ♖hg8 17.d3 ♖g4

This only forces h2-h3, which is beneficial for white; black surely couldn't have seriously hoped for 18.♖xg4? hxg4 19.♕xg4?? ♘f4+. But black had no useful moves anyway.

18.h3 ♖g7 19.♖h4 ♖dg8 20.♔f1!

White calmly gets the king out of the danger zone and will eventually capture the stray pawn on h5.

20...♕d6 21.♔e2 b5 22.♕e4 ♗g5 23.♖xh5 ♗f4 24.♔d1 ♗xg3

Desperation. Rauzer played simply and energetically in the ending.

25.fxg3 ♖xg3 26.♘d4! ♘xd4 27.♗xd4 e5 28.♗f2 ♖3g6

28...♖g2 doesn't work due to 29.♖h8!

29.♔c1 a5 30.d4 ♖e8 31.dxe5

Black resigned.

No. 69. French Defense
Rauzer – Lilienthal
10th Soviet Championship
Tbilisi 1937

1.e4 e6 2.d4

The jury is out – is 2.d3 perhaps better, going for King's Indian structures (2.d3 d5 3.♘d2 c5 4.♘gf3 ♘c6 5.g3 etc.)? White's scores are generally better than after the classical 2.d4. Maybe this happens because black has fewer theoretical guidelines after 2.d3, and, therefore, there's more space for independent creativity? But that's a different topic for a different time.

2...d5 3.♘c3 ♘f6 4.♗g5 ♗e7

For a long time, A. Alekhine favored the system 4...dxe4, defusing the tension in the center and developing the unfortunate c8 bishop as soon as possible. The classical system (4...♗e7) has featured strong proponents in different times, but it has an organic defect – white is able to follow well-studied lines, where black's weak dark squares play a key role. This is noticeable in the present game as well.

5.e5 ♘fd7 6.♗xe7 ♕xe7 7.f4 a6 8.♘f3 b5 9.♗d3 c5

How necessary was this move now? After trading on c5, white gets a clear goal – seize the d4 outpost in the middlegame or endgame (for the knight, or, after numerous trades, for the king! This strategy is known from various predecessor games). Perhaps the simpler plan – 9...♗b7, then ♘c6 and 0-0-0 – was more promising and, at any rate, posed new problems for white.

10.dxc5 ♕xc5 11.♕d2 ♘c6 12.a3 ♗b7 13.♕f2! ♖c8

In the fight for the central dark squares, black has little hope of maintaining equality. It was somewhat better to retreat to a7 with the queen (now or on the next move).

14.♘e2 ♕xf2+(?) 15.♔xf2 ♘c5

Black follows a well-trodden line towards a standard yet very difficult endgame, where the weakness of dark squares and a bad bishop (despite all Lilienthal's tactical prowess!) leave him no hope for survival. Of course, ♘xd3 is not a threat.

16.♘ed4 ♘e7 17.♔e3 h5

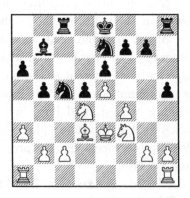

Placing the pawns on light squares (the next move is 18...g6) only exacerbated black's troubles. After the queen trade, he failed to find any acceptable defensive plan. Perhaps there really wasn't one.

18.♘g5

Preventing f7-f6, but white could also play 18.g3 immediately, then h2-h3 and g3-g4.

18...g6 19.g3 ♘f5+ 20.♗xf5 gxf5 21.h3 ♔e7 22.g4! hxg4 23.hxg4 fxg4

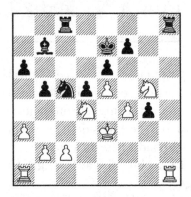

After opening the g- and h-files, white easily increases his advantage, because his attack is more or less a matter of technique now. The mighty d4 knight is very important; white also constantly threatens a king incursion through e3-d4-c5-b6.

24.♖ag1 ♘d7

24...♖xh1   25.♖xh1   ♘e4 26.♘gxe6! fxe6 27.♖h7+ and ♖xb7 was hopeless.

25.♖xh8 ♖xh8 26.♖xg4 ♖h1

Black has some hope for this rook, but white simply trades it.

27.♘gf3 ♔f8 28.♖h4 ♖xh4

Or 28...♖b1 29.♖h8+ ♔e7 30.♖h7 and ♘g5. After the rook trade, black manages to prolong the struggle, but it's now only a matter of time – the game cannot be saved.

29.♘xh4 ♚e7 30.♘hf3 f6

White threatened to invade with the king after ♘b3, ♚d4 and ♚c5. Black weakens the e5 pawn, and then tries to revive his bishop with a pawn sacrifice (d5-d4).

31.♘b3 fxe5 32.fxe5 d4+

There's nothing better. For instance, 32...♗c8 33.♚d4, then ♘c5.

33.♘bxd4 ♗d5 34.b3 ♚d8 35.♚f4 ♚e7 36.♘e1!

The decisive maneuver! From d3, the knight will threaten to invade through c5 or b4. The rest of the game needs no explanation.

36...♘f8 37.♘d3 ♘g6+ 38.♚e3 ♚d8 39.♘c5 ♘xe5 40.♘xa6 ♗c6 41.♚f4 ♘g6+ 42.♚g5 ♗e8 43.♘xe6+ ♚e7 44.♘ec7 ♗c6 45.♚xg6♗e4+ 46.♚g5 ♗xc2 47.b4 ♗d3 48.♚f4 ♚d6 49.♚e3 ♗f1 50.♚d4 ♚c6 51.♘e6 ♗e2 52.♚e5 ♗f1 53.♘ac5 ♗c4 54.♘d4+ ♚b6 55.♘e4 ♗f1 56.♘d6

Black resigned.

No. 70. Queen's Gambit Accepted
Levenfish – Rauzer
10th Soviet Championship
Tbilisi 1937

This game was played towards the end of the tournament, when excitement about the outcome had reached its peak. To deviate from theoretical variations – G. Levenfish was an openings expert himself, but, of course, he was less well-versed in them than Rauzer – white developed the king's rook to e1, not to d1, like in game 46. This time, such an approach proved justified.

Rauzer, instead of completing the mobilization of his forces (12...♘bd7 and ♘b6), played 12...b4 prematurely, launching a queenside attack. He met the 13.♘a4 retreat with 13...♗d5. Rauzer decided against the defense 13...♕a5 as inconsistent with the spirit of the system due to 14.♘e5! ♗d5 15.♘c2!, increasing pressure on the opposing king's position. However, even after the game move, white's cunning maneuvers (14. ♗xf6!, 16.♕c2!, and 21.♖xc6!) gave him a clear advantage. In the resulting difficult endgame, Rauzer put up heroic resistance, but this only allowed him to hold until the 92nd (!) move, and he could not save the game. This is the longest known game played by Rauzer.

Thanks to this win, Levenfish managed to reach first place, which he held onto until the end. The defeat didn't dishearten Rauzer, however. He played the final games very energetically, winning two and drawing two others and securing a top-8 finish.

1.♘f3 d5 2.c4 e6 3.d4 dxc4 4.e3 c5 5.♗xc4 cxd4 6.exd4 ♘f6 7.0-0 ♗e7 8.♘c3 0-0 9.♕e2 a6 10.♗g5 b5 11.♗b3 ♗b7 12.♖fe1

12...b4 13.♘a4 ♗d5 14.♗xf6 ♗xf6 15.♗xd5 exd5 16.♕c2 a5 17.♖ac1 ♖a6 18.♘c5 ♖c6 19.♕a4 ♕c7 20.♘b3 ♖c8 21.♖xc6 ♘xc6 22.♘xa5 ♕xa5 23.♕xc6 ♕a8 24.♕xa8 ♖xa8 25.♔f1 ♔f8 26.♖a1 ♖c8 27.a4 bxa3 28.bxa3 ♔e7 29.a4 ♖c6 30.♔e2 ♔d6 31.♔d3 ♗d8 32.♘e5 ♖c7 33.♖a2 f6 34.♘g4 ♖a7 35.♘e3 g6 36.♘d1 ♗a5 37.♖b2 ♔c6 38.♖b5 ♗e1 39.♔e2 ♗a5 40.♔d3 ♗e1 41.♔e2 ♗a5 42.♖c5+ ♔d6 43.♖b5 ♔c6 44.♔d3

The tournament book adds a move repetition: 44.♖c5+ ♔d6 45.♖b5 ♔c6.

44...♗e1 45.♔e2 ♗a5 46.♖c5+ ♔d6 47.♖b5 ♔c6 48.♔d3 ♗e1 49.♖c5+ ♔d6 50.♔e2 ♗a5 51.♘e3 ♗b6 52.♖xd5+ ♔c6 53.a5 ♖xa5

54.♖xa5 ♗xa5 55.♔d3 ♗c7 56.h3 ♗a5 57.♘g4 ♗d8 58.♔c4 ♔d6

59.♘e3 ♗a5 60.♘d5 f5 61.♘f6 ♗e1 62.f3 h5 63.♘d5 ♗d2 64.♘c3 ♗e3 65.♘b5+ ♔c6 66.♘a3 ♗f2 67.♘c2 ♔d6 68.♔d3 ♔d5 69.♘e3+ ♔e6 70.♔e2 ♗g3 71.♘f1 ♗c7 72.♔d3 h4 73.♘e3 ♗f4 74.♘d1 ♔d5 75.♘c3+ ♔c6 76.♔c4 ♗e3 77.♘d5 ♗g5 78.f4 ♗d8 79.♘b4+ ♔d6 80.♘d3 g5 81.♘e5 ♔e6 82.d5+ ♔f6 83.♔c5 gxf4 84.♘c6 f3 85.gxf3 ♔g5 86.♘xd8 ♔f4 87.♘e6+ ♔xf3 88.d6 f4 89.♘xf4 ♔xf4 90.d7 ♔g3 91.d8=♕ ♔xh3 92.♕g5

Black resigned.

No. 71. Caro-Kann Defense
Rauzer – Chekhover
10th Soviet Championship
Tbilisi 1937

1.e4 c6 2.♘c3 d5 3.♘f3 ♗g4 4.h3 ♗xf3 5.♕xf3 e6 6.b3

Despite his adherence to classical methods of piece development, Rauzer often fianchettoed bishops in the Caro-Kann. See, for instance, his games against I. Rabinovich in the 8th Soviet Championship (game 33) and Budo in the 10th (game 68).

6...d4

Closing the center is far from the best decision. The resulting pawn structure is well-known from numerous won games by M. Chigorin. White's pawn chain (from c2 to h3!) is very mobile and allows him to seize the initiative. Thus, it was better to play simply 6...♘f6 or 6...dxe4 7.♘xe4 ♘d7, then ♘gf6, fighting for the central squares. Of course, white had some hopes thanks to his bishop pair, but if black was prudent enough, this was not dangerous.

7.♘e2 c5 8.♘f4

Rauzer plays the opening freshly and originally – he's ready to parry sorties by the black queen's knight (♘b8-c6-e5 or b4) with the maneuver ♘f4-d3.

8...♘c6 9.♘d3

It was simpler to play 9.d3 or 9.♕e2 with the subsequent development of the bishop on g2.

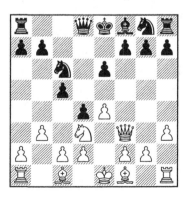

9...♘f6

9...e5 looked obvious. However, white's plan would have been very simple in this case: ♕e2, g2-g3 and ♗g2, then 0-0 and f2-f4, grabbing kingside space. Chekhover relied on the mobility of his knights, and his ideas were partially justified in the subsequent play.

10.g3 ♗e7 11.♗g2 0-0 12.e5

Here, 12.♕e2! with the subsequent 0-0 and f2-f4 was fully possible as well, preventing the black knight from reaching d5.

12...♘d5

Another plan involved the moves 12...♘d7 13.♕e4 ♕c7 14.f4 ♖ac8 15.0-0 b5, thereby ensuring c5-c4.

13.♕e4 ♖c8 14.0-0

14...b6

Here, 14...b5! was still more logical (15.a4 a6, and black also gains a strong outpost on b4) with the same purpose – to play c5-c4, then ♕b6. White still had a lot of work to do to create the e5+f5 phalanx (♘d3-e1, f2-f4, ♘f3, g3-g4).

A complicated struggle would arise, where black's chances were not to be underestimated.

15.♗b2 ♘db4

It was still necessary to play 15...b5 16.♖ae1 c4. Black's cavalry raids are fascinating, but poorly calculated.

16.♘f4 ♗g5 17.a3 ♗xf4 18.axb4 ♗xd2

Black has probably seen that tricks such as 18...♗xe5 19.b5 f5 don't work due to 20.♕e1!

19.bxc5 bxc5 20.♖a6

In the line 20.♕e2 ♗c3 21.♗xc3 dxc3 22.♗xc6 ♖xc6 23.♖xa7 c4, with all six major pieces still on the board, the entire struggle would have still been ahead.

20...♘b4 21.♖xa7

At this moment, black had a wide choice of continuations:

I. 21...♗c3 22.♗c1 d3! 23.♖d1 d2 24.♗xd2 ♗xd2 25.♕e2 ♘xc2 26.♖xd2 ♘d4, and with such a strong knight, black can withstand a lot.

II. 21...♘c6 22.♖aa1 ♘e7, and

black should be satisfied with his position.

III. 21...♘d5 22.♕e2 ♗c3 23.♗xd5 ♗xb2 24.♗e4 g6 or 24.♗c4 ♖a8 etc.

As we can see, black gets good counterplay in lines I and II. Of course, such calculations require a lot of time and energy. The move chosen by V. Chekhover was elegantly refuted by white.

21...c4 22.♖d1 c3 23.♗a3! ♘c6 24.♖a6 ♘b8 25.♖a4 d3

With a naive hope for 26.♖d4 dxc2!.

26.♗xf8 dxc2 27.♕xc2 ♕xf8

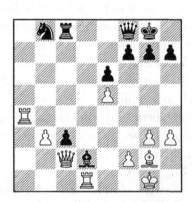

28.♖xd2! cxd2 29.♕xd2

Black's last hopes, the bishop and passed pawn, are eliminated, and Rauzer calmly overwhelms the resistance of his opponent, helped by his own passed pawn supported by the long-ranged bishop.

29...♘c6 30.♕d6 ♘e7 31.♖a7 ♘f5 32.♕xf8+ ♔xf8 33.♖a8 ♖xa8 34.♗xa8 ♔e7 35.♗e4 ♘d4 36.b4

The first step is made.

36...h6 37.♔f1 f5 38.exf6+ gxf6 39.♔e1 f5 40.♗d3 e5 41.♔d2 f4

There's no defense against the march of the king and passed pawn.

42.♗e4 fxg3 43.fxg3 ♔d6 44.♔d3 ♘e6 45.h4 ♘g7 46.g4 ♘e6 47.♔c4 ♘d4 48.b5 ♘e6 49.b6 ♘f8 50.♗f5

The knight is cut off, the b6 pawn distracts the black king, and the white king dominates.

50...♔c6 51.b7 ♔xb7 52.♔d5 e4 53.♔xe4 ♔c6 54.♔e5 ♔c5 55.♔f6 ♔d6 56.♔f7 ♔e5 57.♔xf8 h5 58.gxh5 ♔xf5 59.♔g7

Black resigned.

No. 72. Caro-Kann Defense
Rauzer – Konstantinopolsky
10th Soviet Championship
Tbilisi 1937

1.e4 c6 2.♘f3 d5 3.♘c3 dxe4 4.♘xe4 ♘f6 5.♘xf6+ gxf6

Back in 1937, I had already come to the conclusion that this line was better than its reputation suggested. Of course, black's pawn structure is somewhat weakened, but he can easily and comfortably develop his pieces and, at any rate, has good chances in the middlegame. To neutralize the possible pressure along the g-file (♖g8), white has to play g2-g3, which weakens his kingside somewhat. All in all, there's a struggle ahead, and white needs to play with absolute precision to retain the advantage of a better pawn configuration that can manifest itself in the endgame. In later years, this evaluation was seemingly confirmed.

6.g3 ♗g4

I think that this is more active than 6...♗f5 (with the subsequent ♕d7 and ♗h3), as A. Budo played against Rauzer in the same competition. The f3 knight may as well be kept pinned to increase the threat h7-h5-h4. If white kicks the bishop with h2-h3, then, if the queen is on d7, he won't be able to castle short.

7.♗g2 ♕d7 8.h3

Rauzer considered this a mistake. But after 8.0-0 h5!, white also faces challenges: black threatens h5-h4, the move 9.h4 weakens the king's position, and 9.♕e1 is still met with 9...h4! 10.♘xh4 ♘a6, then 0-0-0 with an attack that's worth the sacrificed pawn. These considerations speak in favor of 6...♗g4.

8...♗e6!

Only here. The bishop would be worse on f5, since white would constantly threaten ♘h4 or (after b2-b3 and ♗b2) ♘d4.

9.b3

Rauzer uses the same development system as in his games against Budo (the Leningrad, tournament featuring R. Fine, and the 10th Soviet Championship).

9...♘a6 10.♗b2 0-0-0 11.♕e2 ♗h6

White should meet 11...♘b4 with 12.d3 (12.♕e4 c5, threatening ♗f5) 12...♗h6 13.♘d4 ♗d5 14.0-0. Still, black's chosen continuation (♗h6) is not too bad for him.

12.0-0-0 ♕c7

Preparing to double rooks along the d-file and transfer the queen to a5.

13.♖he1

Both here and on the next move, white probably should have played 13.♘d4, forcing the bishop trade (after 13...♗d5) and decreasing the danger of an attack on the king.

13...♖d7 14.♔b1 ♖hd8 15.d3 ♕a5

Now black has the initiative (he threatens ♘b4).

16.♕e4

After this poor move, black could immediately start an attack with 16...♘b4!, analyzed in the note to black's 17th move.

16...♗f5 17.♕h4

White doesn't sense the danger. He should have played 17.♕a4,

not fearing the doubled pawns and liquidating the threats to the king. Still, after 17...♕xa4 18.bxa4 ♘c5 19.a5 ♘a4, black's chances are better. And in case of 19.♗a3? ♘xa4 20.♗xe7 ♖xe7 21.♖xe7 ♘c3+ and ♘xd1, white is worse.

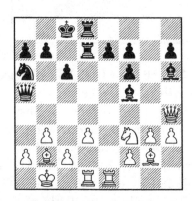

17...♗g5?

After getting a brilliant attacking position, black starts to play very weakly. Here, he should have played 17...♘b4! with a very strong attack. For example:

I.   18.♕xh6 ♕xa2+ 19.♔c1 ♘xc2! 20.♔xc2 (other moves are no better) 20...♖xd3 21.♖xd3 ♖xd3 22.♘d2 (22.♔c1 ♖c3+!) 22...♖xd2+! 23.♔xd2 ♕xb2+ 24.♔e3 ♕c3+ 25.♔f4 ♕xe1 26.♔xf5 ♕xf2+ and ♕xg2.

II. 18.a3 ♘xc2 19.♕xh6 (19.♔xc2 ♖xd3) 19...♖xd3, and black should win (20.♖xd3 ♘xe1).

Instead of this natural continuation, black, after spending a lot of time calculating the immediate rook sacrifice on d3 (which had a refutation), trades a valuable bishop and allows white to seize the initiative.

18.♘xg5 fxg5 19.♕a4!

Of course, not 19.♕xg5? ♖xd3 20.♖xd3 ♕xe1+.

19...♕xa4

Not 19...♕b6 20.♖e3, and white is better. Still, even in the endgame, white has winning chances thanks to his strong bishop pair and black's weak kingside pawns.

20.bxa4 f6 21.♖e3 e5

Now the f6 pawn is weak. At any rate, white cannot immediately play 22.♖f3 due to 22...♗e4.

22.♖f1!

Threatening both ♖f3 and f2-f4. 22.♖de1 was also good.

22...♘b4 23.♖f3?

A risky venture. 23.a3 ♘d5 24.♖ee1 ♘b6 25.a5 was more solid.

Instead of 25.a5, there's a much stronger move: 25.f4.

23...♗g6 24.♖xf6

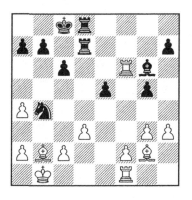

24...♘xd3?

This loses. The move 24...♖xd3! (pointed out by Grandmaster A. Lilienthal), on the other hand,

gave black an advantage. For example, 25.cxd3 ♗xd3+ 26.♔c1 ♘xa2+ 27.♔d2 ♗xf1+ and wins; or 25.♖xg6 ♖d1+, winning an exchange. White is bad after other continuations as well.

25.♗a3!

An important Zwischenzug. If white plays 25.♖xg6 immediately, then 25...♘xb2 26.♖xg5 ♘c4 (26...♘xa4 is also possible), and the fight continues. Of course, 25.cxd3 is bad due to 25...♗xd3+ with the subsequent ♗xf1 and ♖d1+.

25...♖d4

The knight cannot retreat.

26.♖xg6 hxg6 27.cxd3 ♖xd3

Despite the relatively small material losses, black's position is hopeless because of the white bishops' colossal strength.

28.♗c1 g4

28...♖d1 is bad too: 29.♖xd1 ♖xd1 30.♔c2 ♖g1 31.♗e4 etc.

29.hxg4 ♔c7 30.♗e4 ♖3d4 31.f3 ♖b4+ 32.♔a1 ♖h8 33.♗b2 ♖xe4

It was time to resign, but black misses this "opportunity" in time trouble.

34.fxe4 ♔d6 35.♗a3+ ♔e6 36.g5 ♖h3 37.♖f6+ ♔d7 38.♖xg6 ♖xg3 39.♖g7+ ♔c8 40.♗d6 ♖g4 41.♖c7+ ♔d8 42.♖xb7 a5 43.♗xe5 ♖xe4 44.g6 ♖e1+ 45.♔b2 ♖e2+ 46.♔b3 ♖e3+ 47.♗c3 ♔e8 48.g7 ♖g3 49.♖b8+

Black resigned.

I remember well that I was more upset with the missed combination than with the lost point!

No. 73. French Defense
Rauzer – Rovner
Leningrad (m/2), 1937
Annotated by V. Rauzer

1.e4 e6 2.d4 d5 3.♘c3 ♝b4

A very fashionable move, which was declared by me in 1933 (to stir more controversy!) a 'blunder' that weakens the dark squares. I can attest that I managed to prove my paradoxical statement in important games. From this point of view, this game is theoretically significant. The entire match is theoretically significant, because Rovner and I argued a lot in 1935 over whether a third move in the opening could be considered a mistake, especially such a move as 3...♝b4. In such arguments, we couldn't agree on anything. Of course, it's possible that in the next few games black will take his revenge in this line, but I am deeply sure that white will have the last word!

4.e5 c5 5.a3 ♝xc3+

Black tried 5...♝a5 in the fourth game, but unsuccessfully.

6.bxc3 ♛c7

Rovner's own move, recommended by P. A. Romanovsky. However, black got a very difficult position just ten moves later in that earlier game.[17]

---

[17] Romanovsky recommended it in *Shakhmaty v SSSR* No. 3, 1936. Rovner's game referred to occurred that same year at the VTsSPS championship.

7.♛g4

Another good system here is 7.♘f3, then, after preparation, a3-a4 and ♝a3.

7...f5

Rovner's idea is to defend the g7 pawn with a tempo. This, however, weakens the e6 pawn and takes the f5 square away from the black knights.

8.♛g3 cxd4 9.cxd4 ♘e7

9...♛xc2 would have been met with 10.♝d2, threatening 11.♛xg7 and 11.♜c1. For the backward c2 pawn, white would get some tempi and the c-file.

10.♝d2 ♘bc6 11.♘f3

11.♛xg7 ♜g8 and 12...♘xd4 is no good.

11...0-0 12.♝d3

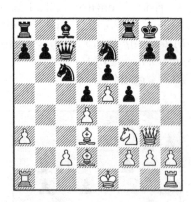

This bishop pair, which is not easy to trade off, ensures white's kingside initiative. The f5 pawn closes the diagonal for the d3 bishop, but allows white to open the g-file with g2-g4.

12...♝d7

12...♛b6 was stronger. For instance, 13.c3 ♘a5 14.0-0 ♛c7 15.♜ab1 ♘c4 16.♝c1, etc.

13.h4 ♔h8

It's dangerous to allow the white pawn to reach h6: white will control all dark squares on the kingside afterwards.

14.h5 h6

This prophylaxis creates a new weakness on g6.

15.♕f4

Preparing to push the g2 pawn.

15...a5

Black correctly seeks chances on the queenside. 15...♘a5 is met with the unpleasant 16.♗b4. On the other hand, black's pawn charge cuts off his pieces' access to white's queenside.

16.♘h4?

After playing all this in three minutes, white misses an important detail: the intended move g2-g4 is impossible as long as the rook remains on a1, because 17.g4 is met with 17...fxg4 18.♕xg4 ♘xe5! 19.dxe5 ♕xe5+ and 20...♕xa1. The correct move was 16.♖b1!, preventing b7-b5 in the meantime.

16...b5 17.♖b1

17.♘g6+ ♘xg6 18.hxg6 ♗e8 19.g4 ♗xg6 20.g5 h5 21.♗e2 ♕f7 22.♗xb5 was not bad either. It seems that black's position is so poor that white can afford to choose various continuations and make some inaccuracies.

17...b4 18.a4 ♔g8

Black decides that his king should escape to the queenside. This is, of course, a desperate measure, but the possible queenside counter-attack also came too late. For instance: 18...♘a7 19.g4 fxg4 20.♕xg4 ♗xa4 21.♘g6+ ♘xg6 22.♕xg6 ♖f5 23.♕xe6 etc.

It's hard to improve this line for black, but white's attack can be made significantly better, for instance, with 22.hxg6, and the bishop sacrifice on h6 quickly decides matters.

19.♖g1 ♖f7 20.g4

20...♔f8

It wasn't too late for black to put up some resistance with 20...fxg4 21.♕xg4 ♘f5. After the actual move, however, the game is over.

21.g5 hxg5 22.♖xg5 ♘g8

Black's position is so unsightly that it's hard for the commentator to find any acceptable moves for him.

23.♘g6+ ♔e8 24.♘h8 ♖e7 25.♔e2 ♔d8 26.♖bg1 ♗e8 27.♘g6 ♖f7 28.♗e3 ♘b8

Both knights are back home!

29.♕h4 ♔c8 30.♘f4 ♕e7 31.♕g3

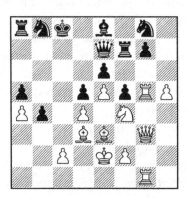

The diagram is quite amusing: white pieces occupy the best possible positions, while the black pieces are positioned almost as poorly as possible. After 31.♕g3, black cannot avoid material losses, because 31... ♖a7 is met with 32.♖g6, and one of the pawns – g7 or e6 – falls.

31...♗xa4 32.♖xg7 ♘h6 33.♖g6 ♘g4 34.♖xe6 ♕f8 35.♘xd5 ♘d7 36.♖a1 ♘xe3 37.fxe3 b3 38.cxb3

This also wins a piece, but prevents the pesky pawn from reaching b2.

38...♗xb3 39.♖c6+ ♔b7 40.♖c7+ ♔b8 41.♖b1 a4 42.e6

Black resigned.

42...f4 is met with 43.♘xf4, and if 43...♔xc7 then 44.♘g6+ ♕d6 45.♖c1+, winning the queen.

No. 74. Ruy Lopez
Rovner – Rauzer
Leningrad (m/13), 1937

1.e4 e5 2.♘f3 ♘c6 3.♗b5 d6 4.d4 ♗d7 5.♘c3 ♘f6 6.0-0 ♗e7 7.♖e1 exd4 8.♘xd4 0-0

9.♗xc6

D. Rovner played more solidly in the ninth game of the match in the same line: 9.♗f1 ♘xd4 10.♕xd4 ♗c6 11.b4 ♘g4 12.♗b2 ♗f6 13.♕d2 ♖e8 14.h3 ♘e5 15.♖ad1 a6. After 16.a3 ♖b8 17.♘d5 ♗xd5 18.exd5 a5 19.♗d4 axb4, the opponents quickly agreed a draw. There's no sense in prolonging the battle further due to full equalization of chances (and probably ambitions!).

Nobody except Rovner could tell why he decided to repeat this line. The attempt was ill-advised and quickly led to a catastrophe.

9...bxc6 10.♗f4 ♖b8 11.♖b1 ♖e8 12.e5? dxe5 13.♖xe5 ♗d6 14.♖xe8+ ♕xe8 15.♕f3

Only this blunder leads to white's

defeat. The position was roughly equal.

15...♖xb2! 16.♖c1 ♖b4 17.♗e3 ♕e5

White resigned.

No. 75
Rauzer – Zinder
Inter-Union Tournament
Kiev 1926
Annotated by V. Rauzer

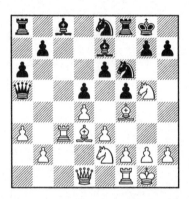

The e6 pawn is the cornerstone of black's pawn structure, and the whole "stonewall" crumbles after it falls. This pawn is only protected with the light-squared bishop. Of course, white decides to eliminate it.

15.♖xc8! ♖xc8 16.♘xe6

White has an initiative.

16...♖f7 17.♘g5

17.♗xf5 was good, too.

17...♖f8

Black doesn't want to return the exchange. After 17...g6 18.♘xf7 ♔xf7, he could have resisted for a while.

18.♗xf5 ♖a8 19.♕c2 g6

Black could avoid the bishop sacrifice with 19...h6, but after 20.♗e6+ ♔h8 21.♘f7+ ♖xf7 22.♗xf7, the game's result is beyond doubt.

20.♗xg6! hxg6 21.♕xg6+ *Black*

probably saw the sacrifice and thought that he had enough pieces around his king to protect it.

21...♔h8

21...♘g7 is also met with a mating attack.

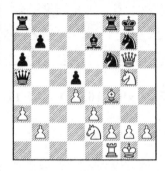

22.♘g3

This is not the only way to win, but it's the most efficient one. 22... ♗d6 23.♘h5 ♕c7 24.♗xd6 ♕xd6 25.♕xg7#

22.♗e5!

This modest yet decisive move only emphasizes the poor position of the black pieces, and he resigned.

After 22...♘g7 23.♗xf6 ♖xf6, black gets checkmated: 24.♕h7#

The game was found in the *Globus* magazine, No. 6, 1926.

No. 76. Queen's Gambit
Rauzer – Romanovsky
5th Soviet Championship
Moscow 1927
Annotated by V. Rauzer

1.d4 ♘f6 2.c4 e6 3.♘c3 ♗b4 4.♕c2 d5 5.♘f3 0-0 6.♗g5 ♘bd7 7.cxd5 exd5 8.e3 h6

This move allows white to launch a kingside pawn attack after playing 0-0-0.

To deprive white of this opportunity, black usually plays 8...c5 with the subsequent ...♕a5.

9.♗xf6 ♘xf6 10.0-0-0

10.♗d3 was more precise.

This prevents the subsequent liberating maneuver by black.

10...♗xc3 11.♕xc3 ♘e4 12.♕c2 ♗f5 13.♗d3 c5

This gives away the good d4 square for the white knight.

However, black gets some nice play, too.

14.dxc5 ♖c8 15.♔b1

If the white king were not on the queenside, white could play 15.b4 a5 16.a3, however, in this position, the king is in danger after 16...b6.

15...♖xc5 16.♕e2 ♕b6 17.♔a1 ♖fc8 18.♘d4 ♗g6 19.♗xe4

If 19.f3, then 19...♘f2! 20.♗xg6 ♘xd1 21.♗b1 ♖c2, and black wins.

19...♗xe4 20.f3 ♗g6 21.♕d2 ♖8c7

Rauzer thought that 21...♕a6 was better.

22.h4 ♖a5 23.♖c1

23...♖ac5

Black could give perpetual check here: 23...♖xa2+ 24.♔xa2 ♕a6+ 25.♔b3 ♖c4 26.♖xc4 ♕xc4+ etc.

24.♖xc5 ♕xc5 25.g4

The position is roughly equal, but it's easier for white to attack on the kingside, not having to fear for his king's safety.

25...h5 26.gxh5 ♗xh5 27.f4

A poor move that weakens the light squares in white's position, which was immediately exploited by black. Rauzer thought that 27.♖g1!? could improve white's attack.

27...♕e7 28.♕d3 ♗g6 29.f5 ♗h5 30.a3 a6

White recorded the move 31.♕b3, but agreed to black's draw offer.

Rauzer's annotations were published in *Proletarskaya Pravda*, 9th February 1928.

No. 77. Queen's Gambit
Rauzer – Russo
Ukrainian SSR championship
Odessa 1928
Annotated by V. Rauzer

1.d4 d5 2.c4 e6 3.♘c3 ♘f6 4.♗g5 ♘bd7 5.e3 ♗e7 6.♘f3 0-0 7.♖c1 ♖e8 8.♕c2 c6 9.a3 a6 10.cxd5 ♘xd5 11.♗xe7 ♕xe7 12.♘xd5

This trade, which improves black's position and restores his pawn center, was not necessary. The immediate 12.♗d3 was better.

Bogoljubov played the recommended move a year earlier: 12...h6 13.♘e4 e5 14.♘g3 exd4 15.♘xd4, and white pieces got into active positions that allowed him to play in the center and on the kingside (E. Bogoljubov – W. Von Holzhausen, Bremen, 1927).

12...exd5 13.♗d3 g6 14.0-0 ♔g7 15.♕c3 f5?!

An erroneous plan. This move gives the important e5 square away to the white knight, and the game is beyond saving after that.

16.b4 ♘f6 17.a4 ♘e4?! 18.♗xe4 fxe4 19.♘e5

Thanks to black's poor 15th and 17th moves, the white knight can "camp" on e5 indefinitely.

19...♗d7

Black is trying to prevent b4-b5. Rauzer thought that the immediate 19...♗e6 was better. In this case, however, white still breaks up black's pawn chain with b4-b5.

20.♕c5 ♕xc5 21.♖xc5!?

If 21.bxc5, then 21...♗e6 22.♖b1 ♖e7 23.♖b6 ♖c8 24.♖fb1 ♖cc7 with a draw.

Another defensive structure was also possible: 21...♖ad8 22.♖b1 ♗c8.

21...♗e6?!

Black decided to protect the d5 pawn, which can remain defenseless after the b4-b5 breakthrough. However, this move allows white to execute immediately his main idea of a pawn minority attack, b4-b5. 21...♖e7 was worth considering, forcing white to delay his breakthrough for a time: 22.b5?! is met with 22...axb5 23.axb5 b6!. Black sacrifices a pawn and goes for a rook endgame with active rooks. 24.♖c2 c5 25.♘xd7 ♖xd7 26.dxc5 bxc5 27.♖xc5 ♖a2, *putting the rook onto the second rank and intending d5-d4.*

22.b5! axb5 23.axb5 cxb5 24.♖xb5

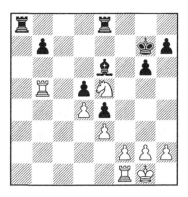

White has achieved the main goal of his pawn minority attack: black now has two weak pawns, on b7 and d5, and the bishop is rather restricted in its activity as it's forced to protect these pawns.

24...♗e7 25.♖fb1 ♖a7

Black is tied up in passive defense, and white launches a kingside attack.

26.f4

The computer prefers 26.h4!? with the subsequent g2-g4, moving the king closer to the front lines, and only then playing f2-f3. In this line, white does not obtain two connected passed pawns, but he gets some active play on the kingside.

26...♖c7

After 26...exf3, white would later get two connected passed pawns.

An interesting point. Rauzer thought that the two connected

passers were a decisive factor. The computer, on the other hand, considers this continuation the strongest for black, and dismisses the game move as poor. A task for self-study: who is correct?

27.g4 ♔f6

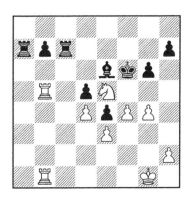

28.♖1b2!?

A good prophylactic move. Rauzer doesn't want to interpose with the rook after, say, 28.♔f2 ♖a2+, preferring to preserve both rooks on the board. After 29.♔g3 ♖e2 30.♖1b3, black would get some chances to save the game after doubling rooks on the second rank.

Rauzer thought that the game move was "necessary" and showed the following line: If 28.♖b6, then 28...♖a2 29.f5 ♖cc2 30.♖xe6+ ♔g5, and white cannot avoid perpetual check.

Instead of 29.f5, white should play 29.♖xb7!, and 29...♖cc2 gives black nothing due to 30.♖xh7. The readers can see for themselves that white is better in this line.

28...♔e7 29.♔g2 ♔f6

Black is completely helpless and can only wait passively for the end.

30.♖b6 ♔e7 31.♖f2 ♖a3

31...♖a6 was more resilient.

32.f5 gxf5 33.gxf5 ♗g8

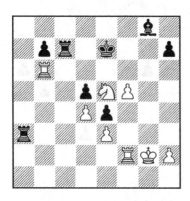

34.♖h6

f5-f6-f7 etc. was simpler.

34...♖ac3

Black had an opportunity to set a cunning trap: 34...♖xe3 35.f6+ ♔e8 36.f7+ ♗xf7 37.♖xh7 ♗e6! 38.♖xc7?? ♗h3+ 39.♔g1 ♖e1+ 40.♖f1 ♖xf1#

35.f6+ ♔e8 36.h4 ♖c2 37.f7+ ♗xf7 38.♖xh7 ♗e6?

Black had a last chance to prolong the struggle with 38...♖xf2+ 39.♔xf2 ♔f8 40.♔g3 ♔g8. After the game move, everything ends quickly.

39.♖h8+ ♔e7 40.♘g6+ ♔d6 41.♖d8+ ♗d7 42.h5 ♖c8 43.♖xc8 ♖xc8 44.♖f6+ ♔c7 45.h6 ♗e8 46.♘e7 Black resigned.

Rauzer's annotations were published in *Proletarskaya Pravda*, 8th July 1928.

No. 78. Queen's Gambit
Rauzer – Rosenstein
Ukrainian SSR championship
Odessa 1928
Annotated by V. Rauzer

1.d4 d5 2.c4 e6 3.♘f3 ♘d7 4.♘c3 ♘gf6 5.♗g5 c6 6.♖c1 ♗e7 7.e3 0-0 8.♗d3 dxc4 9.♗xc4 ♘d5 10.♗xe7 ♕xe7 11.0-0 ♘xc3 12.♖xc3 e5 13.d5

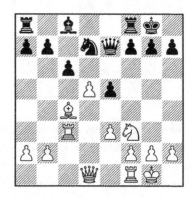

Up until now, the game has followed well-trodden paths. With 13.d5, white avoids theory.

13...e4 14.♘d4 cxd5?!

14...c5 was much better, as Shapiro played against Grigorenko in the same tournament.

15.♗xd5 ♘f6 16.♗b3 ♗g4 17.♕c2

17.♕d2!?

17...♖ac8 18.h3 ♖xc3 19.♕xc3 ♖c8

There was nothing better than returning the bishop to c8. Now black loses a pawn without any compensation.

In this case, however, white's

plan was rather simple, too: 19...♝c8 20.♜c1 h6 21.♛c7 ♛xc7 22.♜xc7, and black has no good moves, while white threatens to play the knight maneuver: ♞d4-b5-d6 or ♝xf7+.

20.♛a5 b6 21.♛a6 ♝d7

The only move that protects the c8 rook.

22.♛xa7 ♛c5 23.♞e2 ♜c7 24.♛b8+ ♜c8 25.♛f4 ♛a5 26.♞c3 ♝b5 27.♞xb5 ♛xb5 28.♜d1 h6 29.♛d6 ♛a5

The attack on the f7 square could be prevented with 29...♛c5, but after 30.♛xc5 bxc5 31.♝c4, the a-pawn is ready to go. In this case, the advantage of the bishop over the knight tells. It supports the movement of the a-pawn, attacks the f7 square and restricts the knight's activity at the same time.

30.♛e7 ♛h5

If 30...♜f8, then 31.♝xf7+ ♜xf7 32.♜d8+ ♚h7 33.♛xf7 ♛e1+ 34.♚h2 ♛xf2 35.♜d7! etc.

31.♛b7

The simple 31.♜d8+ ♜xd8 32.♛xd8+ ♚h7 33.♛xb6 wins without any tricks.

31...♜c5 32.♚f1 ♞d5

An ingenious defense... but only for a single move.

33.♚e1

Already threatening to capture the knight.

33...♞xe3

Desperation, but material losses are unavoidable anyway.

34.♝xf7+!

Black resigned. *34...♛xf7 is met with 35.♜d8+, winning the queen.*

Moral: it's simply impossible to protect the accursed f7 square completely! (Savielly Tartakower)

The game was found in the *Globus* magazine, No. 6, 1926

About My Father

Mark A. Konstantinopolsky

This book is dedicated to the life and legacy of Vsevolod Alfredovich Rauzer, whom Alexander Markovich Konstantinopolsky (1910-1990), my father, considered his best friend, mentor and chess partner, highly valuing both his human qualities and theoretical discoveries in chess. This book is not solely about chess – it's about the great friendship between two famous masters who were selflessly devoted to the game, who befriended each other and worked together as only young people who are passionate about a common goal can.

My father was born on 19 February 1910 in the Ukrainian city of Zhitomir. His father, my grandfather Mark Lvovich Konstantinopolsky, was born in either 1886 or 1888 (there are contradictory sources). Before the October 1917 Revolution my grandfather taught Greek in a high school, and was later a Professor at Kharkov University. After graduation and when my grandfather was still young, in 1910-1917, he went to Dresden, Germany, to collect literature for his doctorate on cultural and religious traditions of Persia.

My father's family lived in Dnepropetrovsk (now Dnipro) until 1922. After that, my father and his mother Olga Mikhailovna (1892-1941) moved to Kiev (now Kyiv), while his father moved to Kharkov, probably as he was working there. In any case, the family split up at that time and my father lived in Kiev with his mother right until 1941.

My father recalled that they had a big library at home with his father's books. My grandfather knew 16 languages according to my father. Alik, as my father was known to his family and friends, learned to read early and would even read the Odyssey and the Iliad in Greek at the age of 4-5.

Later, during my own childhood, my father would subscribe to many foreign chess magazines as required by his work: in Serbian, Croat, Czech, Polish, Bulgarian, German, English and even Hungarian. He possessed an excellent memory, which enabled him to study and understand diverse foreign languages, just like he recalled a huge volume of chess information – games, variations, names and dates.

My father adored his mother, who had mostly brought him up on her own. He said she was kind, tactful, fair, loved him dearly. She fully supported his interest in chess and was proud of his success. Olga Mikhailovna worked as an accountant and also farmed her land plot. Since my grandfather left them, in 1922, my father and grandmother lived modestly.

My father finished studies at a chemistry college in 1931 and then worked in this sphere until February 1934. Many of his achievements as a chess player belong to the 1930s. He won five Kiev championships in 1932–1936, and took prize places at the Ukrainian championships in 1937 and 1938 (3rd place) as well as in the 1937 Soviet Championship (2nd–3rd place). He became a chess administrator and coach at the Pioneers Palace and other clubs in Kiev in 1933 and worked there until 1941.

Everything was fine in this little family of two, until the Nazis invaded in June 1941. My father was conscripted to the army, trained as a combat medic and then sent to the front the same year. Then, from 1942 to 1944, he was engaged in evacuation hospitals for the wounded soldiers to raise their spirits by playing chess with them.

My grandmother remained in Kiev, and in autumn 1941 was murdered by the Nazis at Babi Yar. My father only learned about this in 1944, when he returned to Moscow. It was a huge tragedy for him. The loss of his mother was so unbearable that he hardly ever mentioned these terrible events.

Alexander Konstantinopolsky preferred to recall the happy years he had spent with his mother in Kiev. He spoke of how she would never punish him for being naughty, but encouraged him to enjoy the beaches of the Dnipro River in Kiev as well as chess. I think that those were the happiest years of his life. He recalled the "chess fever" that gripped the country when the Moscow International Tournament was held, when he was fifteen years old. That was when he met Vsevolod Rauzer, his true friend, chess partner, first and only coach, who although being just a few years older than my father had already gained a reputation of an experienced player and mentor. Together they would often spend a lot of time by the river, not only sunbathing, but playing and analyzing chess, and developing new opening variations for their future victories.

After the end of the Second World War, Alexander Konstantinopolsky achieved his greatest successes as a coach, holding the important job of head coach of the Soviet women's team from 1954 to 1982. His team won six women's Olympiads during that period. Such famous chess players as Nona Gaprindashvili, Nana Alexandria, Kira Zvorykina, Tatyana Zatulovskaya, Olga Rubtsova, Olga Ignatyeva and others, who were team members during that time, can be considered his wards and pupils. Perhaps the most famous charge of my father, Grandmaster David Bronstein, was a world championship candidate and drew a world championship match with Botvinnik in 1951.

Despite his outstanding coaching career, Konstantinopolsky still considered himself an active player and continued playing in tournaments both in the USSR and abroad up until 1976. My father devoted almost his entire life, from 1925 to his death in 1990, to chess.

Unfortunately, this book was not published earlier, when my father was still alive, because of his declining health and various other reasons that were beyond the author's control. After my father's death, there were offers in the 1990s to submit the manuscript to a foreign publisher to get it to print more quickly; however, remembering my father's wish that this book's first publication should be in his native Russian, I tried to fulfill his request and it eventually appeared in Russian in 2022. I am glad that this book will now find its readers among the English speaking world as well.

15 July 2023

No. A1. Reti Opening
Konstantinopolsky – Goglidze
All-Union Young Masters
Tournament
Leningrad 1936
Annotated by G. Levenfish

1.♘f3 d5 2.g3 ♘f6 3.♗g2 ♗g4
A difficult defense that gives
white the bishop pair advantage in
the best case. It's only appropriate
after b2-b3.

4.c4 c6
It was necessary to trade pieces
immediately. After 4...♗xf3 5.♗xf3
c6 6.♕b3 ♕b6, black can develop
with quiet moves.

5.♘e5

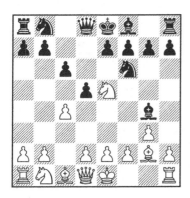

5...♗h5
A careless move. 5...♗e6 was
better.

6.cxd5 cxd5
The last mistake. After 6...♘xd5
7.♕b3 ♘d7!, white has seized the
center, but black avoids an immediate
crushing defeat, which now comes
very quickly.

7.♕a4+ ♘bd7

Black should have come to
terms with losing a pawn after 7...
♘c6 8.♘c3 (8.♘xc6 ♕d7!) 8...♖c8
9.♘xc6 bxc6 10.♕xa7, etc.

8.♘c3 e6 9.g4! ♗g6 10.h4

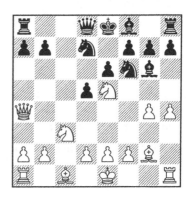

10...b5
In the game Lisitsin –
Konstantinopolsky (VTsSPS
Championship[18]), there followed
10...♗c2 11.♕xc2 ♘xe5, and
black was better, since white's
position was compromised. Later,
Konstantinopolsky found that after
10...♗c2, white got an advantage
with 11.♘xf7! ♔xf7 12.♕xc2
♘xg4 13.♘xd5!. 10...h6 11.♘xg6
fxg6 doesn't save black either –
the weaknesses on e6 and g6 are
impossible to defend. The game
move only relies on 11.♕xb5 ♖b8
12.♕c6 ♖b6 13.♕a4 ♖b4 with a
draw.

**11.♘xb5! ♘xe5 12.♘c7+ ♔e7
13.♘xa8 ♕xa8 14.h5 ♘exg4**

---

[18] Probably the one held in January
1936 in Moscow

14...♗e4 15.f3 ♘exg4 16.fxe4 dxe4 gave black better chances, threatening ♕b8-g3.

15.hxg6 fxg6 16.d4 ♔f7 17.♗f4 ♗e7 18.♖c1 ♘h5 19.♗d2 ♕b8 20.♗h3 ♘hf6 21.♕b3 ♘xf2

The game is already lost, so black's combination doesn't essentially spoil anything.

22.♔xf2 ♘e4+ 23.♔g2 ♘xd2 24.♕xb8 ♖xb8 25.♖c6! ♗f6 26.♗xe6+ ♔e8 27.b3 ♗xd4 28.♖d1 ♗e3 29.♗xd5 ♗g5 30.e3

Black resigned, since he loses a piece.

No. A2
Konstantinopolsky – Smyslov
14th Soviet Championship
Moscow 1945
Annotated by A. Konstantinopolsky

17.♗xh6! ♘f6

After 17...gxf3, white has a pretty win: 18.♗xg7 ♔xg7 19.♕g5+ ♔f7 20.♕h5+ ♔e7 21.♖xe6+! ♔xe6 22.♖e1+ etc.

18.♗xg7 ♕xg7 19.♘g5 g3

Trying to complicate the game. 19...cxd4 then 20.♖xe6.

20.fxg3 ♘g4 21.♕f4 ♕ 22.♗d1 ♕xd4+ 23.♕xd4 c♕ 24.♗xg4 fxg4 25.♖ad1 with a ♕ position. White won after 54 mo

No. A3
Konstantinopolsky – Panov
Moscow 1946
Annotated by A. Konstantinopols

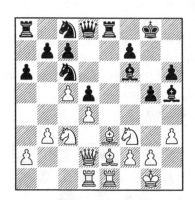

18.♘xg5! ♗xe2

18...♖xe3 doesn't change much: 19.fxe3 ♗xe2 20.♘xf7 ♔xf7 21.♕xe2, and then continuing the attack with ♕h5+ or ♖f1.

19.♘xf7 ♔xf7 20.♕xe2 ♘8e7

20...♖h8 21.♕h5+ ♔g7 22.♘xd5 winning.

21.♕h5+ ♔g8 22.♗xh6 ♕d7

After 22...♗xd4, white wins with 23.♖xd4, while 22...♘xd4 is bad due to 23.♗g5 ♗g7 24.♕g4 ♘df5 25.♘xd5.

23.♖e3 ♘f5 24.♘xd5 ♕xd5 25.♖g3+ ♘xg3

25...♗g7 26.♖xg7+ ♔h8 27.♖g6 is also hopeless.

26.♕g6+ Black resigned.

No. A4. Caro-Kann Defense
Keres – Konstantinopolsky
16th Soviet Championship
Moscow 1948
Annotated by A. Konstantinopolsky

1.e4 c6 2.d4 d5 3.exd5 cxd5 4.c4

This system was developed and introduced to tournament practice by Master Panov. Alekhine considered it one of the best replies to the defense chosen by black. It usually leads to an intense struggle for the central squares. It's probably advisable for black to bolster his stronghold on d5 and prepare to castle.

4...♘f6 5.♘c3 e6 6.♘f3 ♗e7

6...♗b4 often occurs in modern practice, going for Nimzo-Indian-type positions.

7.a3

Probably not the best, because the pawn wedge c4-c5 (prepared by a2-a3) is not dangerous for black. Nevertheless, this plan still has its adherents, and in the 1940s many considered it favorable for white.

7...0-0 8.c5 ♘e4

Since white has removed pressure from the d5 square, black can place an "outpost" knight in the center. The f7 pawn is ready to support it. The only flaw in black's position is the somewhat weak e5 square, where the f3 knight intends to move.

9.♕c2 f5 10.♗e2 ♘c6 11.♗b5

White wants to secure the d4 pawn (black threatens ...♗f6) and remove a defender of the e5 square.

11...♗f6 12.♗xc6 bxc6 13.0-0 g5!

One of my favorite strategic techniques – a blow with a flank pawn.

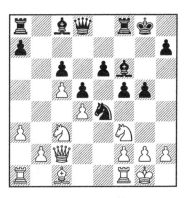

It looks risky at first. However, black can launch a kingside attack with a solid position in the center. Keres tried to prevent this with his knight lunge that now follows. He probably misevaluated the structure that occurred by force – opposite-colored bishops in the presence of all major pieces on the board.

14.♘e5 ♗xe5 15.dxe5 ♘xc3!

If 15...♘xc5 then 16.♘e2!, and white regains the pawn.

16.♕xc3 f4!

Black intends to transfer the queen to g6 (or h5); the a8 rook moves (through b8-b7) to g7, and the bishop will take up a strong position on a6. It's not easy for white to defend against this plan. His bishop has no prospects, and the queenside pawns are blocked. Perhaps such a plan (moves 13–16) is even harder to find than a spectacular combination with a queen sacrifice...

17.♗d2 ♗a6 18.♖fe1 ♖b8 19.♕d4

The d5 pawn has to be blocked.

19...♗c4 20.♗c3 ♕e8 21.♕d1

Preventing ...♕h5 and delegating the blockade of the d5 pawn to the bishop. White will develop his queen's rook to a3 to defend the third rank.

21...♖b7 22.a4 ♕g6 23.♖a3 g4 24.♗d4 ♖g7

Black has concentrated most of his forces on the kingside. He threatens ♖f8-f5-h5 with the subsequent ...♕h6. Other attacks are also possible.

25.f3 h5

Maintaining the pressure and planning ♖f8-f5-g5 with an attack on g2.

26.♖c3

b2-b4 was worth considering, to create some counterplay with b4-b5 as soon as possible.

26...♖f5

Now white can't play 27.♕c2 gxf 28.♖xf3 due to 28...♖xe5! 29.♕x; ♖xe1+ and ...♗f1 checkmate.

27.♔h1 ♖g5 28.b3 ♗a6 29.♖ gxf3

After this trade, black gets very strong e4 square for his qu (and for his bishop later).

30.♕xf3 ♕e4 31.♕f2 ♗d3 32.b4 ♕f5 33.b5

This break is too late, but, due to the threat ♗d3-e4, white has nothing else.

33...♗e4 34.bxc6 ♖xg2 35.♖xg2 ♖xg2 36.♕xg2+ ♗xg2+ 37.♔xg2 ♕e4+ 38.♔f1 f3

Of course, not 38...♕xd4? 39.c7.

White's reply is now forced, because 39.♗f2 is met with 39... ♕e2+ and 40...♕d1+, mating.

39.♗e3 ♕g6 40.♔e1 ♕b1+ 41.♔d2 ♕b2+

41...d4 42.♗xd4 ♕b2+ 43.♔d1 ♕e2+ also won.

42.♖c2 ♕xe5

Black threatens d5-d4, as well as ...♕xh2+, ...♕c7 and ...♕xc6 with the subsequent onslaught of his

ree passers. White tries to revive
s remaining passed c-pawn.

43.c7 ♕xh2+ 44.♔d1 ♕xc7
c6 e5

Preparing   the   winning
bination.

6.♗xa7 d4 47.♗b6

47...d3! 48.♖c1 ♕xb6 49.c7
♕xc7 50.♖xc7 f2

White resigned.

M. Taimanov (white) vs A. Konstantinopolsky (black). Soviet championship.

One of the first postwar tournaments. Masters in play: S. Furman (white), A. Konstantinopolsky (black).

Soviet Team Championship. V. P. Zagorovsky (black), A. M. Konstantinopolsky (white).

Game between A. Konstantinopolsky (white) and E. Geller (black), Soviet Team Championship, Moscow vs. Ukraine, Leningrad, September 1948.

Moscow Team Championship. Bolshevik vs. Krylya Sovetov. Black – Master A. Konstantinopolsky, white – Grandmaster S. Flohr. Moscow, late 1940s.

Soviet Championship. Master I. Kan (black) thinks on his move as A. Konstantinopolsky (white) reads the newspaper. In the background, P. Keres (black) plays M. Botvinnik (white).

A rare photo – participants of a major chess tournament in Sochi, USSR, gathered near the State Theater building, where the tournament was hosted, dated 9ᵗʰ June 1952. Semi-final of the 20ᵗʰ Soviet chess championship. I was only 6 years old, so I'm sorry to say that I remember some faces of the participants, but not their names... Here are the players whom I can identify positively. First row standing, left to right: second – Master V. Simagin, fourth – Master L. Aronin. In the center of the row, wearing a white short-sleeved shirt, A. Konstantinopolsky. Behind his left shoulder, Master V. G. Zak. The tall player wearing glasses, a dark suit and white shirt, Grandmaster G. Levenfish. The young handsome man, below average height, wearing glasses and a gray suit with tie, tournament arbiter I. Berezin. In the bottom row, among those sitting on the ground, third from the left, wearing glasses and a T-shirt, Master B. Baranov.

Game between A. Konstantinopolsky (white) and Master Y. Shaposhnikov (black), Soviet championship semi-final, Sochi, 1952.

A. Konstantinopolsky and P. Keres during the USSR – Great Britain match, London 1954.

Game between A. Konstantinopolsky (black) and O. Moiseev (white). Soviet Team Championship, Riga, Latvia, 1954.

Chess training camp, approx. 1955, with all the strongest woman players of the era. Top row, left to right: A. Konstantinopolsky, his wife L. G. Koshutina, team doctor Stasya (Stanislava Yanovna), second to her right, Master S. Rootare (Estonia), V. Belova on her right. In the center, well-known woman chess player and arbiter T. P. Strandstrom. Far right, Master V. G. Zak, coach.

Second row, left to right: A. Polyak, O. Rubtsova's coach; Master K. Zvorykina; Master O. M. Ignatyeva; Tikhomirova, chess arbiter; Masters L. Rudenko and L. Volpert.

Third row, left to right: unknown master, Master Eliso Kakabadze (Georgia), children of chess players – Mark Konstantinopolsky beside E. Kakabadze, unknown boy, then Misha Rubtsov beside Master T. Zatulovskaya.

I'm sorry that I couldn't recognize or remember everyone, please be kind to a 9 year-old Mark K.

Iceland – USSR team match, Oslo, Norway, mid-1950s. A. Konstantinopolsky, the team coach, watches the game.

Morning walk. Groningen, Netherlands, 1957.

Women's Olympiad in Emmen, Netherlands, 1957. Great interest in the games of the Soviet participants, O. Rubtsova and K. Zvorykina. A. Konstantinopolsky, the team coach, watches play.

Winning the Olympiad, Emmen, Netherlands, 1957. Left to right: O. Rubtsova, K. Zvorykina, coach A. Konstantinopolsky.

The same ceremony.

Another photo from the same ceremony.

At the Abramtsevo training camp, June 1958. The main emphasis was put on physical training.

A rare photo depicting many famous chess players of the 1940s–1950s, participants of a major tournament, probably a Soviet championship. These are the ones I can positively identify: bottom row, left to right, fourth, fifth and sixth persons are Grandmasters V. Ragozin and S. Flohr and Master A. Konstantinopolsky. Top row, left to right, first and second persons are Masters V. Simagin and M. Beilin.

At a 1961 training camp at Pokrovskoe, near Moscow before the 2nd Women's Olympiad. Games analysis. Left to right: Grandmaster I. Boleslavsky, coach; A. Konstantinopolsky, head coach; Master M. Shishov, coach; T. Zatulovskaya, K. Zvorykina, N. Gaprindashvili.

At the same training camp, 1961. A. Konstantinopolsky, his wife L. G. Koshutina and son Mark Konstantinopolsky.

At a Soviet women chess players' training camp, early 1960s. Bottom row, sitting: N. Gaprindashvili and others. Second row, left, at the pillar, Rootare (Estonia); center, N. Konopleva and O. Ignatyeva, then E. Kakabadze, right, at the pillar, K. Zvorykina. Top row, left to right: team doctor M. T. Volodina, Master V. Kozlovskaya, fitness coach Khachaturov, head coach A. Konstantinopolsky.

Rijeka, Yugoslavia, 1963. USSR – Yugoslavia match. Left to right: coach E. Vasiukov, K. Zvorykina, V. Nedeljkovic (Yugoslavia), N. Gaprindashvili, head coach A. Konstantinopolsky.

A training game. White – A. Konstantinopolsky, black – Grandmaster Y. L. Averbakh.

Training camp before the 4ᵗʰ Women's Olympiad, Borjomi, 1969. Left to right: N. Gaprindashvili, Master B. Gurgenidze (coach), N. Alexandria, A. Kushnir, A. Konstantinopolsky (head coach).

Awards ceremony of the 4th Women's Olympiad. First place was won by the Soviet team: N. Gaprindashvili, A. Kushnir, N. Alexandria. Lublin, Poland, 1969.

A. Konstantinopolsky and V. Alatortsev. Burevestnik – Spartak match, 25th February 1976.

At the International Correspondence Chess Federation conference. Left to right: A. M. Konstantinopolsky, a Finnish representative, V. P. Zagorovsky, Jarvenpaa, Finland, 1979.

Vsevolod Rauzer's Tournament Results

Year	Competition	+	−	=	Plac
1923	Rostov-on-Don Championship	7	0	0	1
1925	Kiev Championship	4	1	3	2-
1925	4th Soviet Intercity Championship	6	3	0	2-
	Group tournament, 2nd Winners' Group	6	1	1	2
1926	3rd Ukrainian Championship, Odessa	1	8	2	12
1926	Kiev Championship	8/10			3
1927	Kiev Championship	5	2	3	2–4
1927	4th Ukrainian Championship, Poltava (second to Master Selezniev, who played *hors concours*; awarded the champion's title)	8	1	6	2
1927	5th Soviet Championship, Moscow	5	10	5	18–19
1928	5th Ukrainian Championship, Odessa	4	3	8	3
1929	Kiev Championship	8	1	4	2
1929	Kiev, training tournament	2	4	0	6
1929	6th Soviet Championship, Odessa				
	Group stage	4	1	3	3–4
	Semi-final	3	2	0	3
1930	Kiev Championship	7	1	2	1
1930	Tbilisi. Masters tournament of Transcaucasia, Ukraine and Uzbekistan	4	1	5	1
1931	Kharkov. Ukrainian Championship and qualification tournament for the Soviet Championship	8	3	0	2
1931	7th Soviet Championship, Moscow				
	Group stage	6	0	2	1
	Final	5	4	8	8–9
1932	Kiev. Leningrad – Kiev tournament	6	3	0	2
1932	Kiev Championship	9	3	2	4–5
1933	Kharkov. Ukrainian Championship and qualification tournament for the Soviet Championship	4	2	2	1–2
1933	8th Soviet Championship, Leningrad	10	6	3	6
1934	Baku Championship *(hors concours)*	7	0	4	1–3
1934	Kiev. Training tournament of five city champions	1	5	2	5
1934	Tbilisi. Masters tournament of Soviet republics	5	4	4	3–5
1934	9th Soviet Championship, Leningrad	4	8	7	17
1935	Leningrad, the "Tournament of 12"	4	2	5	3

935	Russian SFSR Championship, Gorky Semi-final Final	3 4	0 3	8 2	2–5 4
36	Leningrad Championship	7	2	5	2
6	All-Union Masters qualifying tournament, Leningrad	7	5	6	5
6	All-Union Young Masters Training Tournament, Leningrad	5	2	7	1–2
37	Leningrad. Tournament featuring Grandmaster R. Fine	0	1	4	4–5
937	Qualifying match for the masters title against D. Rovner, Leningrad	7	3	6	
1937	10th Soviet Championship, Tbilisi	7	5	7	8
1940	Semifinal of the 12th Soviet Championship, Kiev	2	6	8	13–15

Made in the USA
Monee, IL
19 February 2024

53773631R00131